The Irish Revolution, 1913–1923

The Irish Revolution, 1913–1923

Edited by

JOOST AUGUSTEIJN

palgrave

First published 2002 by
PALGRAVE
Houndmills, Basingstoke, Hampshire RG21 6XS and
175 Fifth Avenue, New York, N.Y. 10010
Companies and representatives throughout the world

PALGRAVE is the new global academic imprint of
St. Martin's Press LLC Scholarly and Reference Division and
Palgrave Publishers Ltd (formerly Macmillan Press Ltd).

ISBN 0–333–98225–8 hardcover
ISBN 0–333–98226–6 paperback

This book is printed on paper suitable for recycling and
made from fully managed and sustained forest sources.

A catalogue record for this book is available
from the British Library.

Library of Congress Cataloging-in-Publication Data

The Irish Revolution, 1913–1923 / edited by Joost Augusteijn.
        p. cm.
      Includes bibliographical references and index.
      ISBN 0–333–98225–8 (hardback)   ISBN 0–333–98226–6 (paperback)
        1. Ireland – History – Civil War, 1922–1923. 2. Ireland – History –
Easter Rising, 1916. 3. Ireland – History – 1910–1921. I. Augusteijn, Joost.

DA962 .I77 2002
941.5082′1–dc21   2002025160

10   9   8   7   6   5   4   3   2   1
11   10   09   08   07   06   05   04   03   02

Printed in China

Contents

List of Tables

Preface

The events between 1913 and 1923 have made a huge impact on Ireland and its relationship with Britain. The constitutional changes which accompanied the violent convulsions led to the end of the union between Ireland and Great Britain and the creation of Northern Ireland. The internal politics of the two new states has also been largely shaped by this period. However, despite its importance, debate on it has been very limited. It has even been impossible so far to find a generally accepted term to describe the period as a whole. Although some attempts have been made to find a common denominator, the period is usually described by naming its constituent parts: Home Rule Crisis, First World War, Easter Rising, Anglo-Irish War and Civil War. In recent historiography the previously rarely used phrase the 'Irish revolution' has become more popular to describe the entire period, although, as will become clear from various contributions in this volume, it has not been generally accepted, nor is it clear what the term actually entails. David Fitzpatrick has recently noted in *History: Ireland* that: 'It has become commonplace for historians of Ireland to describe the events of 1912–1923 as a "revolution", typically without attempting to define that term.'[1]

This book is an attempt to do just that. This has been made possible by a number of detailed local and thematic studies that have been published since 1996. Building on foundations laid in the 1970s and 1980s, they have transformed our understanding of the period, replacing a simple narrative approach with a much more analytical method. This has brought us to a point where, even though there are still many blanks in our knowledge, we can now assess what has been done, and try to create an overview of where we are and where we might go in further research.

A great number of fundamental issues regarding the revolutionary period are dealt with in this book, which is composed of thematic essays. These concern themselves with questions such as: was there a revolution in this period and how can it be characterised? (primarily in contributions by Townshend, Hart and Garvin); if so, what kind of revolution was it? (Townshend, Murphy); when did it start and end? (Hart); could it have ended earlier? (Hopkinson); what motivated revolutionaries and those who supported them? (Augusteijn, Novick); how did they operate? (Coleman, Mitchell, Inoue); how did it affect the role of women and other groupings? (Ward, Martin); and what influence did it have on the period thereafter and how did people deal with this past? (English, Dolan). These issues are raised in a variety of ways, from detailed assessments of specific incidents to wide-ranging analyses of themes.

This is therefore not a narrative of the Irish revolution, but a thematic analysis of our interpretation of it. However, if desired, the main events can be traced through the chronology included at the end of the book. Furthermore, to enable the reader to place the various persons mentioned, brief biographical notes on the main players are added to their entries in the index.[2]

This book finds its origin in a symposium held in the Queen's University of Belfast in 1998. Thanks go to all participants in this symposium, and to the departments of Modern History and Politics for their assistance in organising it. We hope that this volume will stimulate and initiate further historical debate on this period and on the phenomenon of revolution in general.

Note

1. David Fitzpatrick, *History: Ireland*, vol. 8, 2 (2000), p. 47.
2. For further details, see P. O'Farrell, *Who's Who in the Irish War of Independence and Civil War, 1916–1923* (Dublin, 1997), and Sean Connolly (ed.), *The Oxford Companion to Irish History* (Oxford, 2002).

List of Abbreviations

AFIL	All for Ireland League
AOH	Ancient Order of Hibernians
APL	Anti-Partition League
BL	British Library
BNL	British Newspaper Library
CAI	Cork Archives Institute
CIR	County Inspector's Report
DMP	Dublin Metropolitan Police
GAA	Gaelic Athletic Association
IHS	Irish Historical Studies
IPP	Irish Parliamentary Party
IRA	Irish Republican Army
IRB	Irish Republican Brotherhood
IUA	Irish Unionist Alliance
IWM	Imperial War Museum, London
KSRL	Kenneth Spencer Research Library
NA	National Archives, Dublin
NLI	National Library of Ireland
OPW	Office of Public Works
PRO	Public Record Office, London
PRONI	Public Record Office of Northern Ireland
RIC	Royal Irish Constabulary
RM	Resident Magistrate
RTE	Radio Telefís Éireann
TCD	Trinity College, Dublin
TD	Téachta Dála, Dáil deputy
UCD	University College, Dublin
UCDAD	University College, Dublin, Archives Department
UIL	United Irish League
USC	Ulster Special Constabulary
UVF	Ulster Volunteer Force

Acknowledgements

The authors would like to thank the staff and trustees of the various libraries, archives and collections for providing access to material in their care.

In particular, Anne Dolan would like to thank University College, Dublin, Archives Department, for providing access to the Ernest Blythe papers, the Mulcahy Trust for permission to consult the Richard Mulcahy papers, and the Cork Archives Institute for permission to consult the Seamus Fitzgerald papers.

Notes on the Contributors

Joost Augusteijn lectures at Leiden University. He is author of *From Public Defiance to Guerrilla Warfare: The Experience of Ordinary Volunteers in the Irish War of Independence, 1916–1921* (Dublin, 1996), and editor of *Ireland in the 1930s: New Perspectives* (Dublin, 1999). He is currently writing a biography of Patrick Pearse.

Marie Coleman is a Government of Ireland postdoctoral scholar at University College, Dublin, currently researching the history of the Irish Hospitals' Sweepstake. She is author of *County Longford and the Irish Revolution, 1910–23* (Dublin, 2002).

Anne Dolan has completed a PhD on the commemoration of the Irish Civil War at the University of Cambridge, and is currently a postdoctoral fellow in contemporary Irish history at Trinity College, Dublin.

Richard English is Professor of Politics at Queen's University, Belfast. His books include *Radicals and the Republic: Socialist Republicanism in the Irish Free State, 1925–1937* (Oxford, 1994), and *Ernie O'Malley: IRA Intellectual* (Oxford, 1998).

Tom Garvin is Professor of Politics at University College, Dublin. His books include *The Evolution of Irish Nationalist Politics* (Dublin, 1981), *Nationalist Revolutionaries in Ireland, 1858–1927* (Oxford, 1987), and *1922: The Birth of Irish Democracy* (Dublin, 1996). He is at present working on a study of politics and economic development in independent Ireland, 1938 to 1960.

Peter Hart is Canada Research Chair in Irish Studies at the Memorial University of Newfoundland. He is the author of *The IRA and Its Enemies: Violence and Community in Cork, 1916–1923* (Oxford, 1998), and the forthcoming books: *British Intelligence in Ireland* and *Guerrilla Days in the UK*. He is currently writing a biography of Michael Collins.

Michael Hopkinson lectures at the University of Stirling. He is author of *Green Against Green: The Irish Civil War* (Dublin, 1988), and editor of *The Last Days of Dublin Castle: The Diaries of Mark Sturgis* (Dublin, 1999). At present he is writing a history of the Irish War of Independence.

Keiko Inoue received an MPhil from University College, Dublin, and is currently a doctoral student at Trinity College, Dublin, working on 'Politics of the Irish in Britain, 1919–25'. She has published articles in *Éire/Ireland*, *Studia Hibernica*, and the *Irish Studies Review*.

Peter Martin received his MA in modern Irish history from University College, Dublin, in 1999 for his thesis on 'Irish Peers, 1909–24'. He is a Government of Ireland Scholar and is studying for a PhD in modern history at Trinity College, Dublin, on 'Censorship in the Two Irelands, 1922–39'.

Arthur Mitchell, a history professor at the University of South Carolina, has a PhD from Trinity College, Dublin, and is author of *Labour in Irish Politics, 1890–1930* (Shannon, 1974), and *Revolutionary Government in Ireland: Dáil Éireann, 1919–1922* (Dublin, 1995).

Brian P. Murphy OSB of Glenstal Abbey, Co. Limerick, is a graduate of Oxford University and of the National University of Ireland. He is the author of *Patrick Pearse and the Lost Republican Ideal* (Dublin, 1991), *John Chartres: Mystery Man of the Treaty* (Dublin, 1995), and *St Gerard's School, Bray: An Educational Initiative* (1999).

Ben Novick is a lecturer in the Residential College at the University of Michigan, Ann Arbor, and the department of history at Oakland University in Rochester, Michigan. He received his DPhil from the University of Oxford, and is the author of *Conceiving Revolution: Irish Nationalist Propaganda during the First World War* (Dublin, 2001).

Charles Townshend is Professor of International History at Keele University; recent books include: (as editor) *The Oxford History of Modern War* (Oxford, 1997, 2000); (with Richard English) *The State: Historical and Political Dimensions* (London, 1999); and *Ireland: The 20th Century* (London, 1999).

Margaret Ward is Assistant Director with the Belfast-based think-tank Democratic Dialogue. Her publications include *Unmanageable Revolutionaries: Women and Irish Nationalism* (London, 1983), and biographies of Maud Gonne and Hanna Sheehy-Skeffington. She is currently co-editing (with Louise Ryan) *Soldiers, New Women and Wicked Hags: Historical and Cultural Representations of Irish Nationalist Women*.

1

Historiography: Telling the Irish Revolution

Charles Townshend

The Irish revolutionary moment has proved hard to fix with assurance. Before the Great War, Patrick Pearse was certain that it had already begun. In 'The Coming Revolution' (November 1913) he asserted – borrowing the Comte de Liancourt's famous epigram – that the founders of the Gaelic League had commenced 'not a revolt, but a revolution'; and he reinforced the point in March 1914 when he hailed the 'existence on Irish soil of an Irish army' as 'a fact which marks definitely the beginning of the second stage of the Revolution which commenced when the Gaelic League was founded'.[1] From the opposite political side, the apostate Catholic controversialist Michael McCarthy deplored the revolution that was underway; and the unionist historian W. A. Phillips seemed equally sure that, by 1923, a revolution had been completed.[2] Admittedly, they seem to have been speaking about different processes. For Pearse the deed, which his generation was required to accomplish, was redemption, the 'realisation of an Irish Nation' which, being divine, might become its own Messiah.[3] For Phillips, the people were sadly short on divinity and dangerously long on gullibility: manipulated by criminal thugs and even, as he darkly hinted, Bolsheviks.[4] (For McCarthy, the Catholic Church was the manipulator.) The upheaval witnessed by unionists such as Phillips was more an aggravated land grab than a spiritual regeneration.

Since then, historians and social analysts have rather fought shy of the term. As Peter Hart notes (see Chapter 2), almost all large-scale comparative studies of revolution have left Ireland out. Not only such

1

tightly conceptualised analyses as Charles Tilly's classic *From Mobilisation to Revolution* (1978), but even James Billington's vast trawl around the metaphor *Fire in the Minds of Men*.[5] There may be a good reason for this. Though nobody could doubt that there was fire in the minds of the Fenian insurrectionists who planned and launched the 1916 rebellion, and also perhaps amongst many of the Gaelic Leaguers invoked by Pearse, there are grounds for doubting whether it was the same 'revolutionary faith', still more whether they and their successors actually achieved a revolution. In recent Irish historiography there is a good deal of slippage in the labels attached to the period around Pearse's great deed – the Easter Rising of 1916 – though there is a general assumption that the years from *c.*1913 to 1923 form a coherent epoch. To take the most salient examples, F. S. L. Lyons preferred the term 'struggle for independence' (his chapter called 'The Road to Revolution' refers only to the 1916 rebellion); Roy Foster speaks of 'rebellion' and 'takeover' rather than revolution; Joseph Lee also of 'rebellion'; Theo Hoppen of 'violence and separatism'; Alvin Jackson prefers 'Troubles' and, like Lyons, 'War'. In all these general works, and others as well, revolution does not figure as a textual topic or an index entry (Jackson's index offers under 'Revolution, Irish', 'see War of Independence'). Hoppen does refer obliquely to a 'constitutional revolution' in making the point that there was no accompanying 'social revolution'.

More specialised studies have used the word more freely, although (and perhaps because) still without much analytical precision. In 1974, following the appearance of an article by Stein Larsen and Oliver Snoddy identifying the 1916 rising as 'a workingmen's revolution', on the basis of a new 'historical–sociological approach to the theoretical study of revolutionary movements', one commentator sharply noted that despite this they 'failed to construct a model of Revolution'. Thus, he added, any conclusion that 'analysts of the 1916–23 period are at last beginning to break away from their traditional analytic myopia and beginning to ground research in a coherent methodological and theoretical foundation … remains premature'.[6] A generation later, a similar verdict might still be brought in.[7]

Of the few books headlining the concept in their title, the most foursquare – *The Revolution in Ireland, 1879–1923*, edited by George Boyce – did not offer a systematic assessment of the revolution, preferring an 'exploration' reaching back into the nineteenth century. The editor dismissed at the outset the 'exercise' of discussing whether the events of 1916–23 could be classified as revolution, and went on to insist that 'nothing in Ireland … conforms quite exactly to the models of revolution constructed by political scientists'.[8] (Some of his contributors who incorporated the word in their chapter titles followed suit by ignoring the issue.) Desmond Greaves' Marxistic *Liam Mellows and the Irish Revolution* offers the proposition that 'the elimination of externally imposed backwardness, isolation, dependence and poverty may be called "the Irish Revolution" in its broadest sense'; but also suggests that the expression can be used of the 'great political upheavals aimed at this object' – whether successful or not.[9] After this vague gesture, Greaves sidelines the concept, and his index references to 'revolution' are for Germany, Russia and France. Others, from Nicholas Mansergh's *Ireland in the Age of Reform and Revolution* (1940) through T. W. Moody's *Davitt and Irish Revolution, 1846–82* (1981) to Léon O Broin's *W. E. Wylie and the Irish Revolution, 1916–1921* (1989), do not identify the revolutionary process as problematic. Senia Paseta's *Before the Revolution* provides an exceptionally illuminating analysis of the home-rule nationalist elite, but is rather mysterious in its signals about the timing of the revolution (since her account ends in 1922).[10] (By contrast, Michael Farry's recent study of County Sligo dates the revolution's 'aftermath' from 1921 – without, once again, saying what the revolution had been.)[11] Elsewhere, 'revolution' sometimes appears as an internal title, but not as a substantive issue: for instance in Michael Laffan's recent large-scale study of the Sinn Féin party;[12] while at the end of his *The Long Gestation* (1999) Patrick Maume offers a chapter of 'Reflections on a Revolution' without having used the term at all in his text. Paul Bew has also offered a rather oblique image of the revolution through the eyes of moderate nationalism.[13]

The clearest specification of an Irish revolution has been made in the work of David Fitzpatrick and some of his research students. In his first book, Fitzpatrick asserted that 'if revolutions are what happens to wheels, then Ireland underwent revolution between 1916 and 1922': 'its major social and political institutions were turned upside down'.[14] The first half of his most recent work addresses the question 'What Revolution?' and offers the answer that 'the alterations in Irish political organisation were sufficiently lasting and profound to merit the term "revolution" '.[15] But Fitzpatrick adds that 'Ireland experienced revolution in several senses,' not all of them equally definite; and in a collection of essays by his research students at Trinity College published under the challengingly curt title *Revolution?* he recognises that 'this book begins with a question which it cannot fully answer'; the best it might offer was 'a richer and more sophisticated notion of forms of revolutionary experience which touched some Irish people between 1917 and 1923'.[16]

Of course it is true that revolution is not a straightforward concept, a fixed template against which any set of occurrences can be measured. Indeed, most writers on the subject have emphasised the problem of definition, and of comparison. Chalmers Johnson, while paying tribute to Crane Brinton's *Anatomy of Revolution*, held that 'precisely because there is so little agreement on how to conceptualise revolution... comparative analyses of revolutions have commonly been a source of further confusion'.[17] None the less, out of the thickets of definition there has undoubtedly emerged a broad consensus about the kinds of processes that the term signals in its modern usage.[18] Revolution means change – not, as the classical and premodern usage had it, reversion to an earlier state.[19] The change is substantial, rapid and violent (although all these qualifications are elastic: Johnson's lucid analysis lays central stress on violence, but also on the fact that 'many revolutions have been accomplished without blood flowing in the gutters'). And finally, the change is located in a discrete political power system: in modern terms, a state. This is clear in the useful 'morphological' characterisation offered by Stanislav Andreski – not unlike the 'marks' of revolution sketched in this volume (Chapter 14) by Tom Garvin:

1. an overthrow of the government from within the state;
2. a replacement of the old ruling elite by the new which has emerged inside the state;
3. mass actions, involving violence or the threat thereof;
4. a transformation of the social system.[20]

Indeed the insistence (notably in the work of Theda Skocpol) that 'the central feature of every true revolution was the transformation of a state', has been the most significant feature of revolutionary studies in the late twentieth century.[21]

From this perspective we can see why Ireland does not feature in the litany of 'modern revolutions': under the Union, Ireland was not a state, but a peripheral part of the United Kingdom. Its leading 'revolutionaries' were principally if not exclusively 'separatists', their transformative vision constructed in negative terms – whether the political 'breaking the connection', or the cultural 'de-Anglicisation'. Their struggle could only be categorised as a revolution in the premodern sense – reversion to an older order of things; in the modern sense it was (as Andreski amongst others insists of the American 'revolution') a 'war of national independence', or 'liberation'. (In his later wide-angle work on *European Revolutions* (1993), Charles Tilly proposed that 'in squinting retrospect, the history of relations between Ireland and England looks like one long nationalist revolution'.[22]) The strong tendency in recent cultural studies to analyse Ireland's relationship with Britain in colonial terms reinforces this view.[23]

So we should not be surprised to find the Irish nationalist movement conforming to the general nineteenth-century nationalist pattern of middle-class orientation, and more or less deep antagonism towards 'social revolutionary' ideas such as class conflict. In the 35 years since Patrick Lynch wrote his path-breaking essay on 'The Social Revolution that Never Was', historians have hammered home his point about the unrevolutionary outlook not only of Sinn Féin but also of the Irish Republican Brotherhood (which started life, it may be recalled, as the Irish Revolutionary Brotherhood).[24] In Irish nationalist terms, 'revolutionary' equalled 'republican', and what 'republicanism' meant was above all 'physical force' – the violent termination of British sovereignty over Ireland. In so far as it represented a future political and social structure, the republic was, as David Fitzpatrick made clear, veiled in an optimistic miasma. After its attempt to promulgate a model republican constitution in the 1860s, the Fenian movement had kept quiet about the substance of independence. And when Sinn Féin was reconstituted in 1917 around a republican programme, it specifically (if bafflingly) allowed that after achieving republican status the Irish people could choose the 'form of government', as if this were a mere detail. Irish republicans have often been labelled 'doctrinaires', but the doctrine offered only the slenderest blueprint for change.

The exception to this conservative nationalism was of course the labour movement. Its leadership before 1916 was working-class, energetic, vocal and unambiguously revolutionary – whether in the syndicalist or the Marxist mode. James Connolly's reputation may have been inflated, but he gave the working class an undeniably radical voice (see Chapter 13). Thanks to the colourful if quirky presence of Countess Markiewicz it also became plausibly feminist. At the height of the Dublin lockout in 1913 there seemed (certainly in the eyes of the bourgeoisie) to be a possibility of 'real' revolution. Ultimately, however, its commitment to class struggle and its internationalism pushed socialism to the margins of Irish political action: in the mainstream, 'Catholicism acted as a cultural vaccine against such ideas.'[25] Moreover Ireland was a peasant society, and peasants have generally not been sable for social revolution – only for 'national liberation'. Though Karl Marx asserted the possibility of an Irish agrarian revolution to aid 'the revolutionary struggle of the English proletariat', Friedrich Engels was sceptical. In 1869 he sardonically observed that 'Ireland still remains the Holy Isle whose aspirations must on no account be mixed with the profane class struggles of the rest of the sinful world.'[26] Whether Connolly himself accepted this has never been entirely clear: his own formulations of the relationship between socialism and nationalism suggest either misunderstanding or self-deception. Until 1915 at least he spoke like a 24-carat Marxist revolutionary, but his commitment to nationalist-led insurrection in 1916 consigned his followers to an auxiliary role in the subsequent nationalist movement.[27]

The defining moment was Labour's decision to stand aside in the 1918 election, and its modest reward in the Democratic Programme declared by Dáil Éireann in January 1919. Thomas Johnson's original draft was shorn of its socialist elements, and although Lynch suggested that the revised draft of the declaration 'remained a radical affirmation of social democratic principles', no specifically socialist points or any hint of class conflict survived Sean T. O'Kelly's surgery. Even Pearse's own assertion (in the *Sovereign People* of 1915) that 'no private right to property is good against the public right of the nation' was excised, along with Johnson's more specific undertaking to nationalise resources that were 'wrongfully used'.[28] All that survived was a generalised commitment to welfare, safely couched in Pearsean nationalist terms. In such terms even the autarchist Arthur Griffith might be seen as a socialist.

At grassroots level, syndicalism reappeared after the war, but in an attenuated form. Although such exotic manifestations as the 'Limerick soviet' of April 1919 were more than enough to satisfy the unionist press that Bolshevism was rampant, they remained localised and transient.[29] Even the more substantial and long-lasting transport strike (an embargo on British security force movements) was a tribute to the spirit of patriotism – and the persuasive power of the IRA – as much as to socialism, and also demonstrated the utter ruin of pre-war internationalist ideals.[30]

To explore the dimensions of the Irish revolution we need to distinguish between aims and outcomes. It is certainly possible to hold that, despite its conventional bourgeois political economy, Sinn Féin's aims were in a vital sense transformative. The changes it envisaged went beyond the transfer of state power from British to Irish hands, to the vague but potent promise of a radically altered way of life. The key to this was cultural. The recovery of the Irish language would enable the nation to find authentic ways of remodelling every aspect of life – from law through economy to architecture.[31] Sinn Féin writings (see Chapter 3) breathed a febrile belief in spiritual regeneration and the rediscovery of the nation's soul. (Other national–revolutionary movements which potently fused regressive with progressive aims, such as Zionism and Nazism, also focused at least as much on psychological as on structural transformation.) In this view, the achievement of political sovereignty was only a stage in the recovery of identity.

Measured on this kind of scale of expectations, Sinn Féin's ultimate achievements were undoubtedly disappointing. Although the ruling elite, in Andreski's formulation, was certainly replaced by a new one that had emerged within the state, the changes that came along with it were limited. Not only at the political level (with the failure to secure an all-Ireland republic), but also in the cultural sphere there was a sense of *révolution manquée* after 1922. Jeffrey Prager's contention that the 1922 Free State constitution represented a serious setback to 'cultural integration' may be over schematic, but it identifies an important issue. Still more significant perhaps was the abandonment of the single most radical innovation of the Dáil regime, the arbitration court system. Again, Mary Kotsonouris's argument (in *Retreat from Revolution*) may be overstated, but there can be no doubt that here a deeply counter-revolutionary impulse made itself felt. What Kevin O'Higgins did when he wound up the Dáil courts in 1923 was effectively to squash the utopian dreams of Gaelicism (the recovery of Brehon law) with the insistence that the British legal system was not just practical but good. This was a total reversal of Sinn Féin ideology.

Still, there has perhaps been a general tendency to exaggerate the extent of the reaction: beyond 'Thermidor' to what Fitzpatrick called 'full circle' – as if Ireland had actually reverted to the pre-war status quo.[32] John Regan's recent large-scale work on *The Irish Counter-Revolution* follows this line, though it neglects the opportunity to establish a clear and comprehensive account of the revolution that was being countered.[33] If there was a counter-revolution, it was, on this showing, fairly unideological and unsystematic. The hard-nosed pragmatism of leaders like O'Higgins and Ernest Blythe (who admittedly seem to have derived a grim *schadenfreude* from each sign of Irish incapacity) seems better described as 'realist' than 'reactionary'. Maybe, indeed, the Irish counter-revolution began in the nineteenth century with the Home Rule movement, with its emphasis on conformity with British methods and standards.

None the less, it remains plainly true that the events of the war and post-war period were felt by their proponents (and, as Phillips shows, their opponents too) to be a revolution. In this sense, at least, the categories of political science are irrelevant to lived experience. Desmond Greaves was right to maintain that whilst 'a revolution cannot be understood without the examination of its base', 'neither can it be understood without sharing the hopes, disappointments, fears and aspirations of its participants'.[34]

As Fitzpatrick says, 'a great many Irishmen behaved during the revolutionary convulsion in a manner inconceivable in 1913'[35] (even though he argues that their attitudes changed less than their behaviour). Most Sinn Féiners and Irish Volunteers certainly felt themselves to be revolutionaries – albeit perhaps for different reasons or in different ways – and the adjectival form 'revolutionary' seems – with its malleable contours – best to convey the Irish experience. Arthur Mitchell's *Revolutionary Government in Ireland* adopts a sensibly practical perspective on the state-building activities of the illegal Republic and the emergence of the new ruling elite. Without too much ado about exact definitions, he showed that the Dáil regime, for all its social conservatism, went some way to realise the Sinn Féin idea of 'achieving self-government by action and self-reliance' – a radical method with at least potentially radical implications.[36] In policy terms, though, it was 'mildly reformist within the parameters of liberal capitalism' (see Chapter 5).

The revolutionary experience can be fruitfully pursued through individual biography, and there has been a welcome if gently-paced enlargement of the field beyond the headline-grabbing trinity of Eamon de Valera, Michael Collins and Constance Markiewicz (despite Ruth Dudley Edwards's biography of Patrick Pearse, Maryann Valiulis's study of Richard Mulcahy and Richard English's of Ernie O'Malley, we still lack modern studies of Kevin O'Higgins and Arthur Griffith; and Roy Foster's 1988 remark that 'there are few worthwhile biographies for the period' remains largely valid); Tom Garvin has added a kind of collective biography in his essay on the cohorts of 'nationalist revolutionaries' from 1858 to 1928.[37] The most constructive developments have been in local and community studies, led by Fitzpatrick's pioneering work on County Clare, followed more recently by Peter Hart (Cork), Michael Farry (Sligo), Marie Coleman (Longford), and Joost Augusteijn's comparative study of five counties.[38]

The key issue raised by this research is signalled in Fitzpatrick's phrase 'some Irish people': the extent of collective mobilisation in the core revolutionary processes of guerrilla action and counter-state formation – Andreski's 'mass actions'. A powerful myth of national solidarity during the 'four glorious years' was generated by the republican campaign, and if anything, perpetuated by its equivocal and, to some, disenchanting outcome. Only when the remarkable archival material compiled by IRA leaders (and civil war opponents) Richard Mulcahy and Ernie O'Malley began to be studied did it become clear that the mobilisation was extremely uneven.[39] Though most attention has been engrossed by areas of intense republican military activity, local studies are demonstrating a complex reality, and exploring the problems involved in measuring and explaining, for instance, Hart's 'rise and fall of a revolutionary family', the Hales of Ballinadee.[40]

Augusteijn chose 'War of Independence' rather than revolution for his title, whereas Hart has followed Fitzpatrick more directly in insisting that a revolution took place. Both, however, are interested in the same process: the generation of a grouping committed to 'separatism' through violent action. Chalmers Johnson's argument that 'non-violent revolution is a contradiction in terms' finds an echo in Hart's assertion that 'What made these changes revolutionary was not just their outcomes, but also their violence.'[41] (Although Johnson's analysis of violence is more complex than Hart's.) The revolutionary process was in part a process of creating revolutionaries – individuals who embraced the time-honoured 'physical force' principle. The central chapter of English's biography of O'Malley, called 'The Revolutionary', makes this particularly clear. O'Malley dedicated himself to the Revolution (capitalised in English's text) as primarily a military task. For O'Malley and many (though not necessarily all) other active Volunteers, this may have spilled over from militarisation – the primacy of military methods – into real militarism – the primacy of military values (though this word has been rather loosely applied). When the IRA journal *An tÓglách* insisted that Volunteers 'should not allow their political activities to interfere with their military duties' it may, in one sense, have simply been making the standard liberal argument that armies should be politically neutral, and in another, sustaining its own contention that 'there was a war on' and thus a need to maximise military effectiveness. But behind all this lay a non-liberal – or even illiberal – conviction, which O'Malley plainly shared, that military values were pure, while political methods were potentially if not inevitably corrupt.

Even a less ideologically freighted form of militarisation required a high degree of commitment that was not always forthcoming, producing sharp imbalances in the activist cohort. These were both geographical and social, reflecting divisions on lines of age and gender, as well as religion, class and occupation. In 1959 Erhard Rumpf offered a pioneering statistical analysis of these variations, in which he established a broad 'east–west gradient' locating the most intense activism in the west. But while he was able to show a degree of congruence over time between the mobilisations of the land war and the republic, it was not decisive, and did not explain some substantial variations in the levels of violence between the Anglo-Irish War and the Civil War. The limitations of his data were subjected to a searching critique by David Fitzpatrick in 1978, and Peter Hart has taken this further, with more sophisticated measurement of a series of variables (such as poverty, 'rurality', agrarian dispute, police effectiveness, and so on). His finding that 'the percentage of national schools in which Irish was taught for fees in 1911 emerges as the best single predictor of republican violence out of over 100 tested variables' supports the more impressionistic arguments of some other writers, such as Conor Cruise O'Brien and Barry Coldrey. But even Hart's calculations, using a fairly selective measure of violence and crude geographical units (counties), may be open to further refinement.[42]

Almost all the individuals committed – or permitted – to use physical force were men. Although works by and about republican women (such as Kathleen Clarke's *Revolutionary Woman* and Margaret Ward's *Unmanageable Revolutionaries*) call these activists 'revolutionaries', they were clearly unable to participate in this central and perhaps defining mode of action. Thus, as Margaret Ward notes (see Chapter 11), the relentless militarisation of the republican movement after 1916 inexorably undermined Sinn Féin's hesitant early feminism.[43] Women participated through a separate organisation, which accepted an auxiliary military function – albeit one that might be categorised in some areas as a semi-combat role.[44] The charisma of Constance Markiewicz guaranteed Cumann na mBan a fairly high profile, but its ultimate achievements remain disputable. (It still lacks a full-scale history.) Margaret MacCurtain, for instance, offered the verdict that it 'effectively radicalised the women towards revolution', yet called it 'essentially conservative in its aims'.[45] And whether Cumann na mBan was designed, as some have argued, to 'compartmentalise' women as a prelude to their political marginalisation, rather than to maximise recruitment into the republican movement, still seems unclear, though Ward concludes that the end result was the reversal of such progress as the women's movement had made during the revolution.

Fitzpatrick's observation that the constitutional revolution 'masked a more far-reaching though informal religious settlement' may carry us closer than any other approach to the substance of the Irish revolution.[46] Though the rhetoric of Irish republicanism was (and remains) secular, the actual behaviour of the IRA in 1919–23 (as now) was fairly nakedly sectarian, and the same of course was true of the various loyalist militias from the UVF through to the USC. Thus the War of Independence was to some extent a religious civil war. The 'pogrom' in Belfast from 1920 to 1922 is all too well known, but recent research has found an equivalent (if smaller-scale: reflecting the greater denominational imbalance in the south) phenomenon in southern Ireland.[47] Even if we do not go the full distance with Peter Hart in characterizing the IRA campaign as systematic persecution and massacre, it is clear that the automatic identification of Protestants as actual or potential enemies of the republic had repeatedly deadly results. The logic was simple: as the West Cork flying column commander Tom Barry put it, 'We never killed a man because of his religion ... but we had to face up to facts.'[48] The most salient fact was that nearly all Protestants were unionists. An analogous argument had been made at the height of what D. P. Moran called 'the battle of two civilizations', to insist that the nationalist movement was practically, if not fundamentally, Catholic. As the residuary legatee of the Irish-Ireland movement, Sinn Féin to some degree projected this assumption. It was inevitable that the revolution would generate a settlement in which, in Fitzpatrick's words, 'the victors self-consciously embodied the religion as well as the political ideology of the majority'; in the Free State 'the new rulers blatantly identified Catholic with national values', and Northern Ireland was created precisely to defend Protestants from that process. It may indeed be that the central function of the Irish revolution was to give political embodiment to the 'devotional revolution' of the nineteenth century.

The eventual form taken by the revolution, though, was determined as much by the incumbent regime as by its revolutionary challengers. To reverse a phrase of Talcott Parsons, the obverse of the analysis of the forces tending to alter a social system is the analysis of the mechanisms by which it is maintained; 'it is impossible to study one without the other'. There is general recognition that the failure of the British state was crucial to the success of Sinn Féin. It is a commonplace, for instance, that the 'draconian' suppression of the 1916 rebellion was the catalyst in the shift of Irish public opinion from bemusement or exasperation to enthusiasm for the insurrectionists – though the mechanics of this shift are still in doubt – and equally that the use of counter-terrorist methods after 1919 destroyed the remaining legitimacy of the British state in Ireland.[49] The bottom line in this was the fact that on 15 January 1922 Michael Collins took over Dublin Castle and most of the British army's barracks for the use of his new Irish national army – an outcome that had been anathema to British governments throughout the period of the Union. The British state project in Ireland had unquestionably failed.

But the British state was not merely a negative factor in the Irish revolution. The nation-building process was profoundly influenced by British political culture. Until recently the discrediting of the 'constitutional movement' after the victory of Sinn Féin in 1918 has been reflected in a tendency to sideline if not to deplore the whole (of what Alan Ward has called the) 'constitutional tradition' in Ireland. Though the persistence of some British practices was indeed due to lack of reforming imagination, it may now be suggested that the core bundle of British values transmitted through the revolutionary process was a positive element in Ireland's emergence as a (moderately) liberal democracy.[50] One of the most vital outcomes, in the light of the incipient militarism of the republican period and the Civil War, was the decisive reassertion of civilian dominance after 1923.[51]

The decline of the British state in Ireland was thus a complex process. Its most dramatic phase was clearly the accelerated erosion if not elimination of its legitimacy after 1916, and the question of how substantial its legitimacy had been is central to the nature of the revolution. Just how public opinion shifted to the side of the republic remains (as does the opinion shift in 1916) unclear. The general assumption has been that British authority was always alien, and that the essence of the Irish revolution was anti-colonial: hence, its eventual demise was unproblematic. It is possible, however, that the legitimacy of the state in its final phase was actually increasing.

From one angle, the rapid final collapse of British government in Ireland was unlikely, because over the previous generation it had carried out an extensive programme of land reform: generally the most effective preventative measure against revolution. Typically, the creation of a landowning peasantry has been the surest bastion of conservatism. The land transfer begun in 1887 and accelerated in 1903 was seen by many observers as a revolution, since it was accompanied by a perceived shrinkage of the authority of the Anglo-Irish landowning class and a real transfer of local power.[52] But it was clearly a government-sponsored one. What did this signify from the stand-point of the state? There is persistent doubt whether the idea of 'constructive Unionism' represented a negation or an intensification of the colonial relationship between Britain and Ireland. At root, this relationship has been the subject of assertion rather than systematic analysis.[53]

The most thoughtful analysis of this issue, by Ian Lustick, has not been as widely noticed by Irish historians as it deserves. In his first comparative study of British rule in Ireland and French rule in Algeria, Lustick argued that the British state-building enterprise was of a piece with that in Wales or Scotland, but was subverted by the inconsistency of British policy and the dysfunctional effect of one of its by-products, the Protestant settler community in northern Ireland.[54] Subsequently he has elaborated a Gramscian analysis, which shifts his focus from 'state-building failure' to the nineteenth-century breakdown of a 'hegemonic conception' (a proposition regarded as inarguable) of Ireland's necessary unity with Britain.[55] Both these concepts can help to illuminate the nature of the Irish revolution – the movement for separation – by relating it to the dynamic of integration.

Lustick's argument about hegemonic breakdown admittedly rests too heavily on the premise that Home Rule in the 1880s was 'sub-stantively similar' to Repeal in the 1840s. In an important sense this is correct, since both projects were studiedly vague about Ireland's ultimate status, and proposed to start by going back to the pre-Union constitution ('Grattan's parliament'). Still, the differences between them were also significant. Not only was Home Rule specifically framed to meet British 'imperial' requirements (thus surely facilitating the paradigm shift on which Lustick focuses), but the national mobil-isation around it in the 1880s was huge and decisive. Where Repeal sank without trace, Home Rule generated an institutional structure that may justifiably be called a proto-state.[56] The political generation that grew up with 'constitutional nationalism', formed a potential rul-ing elite which (especially under the leadership of John Redmond and his heir presumptive, Tom Kettle) was increasingly closely inte-grated into the British world-view.[57] (Sadly, of course, unionists utterly failed to grasp this.) Land reform was buttressed by welfare reform – crucially the introduction of old-age pensions in 1911. Thus it may be that the process of state-formation was still continuing (however inconsistently managed) into the twentieth century; and if so, the Irish revolution was more than a 'war of independence' – it was a real 'internal war' and, to this extent, a 'real' revolution too.

Notes

1. P. H. Pearse, *Political Writings and Speeches*, ed. D. Ryan (Dublin, n.d.), p. 95.
2. W. A. Phillips, *The Revolution in Ireland, 1906–1923* (London, 1923); M. J. F. McCarthy, *The Irish Revolution*, vol. I: *The Murdering Time, from the Land League to the First Home Rule Bill* (Edinburgh, 1912).
3. See S. F. Moran, *Patrick Pearse and the Politics of Redemption* (Washington, DC, 1994), ch. 4: a psychohistorical approach whose parameters are revealed in its subtitle, 'The Mind of the Easter Rising'.
4. 'None could tell what sinister forces lurked behind the self-styled "Republic"' was one of his characteristic insinuations (see Phillips, *The Revolution*, p. 177).
5. C. Tilly, *From Mobilisation to Revolution* (Reading, MA, 1978); J. Billington, *Fire in the Minds of Men: Origins of the Revolutionary Faith* (London, 1980).
6. S. U. Larsen and O. Snoddy, '1916 – A Workingmen's Revolution?', *Social Studies*, II (1973), pp. 377–98; J. Thomas, 'Theory, Method and the Irish Revolution', *Social Studies*, IV (1974), p. 381.
7. Despite its promising title, for instance, C. Kostick's *Revolution in Ireland: Popular Militancy, 1917 to 1923* (London, 1996) is essentially a narrative account. Although it invokes 'European Revolution' at the outset, it does not offer any systematic comparative evaluation.
8. D. G. Boyce (ed.), *The Revolution in Ireland, 1879–1923* (London, 1988), pp. 2, 9–10.
9. C. D. Greaves, *Liam Mellows and the Irish Revolution* (London, 1971), p. 7.
10. S. Paseta, *Before the Revolution: Nationalism, Social Change and Ireland's Catholic Elite, 1879–1922* (Cork, 1999). These dates almost exactly fit those chosen by Boyce for the revolution itself.
11. M. Farry, *The Aftermath of Revolution: Sligo, 1921–23* (Dublin, 2000).
12. M. Laffan, *The Resurrection of Ireland: The Sinn Féin Party, 1916–1923* (Cambridge, 1999).
13. P. Bew, 'Moderate Nationalism and the Irish Revolution, 1916–1923', *Historical Journal*, 42 (1999).
14. D. Fitzpatrick, *Politics and Irish Life, 1913–1921: Provincial Experience of War and Revolution* (Dublin, 1977), p. 232. The significance of the alternative starting dates, 1913 and 1916, is not wholly clarified.
15. D. Fitzpatrick, *The Two Irelands, 1912–1939* (Oxford, 1998), p. 4.
16. D. Fitzpatrick (ed.), *Revolution? Ireland, 1917–1923* (Dublin, 1990), p. 8.
17. C. Johnson, *Revolutionary Change* (Stanford/London, 1983), p. 6.
18. For an account of this, see F. Halliday, *Revolution and World Politics* (Basingstoke, 1999), ch. 2.
19. H. Arendt, *On Revolution* (New York/London, 1963), p. 36.
20. S. Andreski, 'A Typology of Revolutions from a Morphological Viewpoint', in *Wars, Revolutions, Dictatorships* (London, 1992), p. 17.
21. T. Skocpol, *States and Social Revolutions* (Cambridge, 1979); J. Dunn, *Modern Revolutions* (Cambridge, 1989), p. xx.

22. C. Tilly, *European Revolutions, 1492–1992* (Oxford, 1993), p. 139.
23. For example, D. Lloyd, *Anomalous States* (Dublin, 1993); S. Deane, *Strange Country* (Oxford, 1997); T. Eagleton, *The Truth about the Irish* (Dublin, 1999).
24. P. Lynch, 'The Social Revolution that Never Was', in T. D. Williams (ed.), *The Irish Struggle, 1916–1926* (London, 1966); also M. Laffan, 'Labour Must Wait: Ireland's Conservative Revolution', in P. J. Corish (ed.), *Radicals, Rebels and Establishments* (Belfast, 1985), pp. 203–22.
25. T. Garvin, *Nationalist Revolutionaries in Ireland, 1858–1928* (Oxford, 1987), p. 48.
26. See N. Mansergh's pioneering study of 'The Communist International and the Irish Question', in *Ireland in the Age of Reform and Revolution* (London, 1940), pp. 81, 93.
27. See R. English, *Radicals and the Republic: Socialist Republicanism in the Irish Free State, 1925–1937* (Oxford, 1994), ch. 1; A. Mitchell, *Labour in Irish Politics, 1890–1930* (Dublin, 1974).
28. Lynch, 'Social Revolution', pp. 46–7.
29. Kostick, *Revolution in Ireland*, ch. 4; E. O'Connor, *Syndicalism in Ireland, 1917–23* (Cork, 1988); D. Fitzpatrick, 'Strikes in Ireland, 1914–21', *Saothar*, 6 (1980), pp. 26–39; also L. Thomson, 'Strikes in Galway', in Fitzpatrick (ed.), *Revolution?*, pp. 130–43.
30. C. Townshend, 'The Irish Railway Strike of 1920: Industrial Action and Civil Resistance in the Struggle for Independence', *IHS*, XXI (1979).
31. C. Townshend, 'The Meaning of Irish Freedom: Constitutionalism in the Free State', *Transactions of the Royal Historical Society*, 6th series, VIII (1998), pp. 52–7.
32. Fitzpatrick, *Politics and Irish Life*, p. 233.
33. J. Regan, *The Irish Counter-Revolution, 1921–1936* (Dublin, 1999).
34. Greaves, *Liam Mellows*, p. 29.
35. Fitzpatrick, *Politics and Irish Life*, p. 284.
36. A. Mitchell, *Revolutionary Government in Ireland: Dáil Éireann, 1919–22* (Dublin, 1995), pp. 334–5.
37. R. D. Edwards, *Patrick Pearse. The Triumph of Failure* (London, 1977); M. G. Valiulis, *Portrait of a Revolutionary: General Richard Mulcahy and the Founding of the Irish Free State* (Dublin, 1992); R. English, ' "The Inborn Hate of Things English": Ernie O'Malley and the Irish Revolution, 1916–1923', in *Past and Present*, no. 151 (May 1996); *Ernie O'Malley: IRA Intellectual* (Oxford, 1999); Garvin, *Nationalist Revolutionaries*.
38. Fitzpatrick, *Politics and Irish Life*; J. Augusteijn, *From Public Defiance to Guerrilla Warfare* (Dublin, 1996); P. Hart, *The IRA and its Enemies* (Oxford, 1998).
39. See, for instance, C. Townshend, 'The Irish Republican Army and the Development of Guerrilla Warfare, 1916–1921', *English Historical Review*, XCIV (1979).
40. Hart, *The IRA*, ch. 9.
41. P. Hart, 'The Geography of Revolution in Ireland, 1917–1923', *Past and Present*, no. 155 (May 1997), p. 142.

42. E. Rumpf, *Nationalismus und Sozialismus in Irland* (Meisenheim-am-Glan, 1959); E. Rumpf and A. Hepburn, *Nationalism and Socialism in Twentieth-Century Ireland* (Liverpool, 1977); D. Fitzpatrick, 'The Geography of Irish Nationalism, 1910–1921', *Past and Present*, no. 78 (Feb. 1978); Hart, 'Geography of Revolution', p. 170.

43. C. Coulter, *The Hidden Tradition: Feminism, Women and Nationalism in Ireland* (Cork, 1993); also M. Ward, 'Nationalism, Pacifism, Internationalism: Louie Bennett, Hanna Sheehy-Skeffington, and the Problems of Defining Feminism', in A. Bradley and M. G. Valiulis (eds), *Gender and Sexuality in Modern Ireland* (Amherst, MA, 1997), pp. 60–84; S. Benton, 'Women Disarmed: the Militarisation of Politics in Ireland, 1913–23', *Feminist Review*, 50 (1995), pp. 148–72.

44. M. Ward, 'Marginality and Militancy: Cumann na mBan, 1914–1936', in A. Morgan and B. Purdie (eds), *Ireland: Divided Nation, Divided Class* (London, 1980); A. Sheehan, 'Cumann na mBan: Policies and Activities', in Fitzpatrick (ed.), *Revolution?*, pp. 88–97.

45. M. MacCurtain, 'Women, the Vote and Revolution', in M. MacCurtain and D. Ó Corrain (eds), *Women in Irish Society* (Dublin, 1978), p. 54.

46. Fitzpatrick, *Two Irelands*, p. 3.

47. P. Hart, 'The Protestant Experience of Revolution in Southern Ireland, 1911–1926', in R. English and G. Walker (eds), *Unionism in Modern Ireland: New Perspectives on Politics and Culture* (London, 1996).

48. RTE interview, quoted in Hart, *The IRA*, p. 273.

49. C. Townshend, 'The Suppression of the Easter Rising', *Bullán*, 1 (1994), pp. 27–47; J. J. Lee, *Ireland, 1912–1985* (Cambridge, 1989), p. 29.

50. Compare Townshend, 'The Meaning of Irish Freedom'; T. Garvin, *1922: The Birth of Irish Democracy* (Dublin, 1996).

51. Garvin, *1922*; E. O'Halpin, *Defending Ireland: The Irish State and its Enemies since 1922* (Oxford, 1999).

52. P. Bull, *Land, Politics and Nationalism: A Study of the Irish Land Question* (New York, 1996); W. L. Féingold, *The Revolt of the Tenantry: The Transformation of Local Government in Ireland, 1872–1886* (Boston, MA, 1984).

53. Stephen Howe has recently provided an extended critique in *Ireland and Empire: Colonial Legacies in Irish History and Culture* (Oxford, 2000).

54. I. Lustick, *State-Building Failure in British Ireland and French Algeria* (Berkeley, CA, 1985).

55. I. Lustick, *Unsettled States, Disputed Lands: Britain and Ireland, France and Algeria, Israel and West Bank-Gaza* (Ithaca, NY, and London, 1993).

56. E. Larkin, *The Roman Catholic Church and the Creation of the Modern Irish State, 1878–1886* (Dublin, 1975); also D. W. Miller, *Church, State and Nation in Ireland, 1898–1921* (Dublin, 1973).

57. See Paseta, *Before the Revolution*; also K. Jeffery (ed.), *'An Irish Empire'? Aspects of Ireland and the British Empire* (Manchester, 1996).

2

Definition: Defining the Irish Revolution

Peter Hart

The purpose of this chapter is to examine the Irish revolution in more or less sociological or structural terms. It presents a series of propositions, based on the theory of revolutions and on recent local research, regarding the origins, nature, structure and dynamics of the revolutionary movement, process and outcomes. These are not intended to end discussion but to begin it. Debates have begun on a number of key issues concerning republicanism and the revolution: the social background and motives of the revolutionaries; the nature of violence; the radical potential of social conflict; and sectarianism north and south. However, there has been little critical consideration of equally (or more) fundamental factors such as gender and ethnicity, or of the conceptual terms of the debate itself. What do we call the events of 1916–23? Or should it be 1912–22 or 1917–21? Do these events form a unity or are they better understood discretely, as a succession of crises, rebellions and wars? Was there a revolution and if so, what kind of revolution was it?

Revolution?

General definitions of revolution are many and various. I prefer the simple, useful, and broadly inclusive model put forward by Charles Tilly (and widely endorsed in its essence by other writers):

> A revolution is a transfer of power over a state in the course of which at least two distinct blocs make incompatible claims to control the state, and some significant portion of the population subject to the state's jurisdiction acquiesces

in the claims of each bloc. A full revolutionary sequence thus runs from a sundering of sovereignty and hegemony through a period of struggle to reestablishment of sovereignty and hegemony under new management. We can usefully distinguish between revolutionary situations and outcomes. A revolutionary *situation* consists of an open division of sovereignty, while a revolutionary *outcome* entails a definitive transfer of power.[1]

I would put equal emphasis on the revolutionary struggle or *process* as a component of analysis.

The crucial element here is Tilly's concept of 'multiple sovereignty', whereby incompatible claims on the state and popular loyalty acquire powerful support and split the polity.[2] Situations that do not meet this definition are not revolutionary; revolutionary outcomes that do not arise from such circumstances are not 'full-fledged revolutions'. This excludes social movements, rebellions, and coups d'état as such from the definition (although in practice, the distinctions are often blurred).

By these criteria the United Irishmen of the late 1790s constituted a revolutionary movement and the 1798 rebellion may have created a genuinely revolutionary situation – although only marginally so, given the poor record of the rebels and the weakness of their support at a national level. However, since their efforts fell far short of shifting those in power we cannot speak of a revolution as such occurring. The Land War of 1879–82 accompanied the rise and fall of a powerful social movement – the Land League – but neither it, nor the crisis it produced, nor its resolution could be deemed revolutionary in the absence of a serious threat to the state. The Easter Rising was the product of a revolutionary movement (albeit a very small one), but it produced neither a situation nor an outcome of a revolutionary nature as it lacked national strength or support.

From the above follows my first proposition: that the events surrounding southern Irish independence and northern exclusion constitute the only real revolution in modern Irish history. The legitimacy and existence of the British state was directly and forcibly challenged; this challenge was supported by a large proportion of the Irish population; and sovereignty in the 26 counties was ultimately transferred to a new polity and government. This is not the same as saying the rebels were victorious, as the revolutionary outcomes were not the ones envisioned – as is most often the case.

Nevertheless, these events have never been numbered among the revolutions worthy of comparative study, great or small, nor is the term 'Irish revolution' in general or scholarly use. Charles Tilly does not call it such in his survey of Europe, for example. And contrary to the wishful thinking of some of its partisans and chroniclers, the republican campaign did not serve as a model for rebels elsewhere – despite its impressive innovations – as there was no theory or text for them to study. So the honour of inventing modern revolutionary warfare goes to Lenin and Mao, not to Michael Collins and Éamon de Valera.

When did this Irish revolution begin and end? While it might be useful in some respects to speak of a revolutionary decade falling more or less between 1912 and 1922, I do not think the Home Rule crisis of 1912–14 was even potentially revolutionary. Ulster's unionists did raise an army and contemplated a local provisional government but neither was intended to overthrow the existing state. Quite the opposite. Even if fighting had broken out, in so far as it pitted the UVF against the nationalist Volunteers, it would have been little more revolutionary than the standard Belfast riot. If the UVF had faced the RIC or the British army in combat, we could speak of a local rebellion, but not a revolution proper.[3] Only if matters had escalated into either a war of separation from both Britain and Ireland, or a UK-wide Conservative– Liberal power struggle, would a true state crisis have been born.

It was the Great War that added the causal momentum to start the revolutionary clock ticking with the 1916 Rising. It is true that the Easter Rising itself was not a revolution, and that a situation of genuine multiple sovereignty did not arise until early 1920, when real power and legitimacy began to shift to the Dáil ministries while the IRA was defeating the old RIC. This revolutionary moment could be shifted back a year to the formation of the putatively sovereign Dáil by the majority of Irish MPs, but no earlier. On the other hand, in 1916 we do see a preliminary sketch of the revolution to be, complete with a claim to exclusive sovereignty for the insurgent government and army. More importantly, the continuous history of the republican movement, its leadership and ideology, and of revolutionary violence, begins here. This, and not 1912, is Ireland's 1789 or 1917, the GPO its Bastille or Winter Palace.[4]

If the revolution started in 1916, when did it end? Not with the Truce or Treaty of 1921, nor with the formal establishment of a sovereign Free State and self-governing Northern Ireland in 1922. What began in 1916 did not come to a close until the republican armed struggle, having lost most of its popular support, gave up its attempt to dispute the existence of the southern state in the spring of 1923. Only then was the era of multiple sovereignty clearly over.

Why was there a revolution?

Revolutions are never monocausal. A conjunction of necessary conditions is required to break an existing state and make a new one.[5]

Theorists mostly agree on three fundamentals: a (fiscally, politically, or militarily) weakened state, alienated or divided elites, and the effective mobilisation of a challenging movement or coalition with widespread popular support. Different studies emphasise different factors but, generally speaking, all are necessary and none are sufficient.

Rebellions are usually doomed by the odds against them. Governments simply wield too much power to lose. In the Irish case, the failure to defeat the republican movement has been convincingly analysed by Charles Townshend and Eunan O'Halpin in particular.[6] A liberal regime in Dublin Castle, and an Irish Party equally distracted by war, left the Irish Republican Brotherhood free to produce the Rising, and the RIC and DMP incapable of preventing it. From 1916 to 1920 followed the oft-described sequence of conciliation and coercion, undermining the police forces and empowering the republican militant tendency. The end result, in 1920–21, was the ceding to the IRA of territory and initiative, which could only be regained by a politically costly military campaign.

The government's failure was also political, in that it alienated potentially supportive elites and granted popular legitimacy to its enemies. Crucial in this regard was its maladroit handling of the Rising, of Home Rule, and of conscription. These three issues destroyed the moderate IPP, drove the AFIL (All For Ireland League) and other dissidents behind Sinn Féin, and gave the latter command of the nationalist electorate. Divided and radicalised along with its flock, the Catholic Church was likewise lost as a counter-revolutionary bulwark. Much of its personnel was in the separatist camp by 1919.

Finally, the Lloyd George administrations of 1916–22 also faced two important externally imposed political constraints. The first was the Great War and its settlement, which imposed conflicting priorities and bad policy, and exhausted nationalist patience. The second was British public opinion, reinforced by that of other nations, especially the United States, which wanted rid of the problem but would not tolerate ruthless repression. Early mistakes could not be 'fixed' by fighting to win the ensuing guerrilla war.

The state provided the revolutionaries with a unique opportunity but they still needed strong leadership, a powerful organisation, and substantial resources to mount their challenge. All were available for mobilisation in early twentieth-century Ireland. Untapped cadres were to be found in the activist and articulate cultural and dissident sectors of nationalism populated by well-educated and pre-politicised young patriots. Also important were the swelling tributaries of labour unionism. Women were recruited alongside men for the first time in modern Irish history, providing a huge new source of organisational energy. The Easter Rising itself was crucial for transforming many of its participants into an energetic vanguard, and for inspiring other young people to follow their example. They in turn were able to build a sophisticated political machine based on the familiar model and experience of the IPP and its auxiliaries. The guerrilla fringe could tap deep traditional and communal wells of solidarity and resistance. The movement as a whole depended financially on the new wartime wealth of farmers and merchants, and on well-established and well organised emigrant communities in the United States.

Most of these conditions for republican success disappeared in 1922. The apparent opportunity provided by a governmental vacuum and an initially weak successor regime were offset by the Provisional Government's majority support – including from Labour and the Catholic Church – and its lack of constraints or distractions in prosecuting its war. Mobilising for such a fight was far more problematic as the revolutionaries' opponents could claim the same nationalist legitimacy in addition to that inherent in an elected government.

The revolutionary movement

A successful revolution required as broad a movement as possible, accommodated within a variety of specialised organisations: political (Sinn Féin), governmental (the Dáil, its departments, and Sinn Féin-controlled local councils), paramilitary (Irish Volunteers, later the IRA), fraternal/conspiratorial (Irish Republican Brotherhood), boys' (Fianna Éireann) and women's (Cumann na mBan). American and British leagues (the Friends of Irish Freedom; the Irish Self-Determination League) were important. Also, while unions, trades councils, and the Labour Party were not part of the movement proper, the members of the Irish Transport and General Workers Union in particular were often perceived as fellow-travellers, and many candidates in local elections in 1920 ran under both the Sinn Féin and Labour banners. Mention should also be made of the role of the socialist Irish Citizen Army in 1916 as an important part of the original revolutionary coalition.

The movement was male-dominated but far from gender exclusive. In a completely unprecedented wave of inclusion and participation in mainstream politics, women became TDs, cabinet ministers, party officers and activists, and hunger strikers (the latter role having been pioneered by suffragettes). For the first time outside the local arena they were also a potentially crucial electoral constituency. Female TDs formed a key anti-Treaty bloc, and women formed a similarly vital part of Sinn Féin and its public support in 1922 and 1923. Even in 1918, there is reason to believe that Sinn Féin's massive success was due in large part to its enormous advantage in claiming first-time female voters. The IRA and IRB were exclusively male, but the guerrillas required a constant support network of women, organised or active in their own homes, to survive. Revolutionary republicanism is probably the most female-dependent major movement in modern Irish history.

The two most important developments – and analytical issues – here are the evolution of Sinn Féin into a hegemonic nationalist popular front with a republican agenda, and the emergence of the IRA as a guerrilla army. How did the small band of defeated and unrepresentative Easter rebels capture their host organisations – Sinn Féin and the Volunteers – and turn them into successful revolutionary institutions?

The rise of Sinn Féin after the Easter Rising has never seemed especially mysterious. A clear precedent had been established in the nationalist reformation of 1879–82. The geography of its electoral fortunes and membership in large part follow those of its predecessor.[7] Sinn Féin had numerous advantages, including a dynamic and efficient organisation and a multitude of political opportunities afforded by disastrous British policies. The causes of the IPP's rapid decline are equally numerous and well rehearsed, ranging from an exhausted leadership to the countervailing success of parliamentary Unionism. There is thus a retrospective air of inevitability or irresistibility about the extraordinary republican political performance in 1917–18. This achievement required the work and commitment of numerous activists, but the shape and completeness of this political shift, with one monopoly replacing another, suggests it was prepatterned and even determined by the underlying structure and culture of nationalist politics.

Two basic aspects of the phenomenon seem clear. First, Sinn Féin (like the IPP) was a coalition; a flag of convenience as well as of conviction for a spectrum of groups and tendencies. These include old Sinn Féin, the Liberty League, the Volunteers, the IRB, agrarian factions and interests, organised labour, feminists, anti-partitionists, former members of the AFIL and – unofficially – the Gaelic League.[8] It was also a coalition of urban, suburban and rural interests, landed and landless, propertied and unpropertied, farmers and agricultural labourers, shopkeepers and shop assistants. This omnibus 'Sinn Féin' flew a republican flag but it could also mean simple self-government; political and social reform; an end to corruption and profiteering; a voice for youth and women; an alternative to the IPP; a hard line against partition; a prophylactic against conscription; land for the landless; or Gaelicisation.

Secondly, whatever the diversity within the party, its leadership was dominated (when it counted) by republicans who did manage to build a substantial and enduring republican constituency, as the 1920, 1922 and 1923 elections showed. That is to say, a large, enduring and geographically coherent bloc of voters defined themselves against the alternatives of home rule or free state and supported the republic through the Tan and Civil Wars. Thus, although republican cadres built a familiar party monolith on the ruins of the old in 1917–18, they also created within it a new and rigid ideological formation which would ultimately destroy its structural integrity.

The emergence of the IRA as a mature guerrilla force in 1920 was the product of the often piecemeal and gradual reorganisation and radicalisation of the Volunteers.[9] However, these processes do not fully explain the 1920 upheaval any more than they explain that of 1916. In fact, the IRA also grew out of an internal political struggle – beginning in 1916 – to transform the Volunteers into a revolutionary institution in the spirit of Patrick Pearse and Tom Clarke. The Easter Rising had itself been the product of an IRB conspiracy to involve the non-republican and non-revolutionary Irish Volunteers in a separatist rebellion. In the event, only a fraction of the organisation was involved, many of whom were already IRB members.

From early 1917 on, the same process was repeated on a much greater scale within the reconstituted Volunteers. The rejuvenated IRB was once again in the vanguard, but now it could count on a wider radical audience inspired by the Rising. This militant tendency had its agenda – a second round soon – and its own arms, as well as the will to use them, regardless of orders or discipline. Its aims were two-fold: an external campaign of direct action against the state to force a confrontation, and an internal battle to overcome (in Michael Collins' words) 'the forces of moderation'. Both were achieved, against considerable opposition. The result was the winter offensive begun in January 1920, the long-awaited second rising that started the escalatory ball rolling. Armed violence was not merely a symptom of state oppression or political stalemate. It was willed into being, a labour of love.

Thus was born the IRA as a distinct entity, no longer the Volunteers as a public mass movement but instead a much reduced fusion of the IRB and the Volunteers.[10] As Adjutant-General and Director of Organisation of the Volunteers and master of the Supreme Council of the IRB, Michael Collins acted as midwife to this new creation. The creature turned against him in late 1921 and 1922, relaunching the internal struggle for a third time. Once again, a militant minority (this time including most of the veterans of the Tan War) took control of the organisation and weeded out the moderate majority (itself partly a recent product of post-Truce popularity) preparatory to round three of patriotic combat.

The revolutionary process

The revolution began and ended with violence, the product of three interwoven struggles. The first of these was the campaign to overthrow the British state, begun with the Rising and resumed in earnest in 1919. In both cases, the rebels were the aggressors. In 1916 the conspirators within the IRB launched a long-planned surprise attack without provocation. Between 1917 and 1919, the IRA was responsible for over two-thirds of total casualties, and the 1920 uprising pushed this to over three-quarters of shootings. In other words (in terms of armed violence), the rebels started it. However, as in 1916, the 1920 offensive provoked counter-escalation. Government and loyalist forces rose to the challenge, outpacing guerrilla violence over the spring and summer of 1920. This in turn stimulated the republicans to yet greater efforts, so that the IRA's contribution to the casualty lists thereafter held up at slightly over 50 per cent until the Truce. At each escalatory step, violence intended to suppress an enemy rebounded to produce the opposite effect.

Well before this point the cycle of reprisals had acquired a logic and drive all of its own, separate from any immediate military context. Proof of this can be found in the IRA's return to the gun in the first six months of 1922, particularly in the southern provinces. While timing might suggest a 'heightening of tension' progressing toward the outbreak of the Civil War, in fact the great majority of its victims had nothing to do with the Treaty dispute or the establishment of a Free State. They were, rather, the same targets the rebels had been pursuing the previous year: policemen, soldiers and their retired or demobilised comrades, suspected informers and collaborators, and occasionally Protestants in general. Often their alleged crimes had occurred a year or more earlier. Very rarely did the IRA shoot its nationalist political enemies.

This pattern of victimisation shows that revolutionary violence was more than a military competition. In fact by 1921 both the IRA and Crown forces were shooting civilians more often than they shot each other. Unorganised or informal violence was flourishing as well, particularly in Belfast. The potentially heroic 'real war' of ambushes and raids was being overtaken by another reality.

What the second, sustained, rising of 1920 triggered was not just a countervailing state response but also a new ethnic and communal conflict: in effect, a spin-off civil war. Two lines of ethnic division are important here, helping to channel violence towards particular target groups. The first was between the Catholic/nationalist population and the non-Irish forces sent in to combat the insurrection: the ex-soldiers of the Black and Tans, the ex-officers of the RIC's new Auxiliary Division, and the British troops on counter-insurgency duty. These men tended to see most or all Catholics as a racially stereotyped collective enemy, and were in turn viewed as alien invaders, and their actions as brutal and illegitimate. Mutually reinforcing and dehumanising images lowered the threshold of violence, making killing much easier. For a member of the Crown forces seeking a target, almost any young Catholic man might do. For guerrillas, the same could be true of anyone in uniform – or anyone identified with them.

This latter category included, above all, southern Protestants – instinctively identified by many republicans as 'loyalists' in the manner of their northern co-religionists, and targeted with rising vigour by the IRA from the summer of 1920 onwards. Also coming under occasional attack at this time were Ulster Protestants, who saw the republican guerrilla campaign as an invasion of 'their' territory, where they formed the majority. Loyalist activists responded by forming vigilante groups, which soon acquired official status as the Ulster Special Constabulary. These men spearheaded the waves of indiscriminate anti-Catholic violence, which began in July 1920 and continued for two years. This sectarian onslaught was part of an Ulster unionist counter-revolution, whose gunmen operated almost exclusively as ethnic cleansers and avengers. Their activities have yet to be examined in detail: a vital but unenviable task for some future researcher.

The revolution was thus a power struggle, not just between republicans and the United Kingdom, but also between and within communities. Both north and south, this violence was primarily directed at minority groups with the aim of uprooting, expelling, or suppressing perceived enemies within. In the six north-eastern counties this meant that Catholics bore the brunt of the conflict. In the remaining 26 counties, the main target group was the Protestant minority, followed by ex-soldiers, tinkers and tramps, and others seen as social deviants. The forces of the Free State were also intent on removing political deviants, whether strikers or agrarian agitators. Throughout Ireland, political mobilisation, guerrilla warfare, and state repression radicalised all kinds of communal boundaries, leaving those outside the local majority vulnerable to victimisation. Despite the aggression it unleashed, the mentality that lay behind this process was essentially defensive, whether the actors were nationalist, republican, unionist or loyalist. Everywhere, the desire was to impose unity and uniformity on one's 'own people' and to establish or maintain control of territory seen as 'ours'.

It was this communal violence that produced the greatest social change to result from the revolution: the displacement of minority populations. Thousands of northern Catholics and southern Protestants – and considerable numbers of political or social undesirables of other sorts – became temporary or permanent refugees. In the south, a third of the Protestant population in 1911 was gone by 1926. As with loyalist violence, no proper study of Catholic displacement in Belfast and adjacent areas has yet been undertaken.

The third arena of struggle was the revolutionary coalition and nationalist community itself: the site of the Civil War of 1922–3. The question of who was on what side was decided at many different levels, for many different reasons, personal as well as political. Even 'sides' were unclear prior to July 1922, as both pro- and anti-Treaty forces were divided and factionalised.[11] The conflict was not simply the result of decisions made at that time, potentially avoidable if key people had acted differently. Nor do details of personnel matter greatly in structural terms. What was more or less inevitable, given the prior development of republicanism within the IRA and the nationalist polity, was a violent defence of the Republic and of the principles of 1916 by a self-consciously militant minority. Such a response was what had driven the revolutionary process in 1916 and again in 1917. In the ideological terms set by the leaders and circumstances of 1916, the defence of the Four Courts and the anti-Treaty 'Munster republic' was an end in itself, and the transformation of the structure of nationalism meant it would be endorsed by a large section of public opinion.

The revolution and its violence was thus constituted out of three overlapping struggles: anti-British, communal and intranationalist. All three were built into the structure of events. We cannot and should not separate out the anti-British element as if it was the whole, or the 'real' revolution; the consequences and casualties arising from other dynamics were too great. Nor can we draw convenient chronological or geographical lines between them.

The fight over the control and direction of the revolutionary movement runs through the whole of the period. It was one of the main forces driving the revolutionary process. The Easter Rising, the sporadic militant violence of 1917–19 and the creation of the IRA, the Treaty split and the Civil War: none can be properly explained without taking the inner battles into account. The violent character of the movement was inherent in the republican will to revolution. The sectarian division in Irish politics and society and the revolution's central organising principle of nationalist/Catholic ethnicity (along with the role of Protestantism in unionism) inevitably structured the revolution north and south. The violence of 1916 catalysed a new movement. The rise of republicanism meant more violence; this produced official and loyalist reactions in kind; the resulting escalation was significantly ethnic and sectarian in nature.

What sort of revolution?

Not only did the Irish revolution not bring social transformation, there was no socially revolutionary situation in Ireland even in prospect. The republican movement itself had no serious social agenda and was not class-based. Its activists and membership were drawn from a wide variety of backgrounds, forming a predominantly anti-socialist and cross-class coalition, including much of organised labour in the south. Nor did the new Free State – whose establishment was backed by the Labour Party – offer any adjustment to property or labour relations. If the land question had remained unsettled, events might well have taken another turn, but most farmers owned their farms by 1922 (see Chapter 13). Ulster unionism was similarly broad-based and even more conservative and dominated by local elites.

Ireland did share in the international rise in working-class power driven by wartime inflation and shortages. An uncommon level of violence accompanied the many strikes and disputes of the period but organised labour never contemplated an overthrow of the state, except in so far as it supported Sinn Féin in doing so. The few socialists who did think along these lines had neither the numbers nor the influence to do much about it. There was no split in any Irish elite in this regard, nor was there any attempted factional or rank-and-file insurgency within unions or the Labour Party. No workers' militia was formed to replace James Connolly's Citizen Army. Judging by the social background of anti-Treaty republicans and the geography of their violence, the Civil War did not represent an uprising of the poor or dispossessed as is sometimes alleged. The social violence that did occur in the revolutionary years, from sabotage to murder, was as much a by-product of the availability of guns and the absence of a normal police force as of radicalisation. This is not to say that nothing happened in terms of social unrest, or that nothing important happened, but rather that nothing revolutionary happened.[12]

The revolution did not produce an institutional upheaval either, though parts of the *ancien régime* system did crumble or collapse and had to be reconstructed: the police, the judicial system, local government finances. On the other hand there was no uprooting of elites, or purging or forced politicisation of the state on the scale of France after 1789, Russia after 1917 or Algeria after 1962. Much of the civil service remained intact along with its previous ideals and methods. A new political system was introduced, but its differences from the British model were matters of detail rather than principle. What was revolutionary was that Irish people had fought for and won their sovereignty (minor symbolic matters aside). From 1922 on, government in the south would be self-determined.

It was a nationalist revolution, of course, but not simply that. Irish revolutionaries were nationalists, just as unionist counter-revolutionaries were anti-nationalist. But many nationalists were opposed to Sinn Féin and the IRA even before the Treaty split. So while in comparative terms the revolutionary movement was clearly nationalist, in Irish terms it would be more precisely described as republican. Moreover, while the revolutionary movement was a genuinely popular phenomenon, it was not truly 'national'. Unlike the United Irishmen, the Yugoslav communist resistance, the Palestine Liberation Organisation or the African National Congress, republicanism was effectively a monoculture drawn overwhelmingly from the Catholic majority and asserting a separatist and exclusive cultural identity.

Can we then describe the Irish revolution as a whole as 'ethnic' in direction, structure, or outcome? In many ways, yes. Much of its violence (including state violence) was organised along ethnic lines, as were its successor states. The fact of partition, and its openly sectarian border, is evidence of the importance of ethnic identity to its outcome. Equally significant was the displacement of Catholic and Protestant minorities. Nevertheless, we should still be careful in using ethnic categorisations as they easily slip from analytical to pejorative labels. The term 'ethnic' applies to all 'sides' and it is not a fair description of the revolutionaries' ideology or motives. Republican organisations were officially non-sectarian and this had an important part in damping down southern ethnic violence, even though the IRA were its main practitioners. And crucially, neither republicans nor unionists held the goal of an ethnically purified homeland by exclusion or forced assimilation.

Was the revolution democratic or anti-democratic? Its constitutional outcome can be said to have been freely ratified by majorities on both sides of the border in elections in 1921, 1922 and 1923. Partition did not reflect the wishes of the nationalist majority in Ireland but it did reflect the priorities of those in the 26 Free State counties. When offered the option of continued conflict and attempted coercion of northern unionists, neither nationalist voters nor their representatives supported a continued revolution on either side of the border. Even more to the point perhaps, when voters, interest groups and politicians in the south had a chance to raise the issue in late 1921 and 1922 they very rarely did so. Beyond simple majoritarianism, however, the Northern Ireland Government and the Unionist Party certainly failed the democratic test in their sectarianism and drive for one-party rule.

Were the revolutionaries themselves undemocratic in their attitudes or behaviour? Perhaps the best description is Richard English's: they had 'a complicated relationship with democracy'.[13] This captures well the ambivalence and tension between the two republican concepts of sovereignty – of 'the people' (expressed politically in elections) and of 'the nation' (revealed historically and spiritually in heroic rebellions). They were willing to act without an electoral mandate, as in 1916 and 1922, but only in order to uphold the rights of the nation. There was no fascist or communist-style dismissal of electoral democracy, nor was the Republic ever envisioned as otherwise. Republicans never sought to rig or suppress an election or to seize power without the backing of one. Sinn Féin's electoral trickery and intimidation was no greater than the IPP's and was never enough to sway an election result. A republican coup d'état was never seriously contemplated in 1922. Even British politicians were ultimately off-limits for assassination (with the singular case of Henry Wilson excepted). It can also be said that the 'revolutionary moment' of multiple sovereignty was enabled by electoral victory in 1918, and reinforced by further success in local elections in 1920. Sinn Féin's rhetoric and its official platform before and during the first election made its revolutionary intentions plain, so it cannot reasonably be argued that voters were seriously misled, however mixed voters' motives may have been.

Nevertheless, leaving more subjective, ethical or political issues aside, in structural terms it can still be argued that paramilitary and state violence only succeeded in early twentieth-century Ireland when it was used to achieve goals which received a local popular mandate: Irish independence and northern exclusion. Thus Free State repression succeeded where Britain's had failed and the republican resistance collapsed. Much the same tactics were used on both sides as had been employed in 1920–1, but with the opposite results. In the earlier period the guerrillas retained strong popular backing or acquiescence; in 1922–3 it was the forces of the state who held that advantage.

We cannot push this line of argument too far, however. Organised violence is inherently coercive and traumatic and therefore subversive of rational decision-making and political choice. All sides used force to suppress or eliminate opponents, whether constituted by allegiance, opinion or identity. Violence did not gain a hearing for moderation. Moderation was for traitors or spies; and those suspected of 'moderation', whether nationalist or unionist, were liable to have their windows broken, their doors kicked in, their houses burned down. Neither the republic, the Free State nor Northern Ireland was defended by moderate men or means.

A new revolutionary history

All of these propositions are debatable and I hope they will be challenged. The Irish revolution needs to be reconceptualised and to have all the myriad assumptions underlying its standard narratives interrogated. Gender, class, community, elites and masses, religion and ethnicity, the nature of violence and power, periodisation and geography: all need to be explored without compartmentalisation. Violence cannot be satisfactorily understood as a straightforward matter of strategy and tactics. The gender of the revolutionary movement cannot be fully analysed by just adding women to the narrative or by compiling female activist biographies, valuable though these are. Ethnic difference existed beyond the borders of Ulster: it was a constitutive element of nationalism, republicanism and unionism throughout the island. Class was reflected in all mobilisations and coalitions, not just those of land and labour. The IRA, the IRB and Sinn Féin were active throughout the United Kingdom, not just in Ireland. Nor were they just political or military organisations. They were communal entities as well, and responded to local loyalties and drives at least as much as to ideology or orders from above. And it is questionable to what extent the so-called revolutionary 'elite' actually displaced pre-existing social, institutional, bureaucratic and even political elites.

Perhaps most importantly, the revolution needs to be envisioned as a chronological, spatial and thematic unity. The period is commonly divided into the discrete units of the Easter Rising, the Tan War and the Civil War. But what of the months and years lying between these episodes? What of the politics and violence that does not fit this framework, that had different chronologies? Protestants in Cork and Catholics in Belfast, for example, had a very different sense of when the conflict began and ended. How can the 'wars' be explained without reference to their experiences? Similarly, we should not write partitionist histories whereby events north and south are treated independently even before the boundary was drawn. This convention eliminates ethnic conflict and counter-revolution from the 'Irish' narrative of (normal) national liberation and democracy while reducing the 'northern' narrative to a matter of (abnormal) sectarianism.

A new revolutionary history can be built on two great foundations. The first is that offered by the truly extraordinary volume and range of relevant sources. Newspapers, census returns, interviews, memoirs, personal papers, church records, official and organisational documents can be brought to bear on any factual or analytical problem. When nearly every activist and victim can be named, placed and profiled, both macro- and micro-studies can be carried out with great precision. Vast slabs of data can be assembled. Hundreds of social and political variables can be mapped, tracked over time, counted, correlated and regressed.[14] Networks and events can be reconstructed and the progress of the revolution followed, townland by townland, street by street, house by house.[15] Practically the only limit to inquiry is that set by the historian's imagination.

The second foundation is comparative and theoretical. Irish events helped to inaugurate an era of mass movements, citizens' revolts and guerrilla wars of liberation. From Palestine to Nicaragua, these upheavals have been studied and their place in the history and sociology of revolutions argued. Students of the Irish revolution can use these ideas to generate new questions and answers and to engage a broader debate, which would also give Ireland a place in the analytical canon. The Irish revolutionary movement of 1916–23 can lay claim to great originality – and deep comparative interest. Sinn Féin and the Irish Republican Army were the first organisations in the modern world to use a mass political front to build a parallel underground state (see Chapter 5) coupled with sophisticated guerrilla and international propaganda campaigns (see Chapter 6). The accompanying complex of ethnicity, masculinity, violence and state-building prefigured many later such conflicts. The intimacy and precision with which we are able to reconstruct these processes and experiences makes Ireland one of the best historical laboratories in which to study revolution.

Notes

1. C. Tilly, *Popular Contention in Great Britain, 1758–1834* (Cambridge, MA, 1995), p. 237. I have quoted his most recent statements on the subject. For a much fuller analysis, see his *From Mobilisation to Revolution* (Reading, MA, 1978).
2. C. Tilly, *European Revolutions, 1492–1992* (Oxford, 1993), pp. 5–15.
3. For such counterfactual scenarios, see A. Jackson, 'British Ireland: What if Home Rule had Been Enacted in 1912', in N. Ferguson (ed.), *Virtual History* (London, 1997). For a contrary argument that Ulster unionism constituted a second revolutionary movement, see D. Fitzpatrick, *The Two Irelands, 1910–1939* (Oxford, 1998).
4. Not in every sense, of course: 1789 and 1917 saw great shifts in power and authority – 1916 did not.
5. T. Skocpol's is the classic analysis: *States and Social Revolutions* (Cambridge, MA, 1979). See also the more recent work of J. Goldstone, especially *Revolution and Rebellion in the Early Modern World* (Berkeley, CA, 1991); and T. Wickham-Crowley, especially *Guerrillas and Revolution in Latin America* (New York, 1992).
6. See especially C. Townshend, *The British Campaign in Ireland, 1919–1921* (Oxford, 1975); and E. O'Halpin, *The Decline of the Union* (Dublin, 1987).
7. See D. Fitzpatrick, 'The Geography of Irish Nationalism, 1910–1921', *Past and Present*, no. 78 (Feb. 1978); T. Garvin, *The Evolution of Irish Nationalist Politics* (Dublin, 1981); P. Hart, 'The Geography of Revolution in Ireland, 1917–1923', *Past and Present*, no. 155 (May 1997).
8. See M. Laffan, *The Resurrection of Ireland* (Cambridge, 1999).
9. See C. Townshend, 'The Irish Republican Army and the Development of Guerrilla Warfare, 1916–1921', *English Historical Review* (Apr. 1979); J. Augusteijn, *From Public Defiance to Guerrilla Warfare* (Dublin, 1996).
10. See Peter Hart, *The IRA and its Enemies* (Oxford, 1998), for a description of this process in Cork.
11. See J. Regan, *The Irish Counter-Revolution, 1921–1936* (Dublin, 1999).

12. This is a much-discussed issue. See E. O'Connor, *Syndicalism in Ireland* (Cork, 1988); M. Laffan, 'Labour Must Wait: Ireland's Conservative Revolution', in P. J. Corish (ed.), *Radicals, Rebels and Establishments* (Belfast, 1985); and P. Bew, 'Sinn Féin, Agrarian Radicalism and the War of Independence, 1919–1921', in D. G. Boyce (ed.), *The Revolution in Ireland, 1879–1923* (London, 1988).

13. R. English, *Ernie O'Malley: IRA Intellectual* (Oxford, 1998), p. 84.

14. The first example of such an approach was E. Rumpf and A. C. Hepburn, *Nationalism and Socialism in Twentieth-Century Ireland* (Liverpool, 1977), followed by the work listed in note 7. See also P. Hart, 'The Social Structure of the Irish Republican Army, 1916–1923', *Historical Journal*, 42 (March 1999), and ' "Operations Abroad": The IRA in Britain, 1919–1923', *English Historical Review* (Jan. 2000).

15. The great pioneer of such integrated local studies is D. Fitzpatrick in his *Politics and Irish Life, 1913–1921* (Dublin, 1977). The same intensively local focus can be found in Augusteijn, *From Public Defiance*; Hart, *The IRA*; M. Farry, *Aftermath of Revolution: Sligo, 1921–23* (Dublin, 2000).

3

Propaganda I: Advanced Nationalist Propaganda and Moralistic Revolution, 1914–18

Ben Novick

Advanced nationalist propaganda, whether it was newspaper columns, ballad sheets, election material, or speeches and performances, drove the engine of the Irish revolution. In the early years of the revolution (1914–18), propagandists harnessed a growing popular frustration with the war to create anti-British sentiment. This chapter will focus on one particular area of propaganda that intensified during the war: moralistic propaganda that appealed directly to the nationalism of both men and women. The importance of 'moral tone' to Irish revolutionary discourse did not come about as a result of the war, but for advanced nationalist propagandists, the socio-cultural dislocations of war, and the support of the IPP for the British war effort gave new impetus to their campaigns. The highlighting of moral dichotomies between Britain and Ireland was central to the construction of a new revolutionary Irish identity.

Before examining the specifically moralistic propaganda, it is necessary to look at some general aspects of the advanced nationalist propaganda campaign. The first questions we need to answer to be able to assess these forms of propaganda are: who were the advanced nationalist propagandists, and how did they work? From 1917 ephemeral propaganda was produced by a Sinn Féin Department of

Publicity, run by Robert Brennan, ably assisted by Desmond FitzGerald and Frank Gallagher.[1] A recent memoir by Michael Kevin O'Doherty reveals that his father, Seamus O'Doherty, also helped Brennan, and O'Doherty even credits his mother with creating the much-used election slogan 'Put Him In to Get Him Out.'[2] Eamon de Valera, one of the two surviving commanders from the Easter Rising, and after October 1917, President of Sinn Féin, also took an active role in editing election propaganda.[3]

Before 1917, however, newspapers were the main outlet of advanced nationalists. With the exception of Arthur Griffith's short-lived daily *Eire/Ireland* (1914), their papers were either weeklies or monthlies. Weekly papers were finished by Wednesday night or Thursday morning, and published on a Saturday. Robert Brennan, who worked with Arthur Griffith in 1917 and 1918, recalled that Griffith himself wrote most of the leading articles for his newspapers, and this seems to be a consistent pattern with all editors, who both set the general tone and wrote the actual text of these papers.[4]

These newspaper propagandists moved in a small circle of nationalist Dublin. Of the editors whose backgrounds are known, only Herbert Pim, Laurence de Lacey and Terence MacSwiney consistently worked in cities other than Dublin.[5] Pim, a Belfast Quaker who converted to Catholicism in 1912 and took the pseudonym A. Newman, based his work in Belfast and Dublin during the war. MacSwiney split his time between Cork and Dublin, organising for the IRB and Irish Volunteers, editing the Cork-based *Fianna Fáil* until its closure at the end of November 1914 and contributing vitriolic articles to the *Irish Volunteer*. De Lacey, editor of the *Irish Volunteer* until December 1914, had started his journalistic career on the *Enniscorthy Echo*,[6] and printed the *Volunteer* on the presses in Enniscorthy. De Lacey was an active Volunteer and IRB member, but fled to America in February 1915 after police discovered two men in possession of gelignite and seditious leaflets hiding in his home.[7]

Two printers were used regularly by most of these newspapers: Patrick Mahon on Yarnhall Street, whose presses printed the *Irish Volunteer* after December 1914, *Eire/Ireland*, *Sinn Féin*, *Scissors and Paste* and the second series of *Nationality*; and the Gaelic Press, located on Liffey Street, which printed the *Spark*, *Honesty*, and the *Gael*. Mahon was a thorn in the side of British officialdom. When his presses were seized in February 1915 following the closure of *Scissors and Paste*, Mahon successfully sued Dublin Castle and had his material returned after a month.[8] The Gaelic Press was raided in March 1916 following a particularly violent editorial in the *Gael*. Its premises were smashed up, but quickly rebuilt following a fund-raising campaign begun in the *Spark* and *Honesty*.[9]

The support of the editors of the *Spark* and *Honesty* for their fellow journalists in the *Gael* highlights an important element of such propaganda during the Great War – the cooperation between editors of different papers. Newspapers frequently reprinted columns, poems and editorials from other nationalist papers, and new papers were greeted as welcome additions rather than competition. This can be best seen in the close relationship between Pim, Griffith, and Aodh de Blacam.[10] Pim agreed to turn the *Irishman* into a Sinn Féin paper after the Rising, as Griffith was still in prison and unable to resurrect *Nationality*. When de Blacam decided to found *Young Ireland* in April 1917 in order to help mould the nationalist ideals of Irish children, Pim became a prolific contributor of detective stories, gave *Young Ireland* free advertising space in the *Irishman*, and encouraged his readers to subscribe to *Young Ireland*. Griffith in turn allowed *Young Ireland* to use Sinn Féin Headquarters on Harcourt Street as its editorial offices.

The funding for these newspapers reflected the spectrum of political views that they represented. Throughout the war the British Government remained convinced that advanced nationalist papers were funded by 'German gold'. Parliamentary accusations of this nature caused Chief-Secretary Augustine Birrell to approve the first wave of official newspaper closures in late November 1914.[11] (The accusation was never proven, and research for this chapter has uncovered no evidence to support it.) Newspapers were funded in a variety of ways. Official newspapers of various movements received support from their parent organisations. Thus, the *Irish Volunteer* received part of the dues paid into the central committee by Irish Volunteers, and the IRB supported *Irish Freedom*. The IRB also sponsored Arthur Griffith's first series of *Nationality* (1915–16), but he had to rely on private contributions for the second series.[12] Griffith's earlier 1914 papers were supported in part by organisations (*Sinn Féin*), and in part through individual contributions (*Eire/Ireland*). American organisations also supplied funds. The *Hibernian*, mouthpiece of the Ancient Order of Hibernians' Irish–American Alliance wing, was supported by contributions from AOH branches in the United States. All newspapers supported by the IRB were in reality reliant on funds from Clan-na-Gael.[13] In contrast, Labour papers were entirely supported by subscriptions, charity, and occasional union dues. Most other newspapers not linked to an organisation relied on advertisements, and the support of like-minded nationalists, as seen with the launch of *Young Ireland (Eire Og)* in 1917. Despite the variance of political and social beliefs expounded in the newspapers, a close web of support was thus woven between advanced nationalists of all hues.

Advanced nationalists considered this form of propaganda highly effective. The *Irish Volunteer* called Sinn Féin's 1915 national pamphlet series 'The New Weapons' and considered them a 'formidable' part of the arsenal being deployed against British rule.[14] In the *Spark*, Sean Doyle extended the militaristic metaphors, likening the *Spark*'s role on the Dublin scene to a 'man in the gap', fighting to maintain the 'right of Irish Nationalism to print and publish a paper in Dublin'.[15] The National Council of Sinn Féin continually encouraged members around Ireland to publicise their activities, utilising both the advanced nationalist weeklies and the letter columns of daily newspapers. 'There is not a week passes', read a pamphlet produced for Cumainn in 1918, 'but some incident occurs in every county which could be turned to account in driving home the lesson that the country must look to Sinn Féin for its salvation.'[16]

Another argument for the effectiveness of this propaganda is the perception of constant yet ineffectual censorship attempts made by the British Government before the Rising.[17] While closing newspapers and fining proprietors may have had a slightly deleterious effect, the free publicity engendered by such actions in large-circulation papers more than made up for these losses. Trials of advanced nationalists for seditious activity or illegal possession of arms were widely covered in more standard newspapers, and advanced nationalists quickly turned Irish courts into their own bully pulpits.

British political opinion reinforced the idea of the importance of propaganda before the Rising. Enormous pressure was brought to bear on Asquith, Birrell and Nathan in the autumn of 1914, by Tory MPs eager to close down Dublin's seditious press, and the London *Times* and *Morning Post* consistently complained about the widespread printed sedition found around Ireland.

Although British public opinion was crucial to the later efforts of Irish nationalists in the War of Independence, the Great War saw no such equivalent. Nevertheless, Irish propaganda reached newspapers and journals in Great Britain to an unprecedented degree. The *New Statesman* even quoted Griffith's *Nationality* directly, in 1918, to attack the trumped-up 'German plot'.[18] News and information reached British papers through correspondents based in Ireland, most of whom were anonymous contributors,[19] and English journalists had private informants in Ireland as well.[20] Advanced nationalist journals did occasionally reach England. Joe Good, an Irish Volunteer organiser in Great Britain during the war, later recalled reading *Nationality* 'avidly' in London and Salisbury.[21] However, major British papers rarely discussed Irish advanced nationalist propaganda, or its effectiveness. Rather, they used the existence of Irish propaganda as a crutch for their own political views. Conservative papers in 1914 promoted the censorship of Irish advanced nationalist newspapers in order to discredit Asquith's Liberal government. The *New Statesman* and the *Nation* displayed their liberal credentials by complimenting pre-war Sinn Féin doctrine, condemning government coercion in Ireland, and blaming Sir Edward Carson and the Orange Order for Irish problems – all common elements of wartime advanced nationalist propaganda.[22]

The best argument for the effectiveness of pre-Rising propaganda comes from a speech delivered by Justice Kenny at the opening of the Commission for the City of Dublin, two weeks before the Easter Rising. Kenny lashed out at the prevalent sedition in Ireland:

> It is difficult for any movement of that nature [army recruiting] to be a complete success if a propaganda of an openly seditious character, and one which seems to set all authority at defiance, be started in order to counteract it. We read in our daily papers of seditious literature ... and you have in the public thoroughfares of this city what I regard as the most serious attempt to paralyse the recruiting movement – namely, the display of large and attractive posters outside shop doors which must necessarily have a most mischievous and deterrent influence on certain classes of the population. I have seen these posters from time to time. No passer-by could fail to observe them. They purport to represent either the spirit or the contents of some weekly papers.[23]

Propaganda grew even more effective after the Rising. Following on F. S. L. Lyons's earlier assertions,[24] Peter Hart has uncovered primary evidence to help prove that the 'patriotic cult' of the Rising depended in large part on the 'flood of rebel memorabilia, of postcards, mass cards, song sheets, pamphlets, flags, badges, pictures, photograph albums, calendars, and a host of other mass-produced items'.[25] Though self-serving, Major I. H. Price's remarks at the Royal Commission on the Easter Rebellion are worth noting as well. Price claimed that Sinn Féin propaganda cost the British army 50,000 recruits between 1914 and 1916, and focused on the *Irish Volunteer* and the *Gael* as having an especially 'bad influence'.[26]

A final element that supports the effectiveness of war-linked propaganda comes from the results of the eight by-elections in 1917 and

1918 contested by Sinn Féin. Of these eight, Sinn Féin won five (North Roscommon, Longford, East Clare, Kilkenny City, and Cavan). The other three (South Armagh, Tyrone, and Waterford) occurred either in the north, where the unionists and parliamentarians combined forces against Sinn Féin, or in John Redmond's old seat, which was won by his son. Although a detailed assessment of the effectiveness of propaganda used in these elections is impossible, a close study of the existing sources shows that during the run-up to a by-election, Sinn Féin papers and the Sinn Féin Publicity Department concentrated almost entirely on the by-elections. Copies of *Nationality* were distributed for free in polling areas before the election.[27] More speeches and rallies were held in the area, resulting in more arrests for political activity. Similar propaganda was used for many campaigns, with only the names of candidates and counties being changed.

Michael Laffan's work on by-elections in this period supports their centrality to the Irish revolution (see also Chapter 4). To the arguments mentioned above for the effectiveness of propaganda, he adds the high level of organisation among Sinn Féin campaigners, citing the *Irish Independent*'s 1917 report of 'pamphlets ... being handed out by the thousand ... posters ... displayed at every cross-road and village in the constituency'.[28]

Having thus explored the mechanics of the advanced nationalist propaganda war of 1914–18, let us move now to an examination of the specifically moral issues used to attack the British presence in Ireland. In their propaganda the moral probity and purity of Irish nationalists stood as a bulwark against the dangers of British culture. To wartime propagandists, three British *bêtes-noires* in particular threatened Irish culture and the morals of Irish men and women: music halls and salacious literature, drink, and Freemasonry. None of these 'threats' was created by the war, but the war in both practical and emotional ways, heightened concern. The war brought an increase in Irish enlistment, leading more men into the temptations offered by barracks life. The war also increased the mobility of women, exposing them to salacious entertainment far removed from parental or clerical supervision. More importantly, the war amplified fears of alien cultures. Just as Germans were demonised in pro-war propaganda, so too were the immoral figures of British music hall artists and writers symbols of foreign interference in the 'new Ireland'. Freemasonry, long allegedly part of an international anti-Catholic plot, became more threatening when propagandists linked the war to Masonic cabals.

The dangers of drinking were a potent issue for advanced nationalists. Temperance movements had the longest gestation in Ireland, dating back to the mass movement led by Father Theobald Mathew in the 1840s. Strong links between distillers and the IPP were mocked and exploited by these men, some of whom were teetotallers.[29] In the first decade of the twentieth century efforts to ban salacious literature and discourage the appearance of music hall acts had been led by Dublin-based 'Vigilance Committees',[30] which included representatives of the IPP as well as future advanced nationalist leaders. A crusade against Freemasonry was, in turn, part and parcel of Catholic culture at the turn of the century, and had been encouraged in Ireland by organisations such as the Catholic Defence Association, which sought to convince Catholics that Protestants in secret organisations were out to deny Roman Catholics their political and socio-economic rights.[31]

Although the IPP had long been involved in these campaigns, its support for the British war effort made it much more difficult for nationalist newspapers to continue their traditional leadership role on the moralistic propaganda front. Anti-British diatribes in the Home Rule press were toned down, and advanced nationalists created the impression that the IPP could no longer be relied upon to help stop British filth from entering Ireland. This gave them the chance to become the main proponents of moral reform in Ireland. By linking a moral crusade to a political stance, propagandists attained growing clerical and thus popular support for advanced nationalism.

Drink and drunkenness were linked directly to the IPP, considered a main agent by which English customs and manners entered Ireland.[32] Patriotic Irishmen did not drink, or if they did, drinking simply led to the enunciation of anti-British sentiments.[33] The English were depicted as a nation of beer-swilling cowards. Griffith mocked the *Daily Mail* in 1917 for insisting that England needed both 'more men' and 'more beer' to win the war,[34] while Brian O'Higgins linked moral cowardice with drunkenness in his 1915 poem 'A Nail in the Kaiser's Coffin', written in response to an English brewery advertisement which asked people to 'Order a pint of beer and drive a nail into the Kaiser's coffin.' 'When the war is over O', sang the British drunkards of O'Higgins's poem, 'We'll load a train with British beer/And meet the boys at Dover O.'[35]

The threat of drunkenness also permitted propagandists to attack the morals of the wives of Irish soldiers in the British army. Since most Irish recruits were urban and working class,[36] their wives, known as

'Separation Women', survived on the separation allowances provided by the British Government. This class of women was a frequent target for advanced nationalist (although not labour) vituperation. Priests claimed that women who drank this 'blood money' committed the ultimate act of depravity, and would have an awful reckoning on judgement day.[37] A poster for Joseph McGuinness's 1917 by-election contest in County Longford combined the idea of alcoholic and moral/sexual depravity.[38] The dishevelled hoydens shown swilling porter and bearing both Union Jacks and banners for the IPP candidate are marked as libertines by their ragged yet gaudy clothes. Yet, while these women are held as figures of opprobrium, their actions in invading the male sphere of the public house, and socialising rowdily with each other, are all signs of a freedom that was denied the 'purer' female supporters of Sinn Féin.

The enormously popular music hall was also something both male and female nationalists were warned against. Some of these propagandists, especially Arthur Griffith, had been instrumental in leading opposition to the production of Synge's *Playboy of the Western World* at the Abbey in 1907. Thus, opposition to 'immoral' entertainment did not appear overnight. However, most advanced nationalists stopped supporting the vigilance committees and truth societies that led this opposition during the war. The main reason for this was that the IPP's support for the British war effort was thought to compromise their moral stance. The Dublin Vigilance Committee, supposedly influenced by leading member J. D. Nugent's friendship with the French Premier and Freemason René Viviani, was accused of refusing to help nationalist campaigns against smut.[39]

In their own eyes, advanced nationalists' uncompromising anti-British attitude gave them an advantage in the war against immorality. Propagandists insisted that 'smutty papers ... the dirty song, the suggestive film, the indecent revue'[40] were all made in England for exportation to Ireland, and considered Redmondism to be synonymous with vulgarity and immorality.[41]

Protest as they might, advanced nationalists could not deny the popularity of music halls in Dublin.[42] An awareness of its popularity is most visible in the subject matter of some anti-recruiting jokes published during the war. An old lady, stopped with her son in the street by an officer and told that 'The Empire now needs every man', replied 'that she cared nothing about the Empire – her son worked in the Tivoli!'[43] The *Spark* in its turn mocked all the current foibles and activities of the IPP in an August 1915 issue, yet chose to do so by pretending that the parliamentary and English leaders were all appearing in the 'Imperial Theatre of Varieties'.[44]

Advanced nationalists did attempt to present alternative forms of entertainment. This could be the Irish Theatre of Edward Martyn, an English-language theatre which the Gaelic League's *An Claidheamh Soluis* told its readers would 'show them that there is dignity in their Irish nationality'.[45] Readers who wanted to know more about Martyn were encouraged to attend his theatre. There they would learn the truth far better than by reading the 'sultry pages' of the 'godless hedonist' George Moore's *Hail and Farewell*.[46] Aware that Martyn's mixture of Irish translations and repertory theatre might be too high-class for some nationalists, propagandists also promoted concerts at which 'Irish-Ireland Artistes' could appear.[47] Joseph Mulkearns, 'the Rajah of Frongoch', honed his performance in Frongoch, and returned to grace patriotic stages in Ireland throughout the rest of the war. Nationalist concert parties even were formed, touring Ireland in the best tradition of the music hall act. The best known of these was the 'P&Cs', led by Jack O'Sheehan until he was sentenced to two years' hard labour in 1918 for singing 'Felons of Our Land' and 'A Soldier's Song'.[48] Mass entertainments could be even more bizarre. The farewell 'carnival' held for Jim Larkin at Croydon Park in October 1914 before he left for America included speeches, a display by the Irish Citizen Army, and recalling Buffalo Bill's Wild West Show, an 'Attack on an Irish Emigrant Cavern. Rescue by American Army'.[49]

Sean Doyle in the *Spark* was careful to differentiate between music halls and 'West British' music halls. A central place for entertainment was a 'potent instrument of reform, culture, and progress', but the sort of music halls seen in Dublin had become instead 'a blot on civilisation'.[50] The *Hibernian* felt that music halls, and in particular their lurid hoardings, existed only to whet the immoral desires of young men and even young women.[51] But while propagandists blustered about these working-class arenas of amusement,[52] they reserved their wrath for immoral and perverted plays that catered to more middle-class tastes. Herbert Pim blamed the distractions of the war for the production in September 1916 of the musical *My Lady Frayle*, a play that 'abounded in jokes and suggestions of the most immoral character'.[53]

Pim's protest against this play can be seen on two levels. First, and most simply, he objected to the somewhat daring lyrics of the author, Arthur Wimperis, and the plot, a modern retelling of *Faustus*. However, a closer examination of his screed against this play reveals that in fact he was sarcastically attacking British policy in Ireland. By insisting that this sort of play would not have been permitted in Dublin before the war, he argued that the focus of coercion and control in Ireland had shifted from moral control to political control. Propagandists differentiated between the two forms of censorship, going so far as to request the British censor to 'put its foot down on the moral assassins who flood Ireland with filth from the English printing presses … chain up or smother the authors of the indecent songs and "jokes" which you are permitted to *cheer* at the Hippodrome'.[54] Pim asked rhetorically 'whether the theatrical censor and his staff have given up the business and are employed in political censorship'.[55] Pim also protested against the cultural hegemony of Britain. *My Lady Frayle* reached Dublin shortly after its première in London, and it was precisely this sort of importation which propagandists both before and during the war fought so hard against.

Leaving the sub-Wodehouseian world of musical comedy, nationalists also complained about non-musical comedies. 'George Birmingham's' play *General John Regan*, revived by the Abbey Theatre in 1917, was marked in *Nationality* as 'the foulest play ever staged in Dublin'.[56] However, originally written in 1913, Birmingham's comedy about the fictional liberator of Bolivia is completely devoid of any salacious or sexually immoral implications. Most likely, Griffith objected to the author, as Birmingham (Canon James Hannay) was considered a 'great hater of Sinn Féin',[57] and had resigned under a cloud from the Gaelic League when it emerged in 1907 that he and Birmingham were the same man. Secondly, the play depicts Irish life in a small rural town as stultifying, and the main heroes of the play are the men who trick Dublin Castle into providing them with a chunk of money for the purported statue of General Regan. Rather than being 'Sinn Féin' and self-reliant, the characters in this play scheme away and easily find ways to take advantage of the benevolent Union. Griffith would also probably have taken offence to scenes in which the local brass band revealed its ignorance of such patriotic standards as 'A Nation Once Again', and 'Who Fears to Speak of '98'.

Just as specific authors were attacked, so too were specific artists. Sarah Bernhardt was called blasphemous for twisting scripture in her play *Les Cathédrales*, crying 'Father, forgive them not, for they know what they do.'[58] Charlie Chaplin was accused of cowardice and greed,[59] while the Polish Madame Yavorska was condemned for misplaced patriotism after she sang the Russian National Anthem, 'Rule Britannia', and 'God Save the King' to a Dublin audience.[60]

The only specific song that one can find attacked in the advanced nationalist press is *It's a Long Way to Tipperary*. The popularity of this song in the British army, and the idea that *Tipperary* was a proper Irish song, enraged nationalist propagandists around the world. Irish-American writers were especially vituperative about *Tipperary*, and their articles were eagerly reprinted in advanced nationalist journals in Ireland. Writing in the *San Francisco Leader*, Father Yorke summarised the problem of *Tipperary*, stating that it 'is not a song, and it is not Irish. It is a cockney music hall jingle, and its words are a libel even on the stage Irishman.'[61] Propagandists protested especially against the fourth verse, in which 'Paddy' apologised to his 'Molly O' for his atrocious spelling, claiming 'Remember it's the pen that's bad – don't lay the blame on me.' *Tipperary* furthered anti-Irish prejudice, leading Englishmen to think of the Irish as 'grinning baboons',[62] whose lips dripped 'with obscenity and Birmingham-filth'.[63] For Griffith, the song highlighted the immorality of British culture – Piccadilly and Leicester Square, the London highlights of the song, made Griffith think of 'Babylon and Belshazzar'.[64]

The protests against *Tipperary* formed a foundation upon which a form of resistance to music hall entertainment could be built. Advanced nationalists contrasted music halls with the more wholesome forms of entertainment to be found in Germany (or at the very least, the lack of such degraded amusements imported from Germany). Pro-Germanism was encouraged by writers who detested *Tipperary*, and the 'martial vigour' of the German race was linked to songs such as 'The Watch on the Rhine',[65] and the choral training given to conscripts in the German army.[66] Native composers were also encouraged to either write new martial melodies or resurrect old Irish tunes to replace the current 'music-hall rubbish'.[67] Proper military tunes inspired Volunteers to defy the British crown. Terence MacSwiney reported the actions of Cork Volunteers when they escorted J. J. Walsh to the train station,[68] in words that linked songs to violence. The Volunteers, he wrote, had specifically refused to sing *it's a Long Way to Tipperary*; instead, 'they swung on their heels like one man, and in one voice sang "Let Erin Remember the Days of Old." The fire of it! No – we are not terrorised.'[69] Children especially were encouraged to discard 'meaningless jingles depending on the "rattle of the bones" ',[70] and to learn instead the 'exquisite national melodies' of Ireland.[71]

More direct forms of resistance to music hall songs were also suggested. The *Hibernian* encouraged a boycott of all such entertainments, crying 'In the name of God, let us end it or mend it!'[72] The *Gael* recalled the *Playboy* riots, urging its readers to inaugurate a campaign of 'fierce, organised rioting against vile productions'.[73] Nationalists were told to gather outside music halls, and at a given signal from inside the hall, force their way in and physically clear the house. Thus an 'Era of Decency' would appear in music halls and cinemas.[74]

Boycotting was also urged against the popular English literature and newspapers that contributed to the growing immorality of Irish youth. Herbert Pim managed to gain the support of Cardinal Logue in his campaign against 'grossly improper literature' and newspapers such as the *Umpire*, the *Sunday Chronicle*, *News of the World*, *Reynold's Newspaper* and *John Bull*, the majority of which were 'discharged from cross-channel steamers to the sound of church bells on Sunday morning'.[75] Novels and popular children's papers were considered responsible for the presence of 'neurotic children',[76] and writers went so far as to condemn Alfred, Lord Tennyson for having a 'gross mind', and urged school authorities to burn the 'debasing writings' of Tennyson and Macaulay.[77] Mass-circulation papers in Ireland were unable to support such a crusade in good conscience, as their columns were often filled with salacious accounts of divorce, breach of promise, and murder cases, in both Ireland and England.[78] This gave advanced nationalists yet another opportunity to assume a greater leadership role in the fight against immorality.

While some of the resentment felt by propagandists for the immorality of British youth papers may be cynically attributed to professional jealousy (*Fianna* and *Young Ireland* (*Eire Og*) had to convert to adult papers to survive, while *St Enda's*, the children's supplement to *Irish Fun*, lasted only a year), the central fury of propagandists was reserved for one man alone: Alfred Harmsworth (Lord Northcliffe), the press baron who controlled *The Times* and the *Daily Mail*, as well as producing vast amounts of popular and children's newspapers.[79]

Most propagandists conveniently forgot Harmsworth's Irish background,[80] focusing instead on the wickedness wrought by his newspapers. Harmsworth was 'the Cromwell of journaleese [*sic*]',[81] an 'evil genius' who existed only to feed human weaknesses and fill reading hours with 'triviality or gross idiocy'.[82] When Harmsworth was not corrupting morals, he was busy encouraging a 'healthy Imperial outlook'[83] among young readers. If this was not enough to condemn him in advanced nationalist eyes, by January 1916 he had grown blasphemous, printing an article in *Answers* that claimed the Kaiser was the Devil incarnate.[84]

Blasphemy, however, was only what one could expect from a man such as Lord Northcliffe, who among his other faults had joined the Freemasons. Anti-Masonic agitation by advanced nationalists dated from long before the Great War. Encouraged by the support of anti-Masons in the Catholic hierarchy (for indeed, Freemasonry had often been condemned by papal authority), propagandists such as D. P. Moran and Arthur Griffith led the campaign against Masons in public life. The threat of Freemasonry was in part due to its secret nature, in part due to the pre-war scare propaganda of the Catholic Truth Association and other such organisations, and in part due to the anti-Semitic xenophobia felt by many propagandists. Griffith had linked Freemasons with Jewish supporters of the British war effort in South Africa, claiming that inhabitants of 'Jew-Burg' (Johannesburg) wanted nothing more than a Boer defeat in the South African War of 1899–1902.[85] Popular Catholic (and anti-Semitic) publications such as the *Irish Rosary* and D. P. Moran's the *Leader* campaigned for committees of Catholics in business to be set up in order to counteract the influence of Freemasons among the Protestant business community in Dublin.[86]

This paranoia of anti-Catholic plotting continued during the Great War. W. J. Brennan-Whitemore flogged an old horse, accusing the 'Jew-cum-Mason' journalistic agencies, naturally headquartered in London, of circulating 'malicious and abhorrent calumnies upon the Catholics of Ireland'.[87] Thomas H. Burbage, an anti-Semitic columnist for J. J. O'Kelly's *Catholic Bulletin*, laid off condemning the Jews briefly in February 1917 to explain to his readers that Masonic ritual made a mockery of Christian morals, consisting mainly of a 'degenerate and revolting form of phallic worship ... symbolism that fills the mind with impure and obscene imagery'.[88] Such perversions were clearly popular in countries outside Ireland, and Arthur Griffith especially used this as a way of blaming the Freemasons for the suffering of the Great War. After the United States entered the war in April 1917, he turned away briefly from his pro-American stance to prove that Masonry was 'solidly ranged' on the side of the Allies. According to Griffith's calculations, 84 per cent of the known Masons in the world fought on the side of the Allies, as opposed to only 7 per cent with the Central Powers. Since the war was therefore created by Freemasons, and more specifically by the Grand Orient chapter of Freemasons, it should be seen as 'a gratuitous insult to Catholics'.[89] By connecting Freemasonry so directly with the Allied war effort, Griffith clearly defined his anti-war stance as synonymous with his Catholic beliefs, and challenged the overwhelmingly Catholic population of Ireland to go against their own religion by joining the British army.

According to advanced nationalist propaganda, Ireland had better resisted the inroads of Masonry than other European countries, but she was still under threat. Freemasons had infiltrated the educational system, leading to a decline in Irish being taught in the schools.[90] The appointment of the Jewish Sir Matthew Nathan to the position of Under-Secretary helped the Masons achieve a further foothold in Dublin Castle, as it was widely suspected that 'Signor' Nathan was a member of the Grand Orient Lodge.[91] The Reverend F. S. Pollard in the *Hibernian*, a strong crusader against Freemasons and Jews, reacted strongly when Dublin Alderman Alfred Byrne lost a by-election in 1915. Despite Pollard's having ignored the election itself, he saw Byrne's defeat as being caused by a conspiracy between Jews, Orangemen, and Freemasons. Pollard blustered away, threatening the 'hell-hounds' who had been let loose 'to down a Catholic', and insisting that 'someone has got to sup sorrow with a long spoon', before he would let the matter lie.[92]

The IPP was again seen as a primary conduit through which Godlessness and Freemasonry entered Ireland. Joseph Devlin was accused of forming a secret alliance with the Grand Orient via Sir Matthew Nathan,[93] and the advanced nationalist press was outraged in May 1915 when IPP MPs T. P. O'Connor, Joe Devlin, Stephen Gwynn, W. A. Redmond and the Lord Mayor of Dublin (Lorcan Sherlock) met with the socialist French Premier and Masonic leader René Viviani[94] and presented him with the 'sympathy of the Irish people'.[95]

The unholy trinity of threats to the morals of the Irish people did not originate with the Great War, but the events of the war sharpened their danger, and heightened the importance of counteracting them. By blaming the British for the presence of drink and immoral entertainment, and the Freemasons for the slaughter of the war, advanced nationalist propagandists were able to turn the decision to support their views from a political to a moral ground. Devout Catholics saw propagandists such as Griffith, Doyle and Pim take on the mantle of the pre-war vigilance and truth societies, and gain the support of the hierarchy. By so doing, propagandists, whatever their personal views of music halls and drink, presented themselves as champions of decency and morality.

At its most basic level, propaganda directed at people's morals sought to both create an idealised (and fictive) revolutionary, and highlight as a sharp contrast the degenerate and debased nature of British and pro-British people. The construction of idealised imagery helped propagandists exert control over their audiences. Men could be influenced while boys, and women's impulses and desires could be contained through a strictly controlled discourse of sexuality and danger. Clerical support for advanced nationalism came forward first through an alliance forged upon moral grounds, through the crusade against improper literature and entertainment headed by Herbert Pim. By attacking the evils of intemperance and the threat of Freemasons and music halls, advanced nationalists inherited a long tradition of moralistic propaganda. However, the Great War, by increasing the mobility of the population (thus exposing more young men and women to moral danger), by heightening the awareness and hatred of the 'other', and by leading the IPP to be forever associated with British politics, contributed to the transition from moral to political propaganda. When the lines between the two styles blurred, support grew for a set of movements that sought to create in Ireland a revolutionary and yet conservative new nation. In the years following the Great War, the focus of Irish propaganda would switch to a more international and politically-based protest, thus ultimately playing a significant role in the peace settlements that followed the Irish War of Independence (see Chapter 6).

Notes

1. See R. Brennan, *Allegiance* (Dublin, 1950); D. FitzGerald, *Memoirs of Desmond FitzGerald, 1913–1916* (Dublin, 1968); F. Gallagher ('David Hogan'), *The Four Glorious Years* (Dublin, 1953). Herbert Pim, in his unreliable 1920 memoir *Sinn Féin* (Belfast, 1920), p. 23, claimed that 'hundreds of leaflets were distributed, all purporting to come from the "National Council" but really the work of the writer'.
2. M. K. O'Doherty, *My Parents and Other Rebels* (Dublin, 1999), p. 24.
3. Brennan, *Allegiance*, p. 163.
4. Ibid., pp. 207–8.
5. Arthur Griffith's first series of *Nationality* (1915–16) was printed in Belfast, but its editorial department remained in Dublin, see R. M. Henry, *The Evolution of Sinn Féin* (Dublin, 1920), p. 188.
6. A local IPP paper in Wexford.
7. Chief Secretary's Office, Judicial Division: Intelligence Notes, 1915, ff. 33–4, PRO, CO 903/19; *Irish Volunteer*, Feb. 1915 et fl.
8. PRO, CO 904/160/2: Suppression of Newspapers: 'Scissors and Paste', 1914–1915, Letter, Corrigan & Corrigan to Chief Secretary's Office, Dublin Castle, 13 Mar. 1915. See also B. Novick, 'DORA, Suppression,

and Nationalist Propaganda in Ireland, 1914–1915', *New Hibernia Review*, I, 4 (Winter 1997), pp. 41–57.

9. *Spark*, 2 and 9 Apr. 1916; *Honesty*, 8 Apr. 1916.

10. Born Hugh Blackham in London, son of Ulster Protestant Home Rulers, he moved to Donegal shortly before the Great War and gaelicised his name. He continued to be an active nationalist after the revolutionary period.

11. See Novick, 'DORA', pp. 41–57.

12. As part of the IRB's support for the first series of *Nationality*, Griffith had to accept Sean MacDermott as business manager of the newspaper, see P. Colum, *Ourselves Alone! The Story of Arthur Griffith and the Origin of the Irish Free State* (New York, 1959), p. 137.

13. Clan-na-Gael sent $98,297 to the IRB between August 1914 and April 1917; see R. Kee, *The Green Flag* (London, 1972), p. 545.

14. *Irish Volunteer*, 15 May 1915, p. 6.

15. *Spark*, 1 Aug. 1915, p. 4.

16. KSRL (Kenneth Spencer Research Library, University of Kansas), OH Q42:58, Sinn Féin Pamphlets, 'Propaganda', 1918.

17. See Novick, 'DORA'; B. Novick, 'Postal Censorship in Ireland, 1914–1916', *IHS*, XXXI (May 1999), pp. 343–56.

18. *New Statesman*, 25 May 1918, pp. 144–5.

19. Most of the Irish material in the *New Statesman* was written by J. M. Hone or James Hannay (George Birmingham). Before the war, Francis Sheehy-Skeffington also wrote regularly for the journal, but his pacifist stance caused him to lose his position as Irish correspondent upon the outbreak of war.

20. See Memorandum on the State of Ireland, T. Naylor to Ensor, 19 Dec. 1916, Sir R. C. K. Ensor Papers, Box 86, Bodleian Library, Oxford. Naylor blamed British policies for forcing people to support Sinn Féin.

21. J. Good, *Enchanted by Dreams: The Journal of a Revolutionary*, ed. M. Good (Dublin, 1999), p. 12.

22. Compare: *Nation*, 15 June 1915, 17 Feb. 1917, 18 Aug. 1917, 15 Dec. 1917; *New Statesman*, 5 Dec. 1914, 6 Feb. 1915, 6 May 1916, 20 Oct. 1917, 2 Mar. 1918.

23. *Weekly Irish Times*, 15 Apr. 1916, p. 4.

24. F. S. L. Lyons, *Culture and Anarchy in Ireland* (Oxford, 1979), pp. 100–2.

25. P. Hart, *The IRA and its Enemies* (Oxford, 1998), p. 207.

26. *Weekly Irish Times*, 3 June 1916, p. 1.

27. M. Laffan, *The Resurrection of Ireland* (Cambridge, 1999), p. 101.

28. Ibid., p. 100.

29. T. Garvin, 'Priests and Patriots: Irish Separatism and the Fear of the Modern, 1890–1914', *IHS*, XXV (May 1986), pp. 76–7. See also FitzGerald, *Memoirs … 1913–1916*, p. 35.

30. These committees usually consisted of small groups of men and women drawn from the new Catholic middle class. Members enjoyed clerical and press support, as well as close links with the IPP.

31. See S. Paseta, *Before the Revolution* (Cork, 1999).
32. See *Spark*, 11 Apr. 1915, p. 2; *Irish Fun*, Aug. 1917, p. 43. Nevertheless, both the *Freeman's Journal* and the *Irish Weekly Independent* supported the work of the Ulster Temperance Council and the Father Matthew Temperance Union during the war. Compare: *Weekly Freeman's Journal*, 7 Feb. 1915, 4 Mar. 1916, p. 4; *Irish Weekly Independent*, 1915 fl., 4 Mar. 1916, p. 3.
33. See *Eire/Ireland*, 28 Nov. 1914, p. 1.
34. *Nation*, 28 July 1917, p. 6.
35. *Spark*, 28 Mar. 1915, p. 3.
36. See M. Staunton, 'The Royal Munster Fusiliers in the Great War, 1914–1919', MA thesis (University College, Dublin, 1986); T. Dooley, *Irishmen or English Soldiers?* (Liverpool, 1995).
37. *Hibernian*, 30 Oct. 1915, p. 1.
38. KSRL, DK17, Sinn Féin Leaflets, DK17:8:30, 'The Irish Party's Only Props in Longford' (1917).
39. See *Eire Og*, 18 Aug. 1917, p. 4.
40. *Gael*, 5 Feb. 1916, p. 6.
41. *Spark*, 7 Mar. 1915, pp. 2–3.
42. A similar problem dogged the *Freeman's Journal*. Despite the positive coverage given to the efforts of vigilance committees and truth societies, the very popularity of the music hall ensured ample and regular reports in the newspaper about the entertainments on offer in Dublin; for example: *Freeman's Journal*, 3 Aug. 1914, 11 Aug. 1914, 23 Aug. 1914.
43. *Hibernian*, 14 Aug. 1915, p. 4. The four largest music halls in 1914 Dublin were the Royal, the Empire, the Tivoli, and the CYM Pantomime.
44. *Spark*, 21 Aug. 1915, p. 4.
45. *An Claidheamh Soluis*, 14 Nov. 1914, p. 5.
46. Ibid., 9 Jan. 1915, p. 4.
47. KSRL, C3196: Sinn Féin Leaflets (uncatalogued).
48. See *Eire Og*, 14 Sep. 1918, p. 3.
49. *Irish Worker*, 17 Oct. 1914, p. 2.
50. *Spark*, 28 Mar. 1915, p. 4.
51. *Hibernian*, 7 Jul. 1915, p. 1.
52. However, Sean Doyle made sure to insist that he himself was 'not a molly-coddle', and enjoyed 'a man's story' as much as anyone else (*Spark*, 28 Mar. 1915).
53. *Irishman*, 23 Sep. 1916, p. 1.
54. *Spark*, 7 Feb. 1915, p. 1.
55. *Irishman*, 23 Sep. 1916, p. 1.
56. *Nationality*, 1 Sep. 1917, p. 4. This revival received a good review in the *Irish Times*, which remarked that this was 'Irish drama of the best type'. The audience seemed to enjoy it as well, responding quickly to 'the rapid witticisms in which the comedy abounds', *Irish Times*, 28 Sep. 1917, p. 4.
57. *Nationality*, 1 Sep. 1917, p. 4.
58. *Honesty*, 29 Jan. 1916, p. 3.

59. Ibid., 1 Apr. 1916, p. 4.
60. *Eire/Ireland*, 4 Nov. 1914, p. 2.
61. Ibid., 23 Nov. 1914, p. 2.
62. Ibid.
63. *Honesty*, 18 Dec. 1915, pp. 1–2.
64. *Nationality*, 14 Aug. 1915, p. 4.
65. *Eire/Ireland*, 23 Nov. 1914, p. 2.
66. *Honesty*, 18 Dec. 1915, pp. 1–2.
67. KSRL, OH G27: *Fianna Fáil*, 26 Sep. 1914, p. 4.
68. An employee of the Post Office, Walsh had been ordered to take up employ in England after his Volunteer activities came to the attention of authorities.
69. KSRL, OH G27: *Fianna Fáil*, 17 Oct. 1914, p. 2.
70. *Catholic Bulletin*, Aug. 1918, p. 399.
71. Ibid., Feb. 1917, pp. 115–20. Singing these melodies became a widespread form of resistance after the Easter Rising. Prisoners in the dock often sang the 'Soldier's Song' and 'The Wearing of the Green'. For instance, see *Weekly Freeman's Journal*, 17 Nov. 1917.
72. *Hibernian*, 7 July 1915, p. 7.
73. *Gael*, 12 Feb. 1916, pp. 7–8.
74. Ibid.
75. See *Irishman*, 15 May 1916; 21 Oct. 1916.
76. *Gael*, 12 Feb. 1916, pp. 7–8.
77. *Eire Og*, 14 July 1917, p. 3.
78. The *Irish Weekly Independent*, with the largest circulation of weekly papers in Ireland (an average of 50,000–72,000 copies per week in 1914–15; 50,000–69,000 copies per week in 1915–16) was a particular offender, *Irish Weekly Independent*, 30 Sep. 1916, p. 4. See also, 22 Apr. 1916, 25 Mar. 1916, 10 June 1916, and so on.
79. The most important of these papers were *Answers*, the *Magnet*, the *Boy's Friend* and the *Girl's Friend*, and *Home Notes*. Other comic papers for boys included *Chips* and *Comic-Cuts*.
80. The exception being Sean Doyle in the *Spark*, who sarcastically described Lord Northcliffe as 'The "Successful" Irishman', *Spark*, 5 Dec. 1915.
81. *Nationality*, 24 July 1915, p. 5.
82. *Irishman*, 8 Dec. 1917, p. 4.
83. *Spark*, 5 Dec. 1915, p. 2.
84. *Nationality*, 5 Feb. 1916, p. 1; *Answers*, 29 Jan. 1916, p. 211.
85. For more on Griffith's anti-Semitic roots, see B. Novick, 'No Anti-Semitism in Ireland? The Limerick "Pogrom" and Radical Nationalist Stereotypes', *The Jewish Quarterly*, no. 168 (Winter 1997/1998), pp. 35–40.
86. Garvin, 'Priests and Patriots', p. 78.
87. *Gael*, 26 Feb. 1916, p. 5.
88. *Catholic Bulletin*, Feb. 1917, p. 97.
89. *Nationality*, 9 June 1917, p. 1.

90. *Eire Og*, 16 Mar. 1918, p. 1.
91. *Sinn Féin*, 28 Nov. 1914, p. 1.
92. *Hibernian*, 2 Oct. 1915, p. 8.
93. *Sinn Féin*, 28 Nov. 1914, p. 1.
94. Viviani was a great enemy of the Catholic press in Ireland. In 1906 he had championed the secularisation of state education, and in a speech to the French Parliament, boasted that his party had 'extinguished in heaven those lights that never will be relit' (P. Maume, *The Long Gestation* (Dublin, 1999), p. 165).
95. See *Spark*, 2 and 9 May 1915; *Nationality*, 24 Nov. 1917, 2 Feb. 1918. The *Freeman's Journal* applauded the meeting, *Weekly Freeman's Journal*, 2 May 1915, p. 4.

4

Mobilisation: The South Longford By-election and its Impact on Political Mobilisation

Marie Coleman

Advanced nationalism in the shape of Sinn Féin and the Irish Republican Brotherhood was not strong in County Longford prior to the Easter Rising. The dominant political organisation in the county was the UIL, the local organisation of the Home Rule movement. Yet, by the time of the general election in December 1918, the UIL was almost non-existent and the Sinn Féin candidate in the general election, Joe McGuinness, won a resounding victory, gaining 72 per cent of the votes cast, over the longstanding Home Rule MP, J. P. Farrell.[1] The 1918 election was McGuinness's second significant election victory in 19 months; in a by-election in the constituency of South Longford in May 1917 he won the seat by a very narrow margin of 37 votes. The South Longford contest was the second in a series of by-election victories for Sinn Féin in 1917. Earlier, in February 1917, George Noble, Count Plunkett, father of executed 1916 rebel Joseph Mary Plunkett, was elected on a Sinn Féin ticket in North Roscommon; and Sinn Féin followed the South Longford win with victories for Eamon de Valera in East Clare in July and for W. T. Cosgrave in Kilkenny City in August. While the South Longford victory was crucial to Sinn Féin's emergence as an effective political party and its eventual displacement of the IPP, its impact was greatest at local level. This chapter will illustrate the formative effect which the result had on the mobilisation of the organs of advanced nationalism – Sinn Féin, the Irish Volunteers and Cumann na mBan – within County Longford, leading to its emergence as one of the most prominent centres of republican activity during the Irish revolution.

Background to the by-election

Contemporary observers and subsequent historians believed that Sinn Féin was faced with a strong nationalist organisation during the Longford by-election.[2] In fact, the ranch war of 1906–8 represented the zenith of the nationalist movement in Longford and from that time onwards it suffered progressive and sustained decline, beginning with the defection of a senior UIL figure, William Ganly, to Sinn Féin in 1907. For the nationalist movement in the county, 1909 was a year of much turmoil: opposition was voiced to the 'people's budget' and the IPP's support for it; the ranch warriors were dissatisfied with the House of Lords' emasculation of the Land Bill; and a serious political row erupted between the county's two Nationalist MPs, J. P. Farrell and John Phillips, the after-effects of which would still be felt even after Phillips's death in 1917. To such internal dissension was added a complacency derived from the largely satisfactory state of landownership and the prospect that home rule would be achieved by 1914. The result, from 1910 onwards, was a neglect of the local machinery of the party, which was noticeable in the reduction of contributions to the parliamentary fund to pay the IPP's MPs, and a marked and sustained decline in the number of UIL meetings held at all levels of the organisation, as shown in Table 4.1.[3]

Despite the continuing exhortations from Farrell to 'maintain' the nationalist organisation, the UIL's decline became even more pronounced in 1914. This can be explained by competition from the Irish Volunteers and dissatisfaction at John Redmond's support for the

Table 4.1 UIL meetings in Longford, 1908–15

	1908	1909	1912	1913	1914	1915
No. branch meetings	160	189	75	80	60	21
UIL executive meetings	11	6	4	6	5	2
Reorganisation meetings	9	13	1	11	6	18
Other meetings	8	7	1	0	1	1
Total no. UIL meetings	188	215	81	97	72	42

British war effort, which, given the hostile reaction to recruitment in Longford, was not popular in the county. The postponement of home rule for the duration of the war merely served to disenchant nationalist supporters further. It was a combination of these factors that prompted the desertion of another leading Nationalist, Frank McGuinness, by 1916. The Easter Rising, though not widely supported in Longford, accelerated the declining fortunes of the county's Home Rule movement; between April and December 1916 only six UIL meetings were held and a national organiser was sent to the county early in 1917 in an effort to revitalise the League in advance of the expected electoral contest. The death of the ailing John Phillips on 2 April 1917 created a vacancy in South Longford. However, such was the extent of decay that the Nationalists were not even sufficiently organised to hold a selection convention to choose their candidate for the by-election.

Prior to the Rising, Sinn Féin in Longford failed to exploit the declining fortunes of the Home Rule movement. The national decline of Sinn Féin after 1909 did nothing to help the fortunes of William Ganly's largely ineffective Granard branch, and from 1913 onwards its most prominent activists became more involved in organising the Irish Volunteers. Longford was largely unaffected by the Rising, and efforts by some local Volunteers to reach Dublin were unsuccessful. Nor were there many arrests in the county after the Rising. The local police reported that the public reaction to the Rising was muted; the release of some of the prisoners went largely unnoticed and while there was some sympathy with the rebels, the prevailing opinion was that 'the great majority of the people, generally, came to view it as a mad, rash and unwise proceeding in every way'.[4]

The by-election

Failure to hold a selection convention caused much confusion in Nationalist ranks. Paddy McKenna, an activist during the ranch war, was considered to be the favourite choice of the IPP's MPs to be their party's candidate.[5] However, McKenna was not the favoured choice of the influential Bishop of Ardagh and Clonmacnoise, Dr Joseph Hoare, who proposed the nomination of a rival candidate, Joseph M. Flood, instead. The situation was complicated further by the entrance of a third Nationalist candidate, Hugh Garahan, acting Chairman of Longford County Council. In private, John Dillon placed the blame for all the confusion on Bishop Hoare; describing Hoare's conduct as 'outrageous', 'treacherous' and 'scandalous', he made it clear that if Sinn Féin were to win the election he would consider Bishop Hoare to be responsible for the IPP's defeat.[6]

The farcical situation whereby three candidates proposed to stand in the same interest had become so potentially damaging to the IPP that, although reluctant to do so, its leaders were eventually forced to intervene. The three would-be Nationalist candidates were summoned to a meeting in Dublin chaired by Joe Devlin, at which they agreed to accept the decision of John Redmond as to which of them would contest the election on the party ticket.[7] On 24 April, Redmond announced that he had chosen Paddy McKenna as the candidate to represent the party. This decision was accepted without any argument from Bishop Hoare, who even agreed to nominate McKenna.[8]

While Redmond's choice of McKenna helped stem the fragmentation of the Nationalist organisation in Longford, it was unable to undo the damage caused by the initial divisions. The choice of an official candidate was not made until the last week of April, allowing just over two weeks to canvass on his behalf, whereas Sinn Féin had been campaigning on behalf of their candidate since mid-April. The three candidates had been allowed to remain in the field so long that they had all built up strong factions, and the supporters of the two unsuccessful candidates were lukewarm about embracing the cause of Paddy McKenna. The delay and bitterness involved in choosing a candidate was to prove a serious setback to the Nationalist cause, for while the Nationalists had been fighting an election with each other, their opponents had the platform in the real contest to themselves.

Initially, Sinn Féin also encountered some problems in the selection of a candidate to represent them. Within two days of John Phillips's death a group of prominent figures in Sinn Féin, which included Arthur Griffith, Count Plunkett, William O'Brien, Michael Collins and Rory O'Connor, decided that their organisation would contest the election. The candidate suggested was Joe McGuinness, a native of Longford, who was at the time serving three years' penal servitude in Lewes Prison for his role in the Easter Rising. Arthur Griffith was less enthusiastic about this choice, indicating a preference for the republican writer J. J. 'Sceilg' O'Kelly.[9] Opposition to the suggestion of McGuinness's candidature came from the proposed candidate himself and his fellow 1916 prisoners in Lewes Prison, including Eamon de Valera. Thomas Ashe was the only prisoner in Lewes to support the idea. Declining the invitation, issued by Count Plunkett, to contest the election, McGuinness stated: 'I and my comrades here believe that I could not more truthfully represent the national cause of Ireland than in my present position.'[10] The prisoners were concerned about the very real prospect of defeat and the implications this would have for the cause of 1916. They were also suspicious of Count Plunkett, who had issued the invitation, and of Sinn Féin, which still had monarchist connotations in their minds. In spite of McGuinness's firm rejection of the offer to contest the South Longford vacancy, the decision of the Lewes prisoners was ignored and Sinn Féin's Mansion House Committee proceeded with his nomination.

The conditions which had favoured Sinn Féin in the previous by-election in North Roscommon did not exist in South Longford. While a certain level of sympathy could have been conjured up for McGuinness as a prisoner in a British jail, it could not be converted into anything approaching the sympathy vote received by Count Plunkett, the father of an executed 1916 rebel. The after-effects of the Rising had also been felt more keenly in Roscommon, where the fifth highest number of arrests in the months after the rebellion was recorded. In addition, an active separatist organisation under the leadership of Fr Michael O'Flanagan had existed in Roscommon, whereas prior to 1917 Sinn Féin was extremely weak in Longford. However, Sinn Féin had learned much from the campaign in Roscommon and this was used to its advantage in Longford.[11]

Sinn Féin was lucky in that it was given a good head start by its rivals; its canvassers had been campaigning actively for two weeks while the Nationalists campaigned against each other for the favour of the IPP. In a letter to Redmond on 12 April, John Dillon commented that 'The Sinn Féiners ... are extremely active.'[12] The energy and activity displayed by its canvassers characterised the Sinn Féin campaign from the outset. The *Irish Times* commented on the ubiquity of the Sinn Féin machine in the early stages of the campaign: 'The *Sinn Féin* party are extraordinarily active and all parts of the constituency are being visited by them.'[13] The entire area was reported to be littered with the flags and posters of the organisation.[14]

Sinn Féin also had a big lead over the Nationalists in terms of financial and human resources. The South Longford election campaign was estimated to have cost the party £491, which was more than adequately covered by the £1,288 raised by an election fund started by Griffith's newspaper *Nationality*.[15] Contributions to the fund came from many parts of the country;[16] sums of £50 were donated by both

the Working Committee of Limerick Nationalists and the Executive
of Sinn Féin in Cork.[17] In terms of manpower, Sinn Féin also received
help from various parts of the country; supporters were reported as
having come to assist in canvassing from Kerry and Cork, Antrim and
Down, Limerick and Dublin, from where, the police reported, members of the Irish Citizen Army had travelled.[18] In his memoir of the
revolutionary period, the republican activist Frank Gallagher estimated
that 200 election workers travelled from Dublin.[19]

This intense activity on the part of Sinn Féin did not go unnoticed; Paddy McKenna complained: 'Our opponents have been bringing their forces from all over the country in motors etc. trying to
intimidate the people.'[20] Every prominent figure in Sinn Féin went to
Longford to assist in the election effort, including Arthur Griffith,
Count and Countess Plunkett, Mrs Pearse, Kathleen Clarke, and
Darrell Figgis. As Brigid Lyons Thornton, the niece of the Sinn Féin
candidate, later remarked: 'everybody in Ireland that was worth know-
ing came to Longford to help fight the election'.[21]

The intensity of the Sinn Féin campaign certainly provoked the
desired reaction, particularly among the younger generation. All commentators reported the popularity of Sinn Féin with the youth in the
constituency, which appears to have led to some familial disputes; an
Irish Times report stated that 'Sons refuse to help their fathers on the
land unless they exact a promise to support Mr McGuinness, while
daughters decline to pursue their domestic duties without laying similar toll.'[22] According to the *Irish Independent* this dissension had got to
the stage where 'two youths have threatened to "lock up" their fathers
unless they vote for Mr McGuinness'.[23] If it could not persuade the
older generation to transfer its allegiance from the IPP to Sinn Féin
voluntarily, the youth of South Longford was forced to resort to this
type of action to help the cause of McGuinness, because they were
unable to vote in the election themselves. The suffrage was based on the
register in operation at the time of the last general election, which had
been in 1910. Thus, the support that Sinn Féin enjoyed among young
people was useless if not translated into effective pressure to make older
voters, adherents of the Nationalist cause, change their minds.

One section of the younger population which may have had some
influence upon voters was the younger clergy. Many young curates,
and some parish priests, openly supported Sinn Féin and spoke on its
platforms during the campaign, in spite of the explicit Nationalist
sympathies of their bishop. The press, both local and national, also
highlighted the independent stance of the young clergy. A Sinn Féin

demonstration was reported as having been attended by a 'bevy of young priests who filled two or three motor cars'. According to the *Irish Times*, many such priests proudly proclaimed their political allegiance 'by sporting the Republican colours'. That newspaper was convinced that this section of the clergy would influence the result of the election: 'Their attitude is undoubtedly doing harm to the Redmondite prospects, and their influence on voters is not counter balanced by the fact that nearly all the older clergy are supporting McKenna.'[24] Thus, the clichéd distinction between conservative parish priests and rebellious-minded young curates appears to have existed during the South Longford contest.

In stark contrast to the energy and activity displayed by the Sinn Féin machine, the Nationalist electoral organisation, the UIL, was weak, lethargic and disorganised, as illustrated in the controversy that surrounded the selection of a Nationalist candidate. The *Irish Independent* declared that 'as an electoral organisation the League is regarded as practically useless'.[25] The Longford UIL had never undertaken an election campaign, the last contested election in the county having been in 1892, pre-dating the foundation of the organisation. This electoral inexperience, combined with the pathetic state of its organisation and the failure to select an official candidate until two weeks before the election, did not augur well for McKenna's campaign.

Apart from limiting the length of the IPP's campaign, the confusion over selecting a candidate had created so much factionalism within the Nationalist organisation that McKenna was not supported by followers of the unsuccessful candidates, in particular those of Hugh Garahan. In the area around Hugh Garahan's base in Ballymahon, erstwhile Nationalists became staunch McGuinnessites, especially in the case of the Ancient Order of Hibernians. There was also opposition to McKenna from the AOH in Longford town.[26] This defection to the Sinn Féin camp was widespread in the Hibernian organisation in South Longford. The secretary of the Longford county board of the AOH, Michael Cox, publicly declared that, as he had no evidence that Paddy McKenna had been a member of the organisation since 1909, he was under no obligation to vote for him, and announced his intention not only to vote for Joe McGuinness but also to sign his nomination papers.[27] When the national secretary of the Order, John Dillon Nugent, came to Longford to canvass for McKenna the Clonguish and Newtowncashel divisions refused him use of their halls for holding meetings in support of McKenna, while in Ballymahon he was forced to abandon one such meeting by constant interruptions and heckling from the audience.[28]

The head start given to Sinn Féin allowed them to dictate the issues in the campaign. The protraction of the war combined with the introduction of conscription in Britain in 1916 had increased fears of its extension to Ireland, a fear exploited to the full by Sinn Féin. The speeches of all of Sinn Féin's prominent campaigners expounded the allegation that the IPP MPs would support the application of conscription to Ireland, and the only way to stop this was to elect Joe McGuinness.[29] The Sinn Féin press also laid much emphasis on the issue of conscription; *New Ireland* charged that John Redmond had 'temporised with conscription'.[30] This allegation was dishonest propaganda in view of the work of the Irish MPs to prevent conscription being applied to Ireland when it had been introduced in Britain, and the logic of Sinn Féin's assertion that the election of McGuinness was certain to prevent conscription being extended to Ireland is not very clear. Yet, at the time Sinn Féin was spreading this claim the Nationalists were still preoccupied in vying with each other for the prize of officially representing the IPP, and the attempts by John Dillon and others to counter the Sinn Féin charges in the week leading up to the election came too late to have any effect. Sinn Féin had the greatest success in exploiting the conscription menace in the rural areas of the constituency, where farmers feared that their sons, who were needed at home to work on the farms, would be shipped off to France.

The other disaster that would befall Ireland if Joe McGuinness was not elected was partition. Readers of Griffith's *Nationality* were warned that 'Every vote for his opponent … is a vote in favour of the partition of Ireland.'[31] On this issue the Sinn Féin arguments had much more basis than those on conscription, yet, perhaps because it was not so evocative in personal terms, partition was not stressed to the same extent. It, nevertheless, developed into an issue of much greater importance by the day of the election. Another issue which was central to the Sinn Féin campaign was McGuinness's status as a prisoner, and the South Longford by-election quickly became characterised by the slogan 'Put him in to get him out', producing the misleading interpretation that McGuinness's election would secure his release. However, it was felt that McGuinness's election would help to advance the case for the granting of an amnesty to the 1916 prisoners. The timing of the election also helped the cause of Sinn Féin. The campaign straddled the period covering the first anniversary of the Rising and subsequent executions. In conjunction with the amnesty issue, it served to remind the electorate of the cause for which Joe McGuinness was in prison, and the republican press condemned the IPP for its actions after the Rising, implying that they had colluded in the imprisonments and executions.

The South Longford by-election had already been the scene of controversial clerical interference, but the impact of Bishop Hoare's intervention was soon overshadowed by that of his colleague the Archbishop of Dublin, William Walsh. In a provocative letter to the Dublin evening papers on the eve of election day in Longford, Walsh condemned the fact that a partitionist solution to the home rule question still held 'a leading place in the practical politics of today'. His letter concluded with the famous postscript: 'I think it a duty to write this, although from information that has just reached me I am fairly satisfied that the mischief has already been done, and that the country is practically sold.'[32] The information that Walsh claimed to have received alleged that if the IPP won in Longford they were prepared to accept partition and 'to take over the administration of such portion of the country as might be transferred to them'.[33] Sinn Féin was quick to make political capital out of the Archbishop's statement; leaflets carrying the text of the letter were distributed at polling stations throughout the constituency the following day and Sinn Féin cars were covered with posters proclaiming that 'This is a clear call from the venerated Archbishop of Dublin to vote against the Irish Party traitors and vote for Joe McGuinness.'[34]

The Longford election contest had certainly generated much excitement, both locally and nationally. The county's first contested election in 25 years was the cause of great interest among locals, witnessed by a voter turnout of approximately 78 per cent.[35] These factors, combined with the internal disarray of the Nationalists, the energetic campaigning of Sinn Féin, and the controversial involvement of influential members of the Roman Catholic hierarchy, all contributed to the uniqueness of the South Longford by-election campaign. Consequently, the result was eagerly awaited, with both sides predicting victory.

The drama surrounding the announcement of the result was suitably worthy of the eventful campaign that had gone before it. Initially, the returning officer announced a narrow margin of victory, by 12 votes, for Paddy McKenna. However, when the votes received by both candidates were added together the number fell well short of the total number of votes cast, a problem which was solved by 1916 veteran Joe McGrath's discovery of a bundle of uncounted ballots. When these were considered, the final result was announced to be 1,498 for Joe McGuinness, 37 votes ahead of McKenna's poll of 1,461.[36]

Shane Leslie's subsequent judgement that 'By his pen the Archbishop returned the Sinn Féin candidate,'[37] was accepted by commentators at the time and subsequently as the explanation for Sinn Féin's defeat of the IPP in South Longford.[38] Given the narrowness of McGuinness's margin of victory it is most likely that Walsh's intervention was a vital contributory factor. However, to put the Sinn Féin victory down purely to the action of Archbishop Walsh is to ignore the weakness of the Nationalist organisation in the constituency and the energetic campaign fought by Sinn Féin. It is also to ignore the fact that political allegiances were changing rapidly in Longford, especially amongst the younger generation. The London *Times* considered this trend of the younger generation's support for Sinn Féin to be 'the most sinister portent of the South Longford election'.[39]

The Home Rule MP Stephen Gwynn later described the result as 'a notice of dismissal to the Parliamentary Party', while a unionist observer, Sir James Stronge, believed that 'Redmond can no longer pose as the representative of nationalist Ireland.'[40] The impact was as devastating for the IPP as it was formative for Sinn Féin. According to C. P. Scott, editor of the *Manchester Guardian* and a confidant of the IPP leaders, John Redmond considered the defeat to be of such magnitude that he felt his party 'would have to resign their seats in a body and either challenge re-election or else simply retire from political life and leave Sinn Féin and the British Government face to face'.[41] For Sinn Féin the victory vindicated those who had advocated contesting elections in the face of opposition such as that of the Lewes prisoners. This justification of the policy of contesting elections helped forge the emergent and somewhat disparate and loose Sinn Féin organisation into a homogeneous, efficient and effective political party.

Post by-election Longford

The Sinn Féin victory in the by-election rapidly transformed the political landscape of Longford. Only a month afterwards, in June 1917, the County Inspector of the RIC reported: 'Sinn Féinism has increased by leaps and bounds,' and 'The spread of Sinn Féinism is the principal matter calling for reference in the county.'[42] In the same month the separatist press began to report on the foundation of the first post-Rising Sinn Féin clubs in the county.[43] The emergence of Sinn Féin in Longford coincided with its take-off countrywide, which was very extensive between April and July 1917. The release from prison of Joe McGuinness in June 1917 provided an opportunity for a public display of the level of support for Sinn Féin in Longford. A huge rally was held in Longford town on Sunday, 22 July, to mark his first return to his new constituency since his election, at which the attendance was reported to have been between 3000 and 5000 people.[44]

The work of local Sinn Féin activists was boosted by that of prominent national figures in Sinn Féin and the Volunteers – in particular Griffith, Collins and Ashe – who travelled around the country during the summer of 1917 organising branches, making frequent visits to Longford in the process. During one visit to Longford, Ashe addressed a meeting for the formation of a branch of Sinn Féin in Ballinalee. He was subsequently arrested for the use of seditious language at that meeting and sentenced to two years' imprisonment with hard labour in Mountjoy, where he died from the effects of force-feeding on 25 September 1917.[45] After Ashe's death, Collins continued his frequent visits to Longford, especially to Granard where he had by this stage become closely associated with the Kiernan family. He was the principal speaker at a large Sinn Féin demonstration in Ballinalee in October 1917, by which time the local police were becoming aware of his presence.

Between May and October the local press in Longford carried reports of the establishment of Sinn Féin clubs in almost every parish in the county; nearly 30 clubs were formed during this time.[46] At the end of 1917 the Sinn Féin organisation in Longford was very strong. Official party figures indicate that 28 cumainn from the county were affiliated by December, and police figures estimated a membership of around 2,500, although statistics from this source must be treated with caution.[47] The by-election had undoubtedly been the most significant factor instigating this rapid growth. The same effect was seen in almost all of the areas where by-elections took place in that year: when the number of clubs per county in December 1917 is adjusted to take account of the population, three of the counties where there had been elections in 1917 were among the five where the party was strongest; Longford came third, and Roscommon fourth, behind Clare and Leitrim.[48] The reports of the local RIC also serve to indicate the strength of Sinn Féin in the county towards the end of 1917: 'The Sinn Féin organisation is the only one of importance in the county. It is spreading rapidly & the whole county may be regarded as Sinn Féin.' All of the County Inspector's reports for the latter months of

1917 and in early 1918 contain almost identical assessments.[49] This rapid expansion of Sinn Féin was accompanied by the final demise of the already weak Nationalist organisation; according to the County Inspector the UIL existed in name only, and despite the best efforts of J. P. Farrell, the flow of personnel from the Nationalist to the Republican organisation proceeded apace during the latter half of 1917. Although Farrell went on to contest the 1918 general election against McGuinness, by the end of 1917 his organisation had practically ceased to exist.

The attempt to extend conscription to Ireland in early 1918 resulted in a further substantial rise, estimated at 29 per cent by one source, in the national membership of Sinn Féin, and also of the Volunteers, as support for the separatist organisations became associated with opposition to conscription.[50] However, this pattern did not apply to Longford, where the previous year's by-election had already firmly established the Sinn Féin organisation. The benefit that this crisis brought to Sinn Féin in Longford was to enable the momentum generated in the latter half of 1917 to be maintained. The association with resistance to conscription helped the local Sinn Féin branches to hold together and to continue recruiting. The organisation of meetings to mobilise public opposition to the proposed measure provided a new focus of activity.

Attempts to reorganise the Volunteers in the aftermath of the Easter Rising began early in 1917. The first indicators of a revival in Longford came at the time of the by-election. In Ballinalee the Volunteer force was re-formed by Sean Connolly and Sean MacEoin at Easter 1917. The applications for military service pensions made by former Volunteers from Longford indicate that a significant number of Volunteers, especially those in the Longford town battalion, joined during the months of April and May 1917. Of a sample of 406 pension applicants, 184 stated the date at which they joined the Volunteers, and of those, 127 joined in 1917, and only 38 in 1918. Of the 57 who also indicated the month in which they joined, 48 were in 1917, of which 27 joined in April during the by-election campaign. Although the level of response is low, accounting for less than half of the overall sample, the evidence still suggests that the by-election was important in motivating young men to join the Volunteers.

Throughout the latter half of 1917 the growth of the Irish Volunteers in Longford was unable to keep pace with the rapid spread of Sinn Féin. In September 1917 the County Inspector of the RIC still claimed that 'There is no branch of the Irish Volunteers' in the county.[51] While this statement was erroneous, it does illustrate that the Volunteers were not as obvious as Sinn Féin and were still operating more underground. Throughout the country the re-formation of the Volunteers was masked by the ascendancy of Sinn Féin. One reason for this phenomenon was the similarity between the two organisations; because of their shared membership they often appeared to be interchangeable. Such overlap between Sinn Féin and the Volunteers during 1917–18 was very pronounced in Longford, where Michael Collins's frequent visits to the county at that time were concerned with relaunching the Volunteers as well as assisting Sinn Féin. The RIC County Inspector's reports show that the police were unable to discern any significant difference between Sinn Féin and the Volunteers as both terms were interchanged quite often.

After an initial slow start the growth of the Volunteers accelerated towards the close of 1917, prompted by the release of the 1916 internees in June. A second formative occurrence was the death of Thomas Ashe in September 1917. The Volunteer executive responded to the death of Ashe with a show of strength by ordering units to drill in public. His death had particular resonance in Longford as his imprisonment had resulted from a speech given at Ballinalee, and the first accounts of Volunteer drilling in the county appeared in October, when three instances were reported to the Competent Military Authority. The number of cases reported in November was five, and in December there were three.[52] In November the *Roscommon Herald* stated that over 180 people took part in a route march of the Longford town Volunteers, and in the following month the same paper noted 'that the Irish Volunteer movement during late weeks has spread very extensively throughout County Longford and that a Company exists in practically every parish'.[53]

The growth in membership of the Volunteers in Longford continued throughout 1918. The instances of drilling reported by the RIC rose from three in January to seven in February. Police reports also indicated an increase in the number of units in existence in the county: two in January, five in February and seven in March. While these figures underestimate the strength of the force, blurred by its perceived close links with Sinn Féin, they are correct in so far as they highlight the increase in the size of the organisation.[54] During February and March, Michael Collins paid visits to the county to assist in the formation of new Volunteer units.[55] The conscription crisis had a more noticeable impact on the Volunteers in Longford than it had on the county's Sinn Féin organisation, due in part to the fact that the spread of the Volunteers during the latter half of 1917 had not been as extensive as the expansion of Sinn Féin.

There is no evidence of any formal establishment of Cumann na mBan in Longford. It appears instead to have evolved at the time of the 1917 by-election. Correspondence exists from April 1917 between Count Plunkett and the Longford town branch of Cumann na mBan, in which that branch expressed its hearty approval for 'the foundation of Liberty circles for women', presumably an offshoot of Plunkett's ill-fated Liberty League.[56] The by-election appears to have had a similar formative influence on Cumann na mBan as it had on Sinn Féin and the Irish Volunteers. The Ballinalee branch was formed in 1917, and as it was named after Thomas Ashe it was probably formed around the time of his death in September of that year.[57] Branches were also reported to have been established in Granard and Killashee, while some members later stated that they joined branches in Ardagh and Ballinamuck in 1917.[58] Evidence from the applications for military service pensions also indicates that the growth of Cumann na mBan in Longford was substantial during 1917. As the response to the question of when the women joined Cumann na mBan was high, 67 of a sample of 105 applicants, the evidence can be considered reasonably reliable in this instance: 42 of the 67 respondents stated that they joined in 1917; the next highest figure was 16, who joined in 1918.

The secretary's report to the 1918 convention of Cumann na mBan stated that one of the most outstanding features of the organisation during that year had been its rapid growth, the number of affiliated branches having risen from 100 in December 1917 to 600 at the time of the convention in September 1918. The three reasons cited were the spread of republicanism throughout Ireland, the work of travelling organisers, and the conscription threat.[59] This trend reflected the national pattern of growth in the other republican organisations, Sinn Féin and the Irish Volunteers. In Longford, however, the most significant growth in these organisations took place in 1917, with the by-election rather than the conscription crisis acting as the stimulating factor. From the available evidence it appears that the growth of Cumann na mBan within the county followed a similar pattern.

Conclusion

A banner erected outside Birr Castle following Eamon de Valera's election victory in East Clare in July 1917 put the South Longford result into context: 'Irish Party wounded in North Roscommon, killed in South Longford, buried in East Clare. R.I.P.'[60] The South Longford by-election had both national and local repercussions. At the time of the contest Sinn Féin was still a very loose and disparate alliance. Its subsequent transformation into a unified and coherent political party in October 1917 owed much to the by-election victories in Roscommon, Longford, Kilkenny and Clare. From the British Government's point of view, Longford was an indication that Irish public opinion was gradually turning in favour of separatism.

Longford also highlighted a number of important trends that were central to the revolution. The generational divide – both lay and clerical – foreshadowed a development that became noticeable in other parts of the country, as Sinn Féin emerged as the dominant political force in southern Ireland. It was even more marked in Longford a year later when McGuinness had a resounding victory over Farrell during the general election, the margin in this case owing much to a massively increased electorate, including many younger first-time voters. The contribution of the conscription threat to Sinn Féin's victory also serves to highlight the importance of the First World War as a backdrop for the Irish revolution. Redmond's support for the war and the postponement of home rule because of it, both had detrimental effects on support for the IPP. The threat of conscription, in Longford in 1917 and throughout the country a year later, was crucial to the political ascendancy of Sinn Féin and the reorganisation of the Irish Volunteers.

However, it was at local level that the effects of the by-election were greatest; it was the impetus for mobilising both the political and military arms of the revolution in the county, and provided the opportunity to reveal the level of decline which had taken hold in the Home Rule movement over the preceding decade. The rapid displacement of the IPP by Sinn Féin during the second half of 1917 transformed the political landscape of the county. The by-election was the most important event to take place in Longford during the period of the Irish revolution. The seeds of the county's emergence as one of the principal centres of IRA activity during the War of Independence were laid during and directly after the 1917 election.

Notes

1. James Patrick Farrell (1865–1921), founder, owner and editor of the *Longford Leader*; Nationalist MP for Cavan West (1895–1900) and for Longford North (1900–1918); the most influential figure in the Home Rule movement in Co. Longford.

2. Ernie O'Malley papers, UCDAD, P17b/153; D. Macardle, *The Irish Republic* (Dublin, 1951), p. 214; S. Ó Lúing, *Art Ó Gríofa* (Dublin, 1953), p. 284; C. P. Scott, *Political Diaries of C. P. Scott, 1911–1928*, ed. T. Wilson (London, 1970), pp. 289–90; P. S. O'Hegarty, *The Victory of Sinn Féin* (Dublin, 1925), p. 28; D. Hogan (Frank Gallagher), *Four Glorious Years* (Dublin, 1953), p. 9; and W. O'Brien, *Forth the Banners Go* (Dublin, 1969), p. 145.

3. *Longford Leader*. As records for 1910–11 are incomplete, these years have not been included.

4. RIC, CIR, Longford, 1916, CO 904/120.

5. *Roscommon Herald*, 21 Apr. 1917.

6. John Dillon to John Redmond, 12 and 13 Apr. 1917, NLI, John Redmond papers (hereafter JR), ms. 15 182/24.

7. *Roscommon Herald*, 28 Apr. 1917.

8. Bishop Hoare to John Redmond, 26 Apr. 1917, NLI, JR, ms. 15 197(2).

9. M. Laffan, *The Resurrection of Ireland* (Cambridge, 1999), p. 96.

10. J. McGuinness to Count Plunkett, Easter Sunday 1917, UCDAD, Eamon de Valera papers, P150.

11. Laffan, *Resurrection*, pp. 96–103.

12. Dillon to Redmond, 12 Apr. 1917, NLI, JR, ms. 15 182/24.

13. *Irish Times*, 20 Apr. 1917.

14. *Irish Independent*, 1 May 1917.

15. Laffan, *Resurrection*, p. 100.

16. *Irish Independent*, 4 May 1917.

17. *Factionist*, 17 May 1917; *Nationality*, 5 May 1917.

18. *Irish Independent*, 8 and 9 May 1917; C. Townshend, *The British Campaign in Ireland* (Oxford, 1975), p. 4; *Factionist*, 17 May 1917; RIC, CIR, Longford, May 1917, CO 904/103.

19. Hogan, *Four Glorious Years*, p. 10.

20. Paddy McKenna to Mr Mulvihill, 1 May 1917, NLI, ms. 11 379(14).

21. K. Griffith and T. E. O'Grady (eds), *Curious Journey: An Oral History of Ireland's Unfinished Revolution* (London, 1982), p. 108.

22. *Irish Times*, 8 May 1917.

23. *Irish Independent*, 5 May 1917.

24. D. W. Miller, *Church, State and Nation in Ireland, 1898–1921* (Dublin, 1973), p. 354.

25. *Irish Independent*, 1 May 1917.

26. *Irish Independent*, 1 May 1917; *Roscommon Herald*, 5 May 1917.

27. *Irish Independent*, 3 and 5 May 1917.

28. *Irish Independent*, 4, 7 and 8 May 1917.

29. Such speeches are reported in *Roscommon Herald*, 21 and 28 Apr. 1917, and 12 May 1917.

30. *New Ireland*, 5 May 1917.

31. *Nationality*, 5 May 1917.

32. Letter of Archbishop Walsh, reprinted in *Irish Times*, 9 May 1917.

33. P. Walsh, *William J. Walsh, Archbishop of Dublin* (Dublin/Cork, 1928), p. 572.
34. *Irish Independent*, 10 May 1917.
35. *Irish Times*, 10 May 1917.
36. *Irish Independent*, 11 May 1917.
37. Sir S. Leslie, 'Archbishop Walsh', in C. C. O'Brien (ed.), *The Shaping of Modern Ireland* (London, 1960), p. 103.
38. *Irish Independent*, 11 May 1917; *Irish Times*, 11 May 1917; *Freeman's Journal*, 11 May 1917; *Longford Leader*, 26 May 1917; *Dublin Evening Mail*, 11 May 1917; Walsh, *William J. Walsh*, p. 573; Laffan, *Resurrection*, p. 102; Scott, *Political Diaries*, p. 289; Miller, *Church, State and Nation*, p. 356; Hogan, *Four Glorious Years*, p. 10.
39. Newspaper cutting, NLI, ms. 23 064.
40. S. Gwynn, *John Redmond's Last Years* (London, 1919), p. 259; Sir J. H. Stronge to Hugh de Fellenborg Montgomery, 12 May 1917, quoted in A. P. Collins, 'The Decline of the Irish Parliamentary Party, 1910–1918', MA thesis (NUI, Galway, 1986), p. 122.
41. Scott, *Political Diaries*, p. 290.
42. RIC, CIR, Longford, June 1917, CO 904/103.
43. *Nationality*, 16 June 1917; *Roscommon Herald*, 30 June 1917.
44. RIC, CIR, Longford, July 1917, CO 904/103; *Roscommon Herald*, 28 July 1917.
45. *Longford Leader*, 29 Sep. 1917.
46. *Nationality* and *Roscommon Herald*, various issues, May–Oct. 1917.
47. NLI, ms. 11 405; RIC, CIR, Longford, Nov. 1917, CO 904/104.
48. Laffan, *Resurrection*, p. 187.
49. RIC, CIR, Longford, July–Dec. 1917, CO 904/104.
50. D. Fitzpatrick, *Politics and Irish Life* (Dublin, 1977), p. 152.
51. RIC, CIR, Longford, Sep. 1917, CO 904/104.
52. RIC, CIR, Longford, Oct.–Dec. 1917, CO 904/104.
53. *Roscommon Herald*, 10 Nov. 1917, 22 Dec. 1917.
54. RIC, CIR, Longford, Jan.–Mar. 1918, CO 904/105.
55. A. T. Q. Stewart, *Michael Collins: The Secret File* (Belfast, 1997), Doc. 34, p. 90.
56. M. Doyle to Count Plunkett, 24 Apr. 1917, NLI, Count Plunkett papers, ms. 11 383(11).
57. Áine Ní hAodha (Annie Hughes) to Sighile Humphreys, 1 June 1968, UCDAD, P106/1379.
58. RIC, CIR, Longford, Nov. 1917, CO 904/104; UCDAD, P151.
59. *Cumann na mBan Convention Report*, 1918.
60. J. N. McEvoy, 'A Study of the United Irish League in King's County, 1899–1918', MA thesis (NUI, Maynooth, 1990), p. 141.

5

Alternative Government: 'Exit Britannia' – the Formation of the Irish National State, 1918–21

Arthur Mitchell

The ending of the European war of 1914–18 set the stage for the assertion of self-government by a wide range of national groups. Taking advantage of the political and military disruption of the time, they moved rapidly to make good their claims to political authority before the beginning of the conference of Allied nations, scheduled to meet in Paris in January 1919. Among the petitioners were Finland, the Baltic States, Poland and Czechoslovakia, all of which were formerly controlled by one of the defeated belligerents. An exception was Ireland's claim for separation from the United Kingdom, one of the victorious Powers. The Allied leaders at the Versailles Conference had little difficulty and took obvious pleasure in carving up the territory of their defeated foes in Eastern Europe, but obviously Ireland was a very different matter.

The Irish claim was bolstered by recent developments in Ireland. In January 1919 an assembly was formed in Dublin, claiming the right to political authority in that country. This assertion was underpinned by the United Kingdom general election of December 1918, in which supporters of Irish independence won 70 per cent of the parliamentary seats in Ireland. The new assembly, Dáil Éireann, declared that Ireland was an independent state with a republican form of government. The

assembly's assertions were confronted by the twin challenges of impos-
ing its authority and gaining popular acceptance.

Pursuant to achieving political independence, the Irish national
movement employed four methods. First, it participated in open, legal
political activity – organisation, meetings, literature and, most importantly, elections. It also employed physical force; its army, Oglac na
hÉireann or the Irish Volunteers, was not a conventional military
organisation, but a secret, underground body that employed a variety
of devices – intimidation, coercion, arson, murder and, ultimately,
guerrilla warfare. A third method was the obstruction and nullifica-
tion of the existing civil administration of the country. Last, but not
least, it created an alternative government and administration.

This was not the only time the Irish attempted to form their own
government. Faced with the prospect of Irish self-government, Ulster
Unionists had established a 'provisional government' in Ulster in the
summer of 1914. The outbreak of the European war resulted in the
home rule issue being tabled, so the real intentions of the Ulster
Unionists were not put to the test. Yet in July 1917 Edward Carson,
leader of Ulster unionism, threatened to summon the 'Ulster
Provisional Government' and call out his paramilitary ally, the Ulster
Volunteers, if there was any change in the constitutional status of the
province. In the middle of the war the IRB staged a short-lived rebellion, which declared a republic and proclaimed a provisional government. After the 1919–21 campaign, a large section of Irish nationalists
rejected the compromise agreement with the British Government, and
its leadership formed a 'republican government' to act as a political
focus for their opposition. There was, thus, an apparent Irish propen-
sity to form your own government if and when necessary. This could
be viewed as the fruition of Sinn Féin's principle of 'do it yourself'.

The First World War provided the opportunity and stimulus for an
ultimately successful effort to attain Irish self-government using the
aforementioned methods. In the 30 years before 1914 the campaign to
achieve even a limited form of self-government through political pressure in Westminster had foundered on British reluctance to accept the
idea of a separate Irish political identity, the archaic intricacies of the
British constitutional system and the opposition of Irish unionists.

With the outbreak of war, Irish advocates of physical force, led by
the IRB, drew two conclusions. The peaceful constitutional movement
had failed to deliver the goods. Now it was time to revert to physical
force. Secondly, the best time to employ such violence was during a

period of mass-violence. This group, therefore, determined that they would act while the war was on. They were ultimately satisfied that even a mini-revolt would have the same destabilizing effect in Ireland that mass-violence was having on the Continent.

They were right. The 1916 rebellion, although easily contained and suppressed, transformed the political situation in Ireland. George Bernard Shaw saw its importance immediately: 'I remain an Irishman, and am bound to contradict any implication that I can regard as a traitor any Irishman taken in a fight for Irish independence against the British Government, which was a fair fight in everything except the enormous odds my countrymen had to face.' Shaw's statement reflected the eventual public response to the Easter Rising, which shifted from a numbed, adverse reaction, to a growing respect for the courage and dedication of the rebels, to excited support for militant Irish nationalism. This phenomenon can also be seen in three poems of William Butler Yeats (composed in the winter of 1916–17 but first published in 1920) in which he expressed riveting but qualified admiration for the insurgents.[1]

In the course of the European war both sides claimed to be the champions of peoples suppressed by their opponents, causing some stirrings among the subject nationalities. America's entry into the war in 1917 greatly increased this atmosphere of political aspiration. Woodrow Wilson's ringing phrases about making the world safe for democracy, and the right of every people to self-determination, sounded in many Irish ears as siren songs ideally suited to their objectives.

Two inter-related organisations were shaped in the aftermath of the rebellion. The Irish Volunteers (after 1916 popularly referred to as the Irish Republican Army) was revived and greatly expanded. Its objective was an independent republic. The organisation grew to the status of a people's militia, a people's army. The political side of the movement also took form, creating an umbrella organisation under the banner of Sinn Féin. This party had had a marginal existence advocating passive resistance to British control and the formation of alternative indigenous government institutions. When the 1916 Rising was labelled the 'Sinn Féin rebellion' by the press, militant nationalists regrouped in that body. They saw the methods of the Sinn Féin programme as a useful supplement to physical force. The new party was, in fact, a coalition, with its original leaders, principally Arthur Griffith, reluctantly agreeing to accept the new objective of an independent republic. On the other hand, the expanded party retained its original capitalist outlook. Although it advocated a broader role for government in social and economic matters, it argued that the principal reason for Irish under-development was foreign political control.[2]

The two organisations were separate bodies, but with overlapping membership, held tenuously together by the president of both entities, Eamon de Valera. Although new to the leadership of Irish nationalism, he was to demonstrate a capacity that carried him for over 40 years as the dominant political figure in Ireland.

By the end of the war, Europe was saturated by Allied, mainly American, propaganda about freedom, democracy and self-determination. This was an ideal time for Sinn Féin to seek electoral success. Lloyd George and his coalition partners, eager to gain an easy victory by means of a post-war election, provided the opportunity. In its platform, Sinn Féin de-emphasised republicanism, declaring its intention to establish a constituent assembly as the supreme national authority. It stressed the right of self-determination, with its case to be carried to Versailles, whose leading participant would be Woodrow Wilson, champion of that right.[3]

In the election of December 1918, although mustering only about half of the entire vote, Sinn Féin overwhelmed its Home Rule opponents. It did not expect nor receive success in the Unionist areas of Ulster. Having won almost three-quarters of the seats in Ireland, Sinn Féin proceeded to put its programme into effect. In part owing to the absence of essentially moderate but imprisoned leaders, the party went beyond merely forming a constituent assembly to the creating of a national assembly of an independent republic. To critics of Sinn Féin this action was a foolhardy gesture of defiance, grist for mockery and a propagandist posture without substance.[4]

In Sinn Féin's eyes, the country had an ironclad case for self-determination at the post-war conference. Versailles, however, was less a 'peace conference' than a cut and chop operation by the victors in the war. When Sinn Féin failed to impress the Allied representatives, there was disappointment in its ranks, but rejection at Versailles roused a feeling of righteous indignation in the country. The Sinn Féin leadership responded to this rebuff by carrying on an extended publicity campaign on the Continent and by opening up two other avenues of activity – carrying the case of Irish freedom to the United States and creating an effective alternative government at home.[5]

The revolutionary government of Sinn Féin was essentially parliamentary, with a unilateral legislature and an elected executive. Despite pleas that an Irish system should reject the British model, the founders of the new state decided to rely on the familiar. In doing so, they demonstrated political prudence: it would be hard enough to rally public support for the new government without providing their opponents with ammunition for satire by creating an innovative system.[6]

In regard to social and economic orientation, the rebel regime was mildly reformist within the parameters of liberal capitalism. At its first meeting it adopted a Democratic Programme, which anticipated an expanded government role in elevating social and educational standards. The immediate post-war period was an era of lofty rhetoric. Dáil Éireann felt compelled to match the slogan of the Lloyd George coalition of 'a land fit for heroes'. As well, its Labour allies required such commitments to establish the country in the emerging international labour and socialist organisations. In time, the Dáil executive launched modest pilot schemes in housing, land purchase, fisheries and cooperative enterprises.[7]

Dáil Éireann had also to take note of the Catholic Church, very few of whose conservative leaders endorsed the rebel administration.[8] In addition, the Dáil would get nowhere without the financial support of larger farmers and small businessmen. Any taint of radicalism would shut off this vital source. A radical, committed social and economic programme would subject the fledgling government to charges of socialism and Bolshevism. There was nevertheless considerable press commentary that its Labour allies were leading the Sinn Féin government to collectivism. Finally, Dáil Éireann, like its parent party, was not primarily a social or economic movement; its real concern was fostering nationalism.[9]

In its first few months Dáil Éireann had to rely on propaganda to tell the world it indeed was a government (see Chapter 6). At the same time it prepared a modest programme of action. By June 1919 it was ready to proceed. Eamon de Valera, now president of the Dáil executive, went to the United Sates, where in an 18-month sojourn he generated public support and raised a large publicly subscribed loan. At home the Dáil passed a legislative programme creating a rival system of administration, encouraging fisheries and forestry, forming arbitration courts and investigating the nation's resources. It also decreed vague but sweeping land reform.[10]

At this time, Diarmuid O'Hegarty, the head of the embryonic civil service, expressed optimism about the work of the Dáil:

> Actual constructive work will leave a bigger mark on people than *political* work. It makes them think more, and besides it invests the *Government* with tangibility as such. It means that the Dáil has stepped away from the beaten path of political parties and their shibboleths, and that it is functioning as any progressive Government would be expected to function.[11]

Having laid before the public some of its intentions, the Dáil proceeded to launch a loan campaign in Ireland to finance these programmes. Its goal was £250,000, the same amount raised by the anti-conscription campaign in 1918. Its hope to have a large part of that fund's mostly unspent money transferred into its hands did not materialise. Nevertheless, with mounting evidence that the Dáil loan effort was succeeding, Dublin Castle lost its hope and expectation that the campaign would end in a humiliating failure. The prospect of another government in the country roused the unionist *Belfast Newsletter* to question on 9 June 1919, 'Why should the Sinn Féin organization be allowed to exist? Why should a number of men be allowed to call themselves "the Irish Parliament", to elect a "Cabinet" and a "President"?' It concluded, 'The Government will not be successful in enforcing the law so long as it does not suppress the rival Administration.'

In September 1919 Dublin Castle heeded this advice, declaring Dáil Éireann and its supporting organisations to be illegal bodies. Arthur Griffith flung the words of Edmund Burke at the *ancien régime*: 'The government against which the claim of liberty is tantamount to high treason is a government to which submission is equivalent to slavery.' Augusta Gregory recorded what Lennox Robinson, the Abbey playwright, told her about further action against the Dáil in November: 'The Government chose a time just after the two minutes of silence on Armistice Day to make their descent on Dáil Éireann, with soldiers and motors and to arrest its members.' That was not all: Dublin Castle 'had sent a "chit" to the papers forbidding them to publish any of the reports of Dáil Éireann's activities in constructive policy and economics which they are working at, lest they should get credit for it in England'. However, in little more than a year it was the British administration that was humiliated, cordoned off by armed guards and devoid of substantial public support. The situation did not improve. When John French, the embattled Lord Lieutenant, travelled to Belfast in March 1921 to denounce the campaign for Irish independence he arrived in a large motorcade, which included soldiers, armoured cars and a lorry with a mounted gun.[12]

The banning of the Dáil was not its end but really its making. Driving it underground generally was to its advantage. Now Dublin Castle would only have a vague idea of what the rebel government was doing. The leaders of the Dáil, through their membership of the Irish Volunteers, Sinn Féin and the IRB, had a wealth of covert operating experience. Many members of the public had a lively appreciation of the ability of its young men and women to frustrate the efforts of the old order. Rather than merely surviving, the Dáil administration

continued to grow, increasing its employees, extending its programmes and broadening its control of the country.

Its loan drive rolled to success, achieving its goal of £250,000 in
June 1920 and growing to £372,000 when it ended that September.
'The British Government are out after the Loan – neck or nothing,'
Diarmuid O'Hegarty wrote to his colleague in Paris, 'but the Loan
goes merrily along. They appear to have gone into a blue funk about
it, but they cannot stop its progress. Their activities so far have been
an asset.' Not everything went smoothly. The impatient Finance
Minister Michael Collins wrote privately, 'This enterprise will certainly break my heart. I never imagined there was so much cowardice,
dishonesty, hedging, insincerity and meanness in the world.'[13]

At the beginning, most of the public probably shared the scepticism
of the press concerning the rebel government, but when Dáil Éireann
demonstrated that it was serious, there was a shift towards respect and
support. P. S. O'Hegarty, a Sinn Féin journalist, later observed, 'Nothing
was more remarkable ... than the way in which, month after month,
the number of people giving allegiance to the Irish Government,
accepting it, and the British Government in Ireland was over, grew.'
Some 150,000 persons subscribed to the Dáil loan. In local government elections of January and June 1920 Sinn Féin and its Labour
allies won a majority of seats. Nationalists took control of local
government in Derry City and the Tyrone and Fermanagh county
councils, long controlled by Unionists. The great majority of local government outside the Unionist north-east pledged allegiance to Dáil
Éireann. With the driving force being Kevin O'Higgins, the Local
Government Department effectively coordinated the management of
local government. Despite a myriad of difficulties, local government
remained largely under Sinn Féin control.[14]

The Dáil's most striking achievement was its creation of a popular
and democratic judicial system. The effort began at local level, with
the establishment of arbitration courts. Under Austin Stack, the Home
Affairs Department formulated rules for local courts, created a framework of district courts and even a supreme court.[15]

A wide range of journalists provided testimony to the Dáil Government's viability by this time. Others received a very positive gloss on the
Dáil's activities from the London-born Desmond FitzGerald, Director
of Publicity. A *Daily Herald* report declared in November 1919, 'This
invisible Republic, with its hidden courts and its prohibited volunteer
troops, exists in the hearts of the men and women of Ireland, and wields
a moral authority which all the tanks and machine guns of King

George cannot command.' In July 1920, the *Irish Times* asserted that 'an Irish Republic is very nearly in being', noting that the 'Sinn Féin flag flies already over the whole province of Munster, and soon will fly over the whole of Leinster and Connaught and over a large part of Ulster'.[16]

A variety of English visitors were impressed by what they found. Mrs Francis Acland, travelling the country in late 1920, observed, 'Dáil Éireann is respected and obeyed by high and low, although the unimprisoned remnant of that body has to meet in secret and in secret promulgate its decrees.' She also commented: 'We know about those who join the Republican Army, but we know very little about those who are acting as Mayors and County Councillors. Such work is fraught with no little personal risk; perhaps that is why it is being undertaken with the spirit and faith of adventurous crusaders.' In describing the take-over of authority by the Irish Republic, John Hampton Bright, declared that this phenomenon 'resembled the flood of a tide, which Dublin Castle has been as impotent as King Canute to stay'. In Galway a fellow landowner complained to Augusta Gregory about the encroachment of poachers and timber cutters but stated: 'the Sinn Féin Courts were wonderful in keeping order'.[17]

The opponents of Sinn Féin charged that the Irish public did not support the rebel government but was driven into consent by IRA intimidation. The Dáil's relationship with the Volunteers was of crucial importance in the struggle for self-government. The military organisation pre-dated the Dáil, and the relationship initially was distant. De Valera told the Dáil in April 1919, 'The Minister of National Defence is, of course, in close association with the voluntary forces which are the foundation of the National Army.' But the said minister, Cathal Brugha, was determined to subordinate the IRA to the Dáil. In August 1919 he convinced the Dáil to require all Volunteers to take an oath of allegiance to 'the Irish Republic and to the Dáil'. Despite some dissent, almost all IRA men took the oath over the next few months.[18]

The Dáil seldom discussed IRA activities and knew little of its expenses. More than a few supporters of Sinn Féin actually opposed the IRA campaign. It appeared to some that the national assembly did not want to accept responsibility for its violent actions. Arthur Griffith, acting president while De Valera was in America, had long advocated passive resistance. His usual response to reports of IRA attacks was that these were merely reactions to actions of the Crown forces. Ambiguity about this relationship was ended only in March 1921 when de Valera told the Dáil that it 'was hardly acting fairly by the army in not publicly taking full responsibility for all its acts'. The assembly responded by giving the president authority to state publicly that the army was the official instrument of the Dáil. Reinforcing this position, the assembly appropriated $1,000,000 for 'national defence'.[19]

Then there was the matter of Irish unionists, most of whom were concentrated in the four counties of eastern Ulster, descendants of Scottish and English immigrants. Irish nationalism had no attraction for them, and they were not convinced that their civil and religious liberties would be protected by the Irish Republic. Sinn Féin presented itself as a democratic, non-sectarian movement, but was overwhelmingly Catholic and aligned to a violent organisation. The Dáil leadership made no real appeal to northern unionists.

The Dáil and its leaders were fully occupied in making good their authority in the nationalist part of the country; Ulster unionism could be dealt with later. The only member of the Dáil from Belfast was Sean MacEntee, an engineer, whose hard-line republicanism did not reveal the mentality of the Belfast Protestant proletariat. The only other substantial figure from Ulster was Ernest Blythe, a Protestant ex-salesman and Gaelgori. There was no one from the working class; here the absence of Labour Party representation in the Dáil revealed a major gap of opinion and experience in the body. The first Dáil was overwhelmingly lower middle-class.[20]

Sectarian rioting broke out in Belfast in the summer of 1920 and a large number of nationalists were driven from their jobs and homes. The Dáil was finally forced to turn its attention to the North. But its response was entirely negative: it imposed a boycott on mostly unionist-produced goods from Belfast city. Blythe protested in vain about the futility of this policy. The Dáil established an Ulster committee to study the matter of unionist Ulster within the framework of a united Irish state, but that only avoided unpleasant realities. De Valera hinted at federalism or provincial government in a future Irish constitution, but that was all. The revolutionary Dáil had neither time, means or experience to address the Ulster dilemma. With the Government of Ireland Act moving towards completion, which would create a six-county parliament, the most that its rebel opposite in Ireland could hope for was to deal with the matter of Ulster through future negotiations with London.[21]

In October 1921, in the midst of negotiations with London on a political settlement, the Dáil executive finally forwarded a proposal dealing with Ulster unionists – the new six-county parliament in operation for four months would be subordinated under the Irish state. The Ulster unionists were not interested.[22]

From the beginning, the Dáil Government, for its own survival, plotted the destruction of the RIC. In April 1919 the Dáil declared that the RIC was to be 'ostracized socially by the people of Ireland'. De Valera asserted that the force was composed of 'spies in our midst' who were the 'eyes and ears of the enemy'. This policy, supported increasingly by the public, was followed by a concentrated campaign to get RIC men to resign from the force.[23]

The IRA then initiated a campaign attacking policemen, seizing arms and destroying police barracks. When it became clear that British rule was collapsing, RIC resignations increased and recruitment faltered. Many RIC men hung on, however, determined to attain their treasured pension rights. By the summer of 1920 the RIC was isolated and demoralised. Police power, fragmented and rudimentary, passed into the hands of the IRA and its emerging police force, the Republican Police.[24]

By the autumn of 1920 the revolutionary government had adequate finance for its limited but not insignificant programme. Although £372,000 (plus £50,000 from the Self-Determination Fund, largely raised in Britain) was being expended, funds from the loan campaign in the United States began to pour in. Of the $5,000,000 raised there, $1,000,000 had been received in Dublin by the time of the Truce of July 1921. Moreover, the Dáil's money was secure. Directed by intelligence chief Ormond Winter, Dublin Castle's effort to locate the funds ended with a bloody response by the IRA, with only £23,000 being seized by British authorities.[25]

The Dáil executive was slow to spend its money. In the period 1 May to 31 December 1920 its revenue was £356,000 but it spent only £279,000, with £200,000 of that used to provide capital for the Dáil-sponsored Land Bank. The estimate of expenses for the first six months of 1921 was £186,000, but only £110,000 was spent. This was due, in part, to the underdeveloped administrative organisation and the repressive measures of the British forces. But financial restraint was strongly advocated by Collins, who was responsible for the creation of large reserve funds both in Ireland and America. The leaders of Dáil Éireann were planning for a prolonged struggle.[26]

The greatest challenge to the authority of the Dáil Government came not from Dublin Castle but from the land agitation in the west in the spring of 1920. There was a long history of land agitation and disputes coming up to the annual lettings of land in springtime, but this year, with the breakdown of British authority, the turbulence was exceptional.

Art O'Connor, the Dáil's Agriculture Minister, graphically described the situation: 'Power, actual and real, was passing from the British Authorities in Ireland into the hands of the Government of the Republic, but in those days it was in a state of flight and had not yet taken definite rest in its new home.' 'The British were either so frightened or paralysed or unable to read the sign of the times,' he declared, 'that they suddenly ceased to perform the ordinary civil functions of administering law and keeping order. The Dáil itself seemed overwhelmed by the suddenness with which the responsibility of government had been thrust upon it and for a while it seemed to shrink from the duties as one shrinks from the fulfilment of an unexpected joy.' It was the land agitation in the west in the spring of 1920 that roused the Dáil 'from its lethargy like an angry mother to punish an unruly child'.[27]

Flooded with calls for help from landowners, the Dáil executive responded by investigating claims and ordering the IRA to put a halt to land seizures. It also established a Land Bank to provide limited finance for the landless. The land agitation was thus contained.[28]

By mid-1920 it was obvious to most observers that Ireland was lost to Britain. If this was true, the consequences would be far-reaching and ominous. At last, and too late, the British Government turned its full attention to Irish affairs. In the spring of 1920 a new administrative team was brought in to salvage British authority. Dublin Castle was given extraordinary powers. Martial law was imposed in several southern counties. Internment without trial swept thousands of young men into concentration camps. The Dáil courts were driven underground and local government was disrupted. The army was reinforced and re-equipped. To prop up the RIC, British recruits, popularly named the 'Blacks and Tans', were introduced and were supplemented by the 'Auxiliary Division', composed of gun-happy displaced ex-soldiers. Ireland was to get what Winston Churchill called 'rough handling'. Faced with the loss of her first colony, Britannia bared her teeth.[29]

The result was an orgy of violence, with the IRA actively participating. There were many accounts of murder and pillage by agents of the Crown. On 30 October a Doctor Foley came to see Augusta Gregory in Galway:

> He was very excited, and said houses at Ardahan had been burnt down last night and that the Black and Tans are spreading terror and ruin. … At Clarenbridge they got drunk and assaulted a widow. And a man there, Casey, had come to him yesterday saying, 'Don't let your Misses walk on the road, they are out for drink and women', and said he and his son had been dragged from their houses, put up against the wall and held while his two daughters were assaulted.

Armed with a wealth of accounts of Black and Tan violence, Gregory wrote an unsigned series of articles for the London *Nation* in the late autumn of 1920.[30]

Contrary to Richard Mulcahy's later assertions,[31] Irish intellectuals and artists supported the independence movement. Another Galway resident, William Butler Yeats, passionately denounced the Crown forces. Speaking at the Oxford Union in February 1921, he quickly refuted the previous speaker's statement that law and order had broken down in Ireland. Striding up and down waving his arms and shaking his fists, he declared, 'English law had broken down. ... In his own county of Galway such even-handed justice as was administered by the Sinn Féin courts had been unknown in the days of the English ascendancy.' After citing examples of Black and Tan actions – the shooting of 'women, girls and children ... even girls had been outraged', he declared: 'Across the final page of this fearful tragedy might well be written the words "Exit Britannia".'[32] The versatile and prolific George Russell (AE) hammered away at the need for Irish self-government in the pages of his *Irish Homestead*, and provided eloquent if somewhat vaporous arguments in its favour in his book *The National Being* (1918) and a pamphlet, 'The Inner and the Outer Ireland' (1921).

Hamar Greenwood, the Chief Secretary for Ireland, repeatedly claimed that law and order were being restored, while Lloyd George claimed that his government 'had murder by the throat'. At the same time, the British Parliament proceeded, at a most leisurely pace, to produce a new Home Rule Act, the most important feature of which was partition, with a six-county enclave provided for Ulster unionists.[33]

By this time the Conservative-dominated British Government had attained both its vital interests in Ireland. The creation of Northern Ireland enabled the Ulster unionists to build their barricade against the flood of Irish nationalism; while the fear that in future a self-governing Ireland could be used as a base against Britain was addressed by Eamon de Valera's statement in February 1920 that an independent Ireland would not be a hostile base on Britain's Atlantic flank. The makings of a settlement were thus in place by mid-1920, but Britain's political elite hedged (see Chapter 8).

British hope for a more favourable settlement was suggested in a London *Times* report that 'many members of the Coalition believe that the time for negotiation with Ireland will only be ripe when General Tudor and his Black and Tans have done their work and Irishmen have been chastened into acceptance of any way of escape from their distressful plight'. Echoing this position was John Ward, who, in an article in January 1921, vigorously defended the record of the leaders of the British army in Ireland: 'No parley is possible with those who have massacred their officers, or connived at the same. The iron discipline of the Army would be entirely undermined if it could not rely upon full justice being meted out to those who have so treacherously destroyed their comrades.'[34]

Martial law, internment, executions, shooting and burning did not cow the Dáil leadership or the IRA, but they severely circumscribed the Dáil's campaign to replace the *ancien régime*. No meeting of the Dáil or its Cabinet was discovered or substantially disrupted, but the Dáil only met 21 times between its establishment and the Truce of July 1921 (and only 8 times from its suppression in September 1919). To some critics the one-party assembly was little more than a rubberstamp, propagandist body, but propaganda was one of the reasons for its being. Given the difficulty in meeting, and considering that a majority of its members were either under arrest or in the United States, there was a reasonable measure of debate at the Dáil sessions. Michael Collins made the sensible proposal that with the aid of an effective courier system, meetings could be replaced by extensive correspondence. When the underground government began to use IRA dispatch riders, however, there were heated objections, and the Dáil administration was unable to develop a wholly effective system of its own.[35]

The Dáil courts were driven underground and harried, but Collins and Austin Stack laboured to have them continue. The absence of reports about the activities of these courts in this period indicates that at least most of them were, effectively, in a state of suspension. Due to the vigilance of Sinn Féin activists and the IRA, however, the British court system was totally shut down.[36]

The Dáil's leadership struggled to maintain continuity and control. The cabinet held 77 meetings from April 1919 to June 1921. There were 19 ministerial and sub-ministerial positions held by 31 individuals, including Constance Markievicz, the second woman in Europe to hold a cabinet position. Arrested ministers and officials were quickly replaced from a pool of capable Dáil deputies and Sinn Féin members. The key men – Collins, Brugha, Mulcahy and de Valera – evaded arrest until the end, although their administrative activities were disrupted frequently. Dublin Castle could neither discover nor destroy the Dáil organisation.[37]

In the grim month of December 1920 there were indications that the revolutionary government was wobbling. Arthur Griffith and some other leaders had been arrested. Roger Sweetman, TD, publicly advocated negotiations, a position supported by two local bodies in Galway. For a crucial two weeks in late December Michael Collins was acting head of the executive. He issued a 'stand fast' injunction to the public. On Christmas Eve, Eamon de Valera returned to Dublin. He promptly launched a flurry of activity: reports from all departments, the setting up of a presidential office, and a meeting of the Dáil. The incipient crisis evaporated.[38]

Since the end of 1920 a variety of agents, some self-appointed, others sanctioned by the British Government, had gambolled about, seeking clues for a willingness of the Dáil leadership to begin negotiations. For months Andy Cope became Lloyd George's 'man about town' in Dublin. Father Michael O'Flanagan returned to the public arena as a vice-president of Sinn Féin, venturing back and forth to London. Upon his return de Valera ordered a halt to all opportunistic communication of the sort.[39]

By the late spring of 1921 a stalemate had been reached. The Dáil Government summarily rejected the new Home Rule Act, yet Ulster unionists were given their enclave. Elections in May for the two 'home rule' assemblies resulted in a Unionist majority in the northeast but unchallenged Sinn Féin victories everywhere else. Dublin Castle had failed to regain public support or even consent; it ended up besieged. It did, however, prevent the Dáil administration from operating in many areas. British forces could not destroy the IRA, whose activity escalated. Although British military personnel were near exhaustion, the IRA could do little more to uproot British authority. A major factor in the final search for a settlement was the growing British opposition to the campaign of violence.[40]

A truce went into effect on 11 July 1921. Dáil Éireann and its administration came out in public and carried on as the *de facto* political authority in the country. The boys of the IRA came down from the hills to be greeted as conquering heroes. The unionist historian W. A. Phillips lamented, 'The forces of the Republic ... which had almost ceased to exist at once began to recover their vigour. ... Sinn Féin, so recently under the eclipse of defeat, now shined forth with all the prestige of victory.' Subsequent negotiations with the British Government dragged on for six months.[41]

The irrepressible George Bernard Shaw somewhat prematurely celebrated Sinn Féin's achievement: in September he declared that 'the offer of the British Government is not a burst of repentant magnanimity, but a forced capitulation submitted to after Sir Hamar Greenwood has done his utmost in the way of crude reprisal, and the government got the worst of it'. In December he asserted, 'Ireland had made a revolutionary discovery. ... Do not advocate a republic; simply assume a republic, appoint its administration and its Parliament, and carry on. If you are interfered with by ill-disposed persons, appoint your police and army, and defend your extant republic. Very simple, like Relativity and all the other great discoveries.'[42]

To Charles Bay, the US vice-consul in Cork, the future was anything but bright. He reported in October 1921, 'Whatever settlement is arrived at of the Irish situation, the new phase will be the breaking up into political divisions, for the national psychology exemplified in an intense national egotism, attempts to rejuvenate an all but extinct and useless language, and a worldwide agitation will disintegrate into an individual effort to obtain rewards and benefits of office.'[43]

The resulting Anglo-Irish agreement of December 1921 was disappointing to many Irish nationalists but it was seen as a sell-out by a variety of British politicians. Dubliner Edward Carson, champion of Ulster unionism, caustically noted in the House of Lords, 'You know you passed them because you were beaten. You know you passed them because Sinn Féin with the army in Ireland has beaten you.'[44]

Above and beyond everything else, the experience of the revolutionary government of Dáil Éireann demonstrated that the basic premise of Sinn Féin was sound – if you want something, do it yourself. Remembering that a variety of other European countries gained political independence at this time, the realisation of an Irish state does not seem remarkable, but this was achieved in the face of determined opposition from a Great Power, while all the other new nations emerged from the wreckage of mid-European empires. With massive popular support, the underground government of Dáil Éireann combined all methods, including violence, to emerge as the governing instrument of the Irish nation.[45]

Nationalist Ireland was rocked by the Anglo-Irish agreement of December 1921. Despite this, many people could see that the Treaty marked the beginning of a new age, a giant step forward in the struggle for their own people to run their own country. In January 1922 Augusta Gregory stood in a large crowd in Dublin to watch the exit of the 'Black and Tans': 'There was no booing or applause, just a sort of delighted murmur, a triumphant purr.'[46]

Notes

1. *Daily News*, 10 May 1916, quoted in G. B. Shaw, *The Matter with Ireland* (London, 1962), p. 113. The three poems are 'Easter 1916', 'Sixteen Dead

Men' and 'The Rose Tree', the first being published in October 1920 and the last two that November; see A. N. Jeffares (ed.), *Yeats's Poems* (London, 1979), pp. 286–90, 569–71.

2. M. Laffan, 'Sinn Féin from Dual Monarchy to the First Dáil', in B. Farrell (ed.), *The Creation of the Dáil* (Dublin, 1994), pp. 15–30.

3. D. Macardle, *The Irish Republic* (1968), pp. 215–31.

4. Anon., 'The Vagaries of Sinn Féin', pamphlet, NLI; T. P. O'Neill, 'The 1918 General Election', *Capuchin Annual* (1968), pp. 396–403; Anon., 'The Anniversary of the General Election, 1918', pamphlet, NLI, I94 109 P5(15); J. Coakley, 'The Election that Made the First Dáil', in Farrell, *Creation*, pp. 31–46.

5. M. Hopkinson, 'President Woodrow Wilson and the Irish Question', *Studia Hibernica* (1993), pp. xxvii, 89–111; R. Brindley, 'Woodrow Wilson, Self-determination and Ireland, 1918–1919: a View from the Irish Newspapers', *Eire/Ireland*, XXI: 4 (Winter 1986), pp. 62–82.

6. A. deBlacam, 'Berne, the Bolsheviks and Dáil Éireann', *New Ireland*, 12 Apr. 1919; Lector [Alf O Railly], in ibid., 19 Apr. 1919, complained that 'The Dáil is simply Westminster put into Irish.'

7. Dáil Éireann, *Proceedings* (21 Jan. 1919), pp. 22–4; (11 Apr. 1919), p. 78; *The Irishman*, 19 Apr. 1919; A. Mitchell, *Revolutionary Government in Ireland: Dáil Éireann, 1919–1922* (Dublin, 1995), pp. 15–16, 43–9.

8. Ibid., pp. 172–6.

9. Ibid., pp. 43–4.

10. Dáil Éireann, *Proceedings* (18 June 1919), pp. 120–3.

11. D. O'Hegarty to George Gavin Duffy, Duffy Papers, NA.

12. Macardle, *Irish Republic*, pp. 290–7; Arthur Griffith, *Irish Independent*, 7 Sep. 1919; A. Gregory, *Lady Gregory's Journals, 1916–1930*, ed. L. Robinson (London, 1946), pp. 111–12; John French, *Irish Independent*, 3 Mar. 1921.

13. Mitchell, *Revolutionary Government*, pp. 57–65.

14. J. L. McCracken, *Representative Government in Ireland* (Oxford, 1958), pp. 47–8; P. S. O'Hegarty, *The Victory of Sinn Féin* (Dublin, London, 1924), p. 35; J. Augusteijn, *From Public Defiance to Guerrilla Warfare* (Dublin, 1996), table 13, p. 303; M. A. Daly, 'Local Government and the First Dáil', in Farrell, *Creation*, pp. 123–36.

15. M. Kotsonouris, *Retreat from Revolution: The Dáil Courts, 1920–24* (Blackrock, 1994), pp. 20–35, 47–8.

16. Mitchell, *Revolutionary Government*, pp. 154–5.

17. Mrs Francis Acland, 'The Sinn Féin Fellowship', reprint from *Westminster Gazette*, 29 Apr. 1921; Gregory, *Journals*, p. 222.

18. Dáil Éireann, *Proceedings* (10 Apr. 1919), p. 47; (20 Aug. 1919), pp. 151–3.

19. Dáil Éireann, *Proceedings* (29 June 1920), p. 172; (11 Mar. 1921), pp. 278–9.

20. Mitchell, *Revolutionary Government*, pp. 33–5, and appendix 1, pp. 342–4; T. Garvin, *Nationalist Revolutionaries in Ireland, 1858–1928* (Oxford, 1987).

21. Ibid.; John Bowman, *De Valera and the Ulster Question, 1917–1973* (Oxford, 1982), pp. 41–8, 56–7.

22. Macardle, *Irish Republic*, pp. 495, 519, 749, 882.

23. Dáil Éireann, *Proceedings* (10 Apr. 1919), pp. 67–9; 'Resignations and Retirements from Irish Police Force', DE 2/87, NA; C.Townshend, *The British Campaign in Ireland* (Oxford, 1975), appendix I, p. 209; Mitchell, *Revolutionary Government*, pp. 68–74.

24. Ibid., pp. 147–54, 270; Townshend, *British Campaign*, pp. 11, 22, 31, 28, 42, 92, 109, 116.

25. Dáil Éireann, *Proceedings* (29 June 1920), pp. 181–2; Mitchell, *Revolutionary Government*, pp. 199–200, 64, 202.

26. Ibid., pp. 163–5.

27. Dáil Éireann, 'A Brief Survey of the Work Done by the Agricultural Department from April 1919 to August 1921', DE 2/64, NA.

28. Dáil Éireann, *The Constructive Work of Dáil Éireann, No. 1: The National Police and Courts of Justice*; C. A. Maguire, 'The Republican Courts', *Capuchin Annual*, 1969, pp. 378–88.

29. Townshend, *British Campaign*, pp. 73–105.

30. Gregory, *Journals* (27 Oct. 1920), p. 196; H. W. Nevinson, editor of *Manchester Guardian*, to Gregory: 'Those *Nation* articles of yours have been the greatest use', in ibid. (20 Nov. 1920), p. 139.

31. *Irish Independent*, 17 Oct. 1921; Gregory, *Journals* (18 Oct. 1921), p. 161.

32. Yeats at Oxford Union, *Freeman's Journal*, 17 Feb. 1921; E. Cullingford, *Yeats, Ireland and Fascism* (London, 1981), pp. 108–9.

33. A. Jackson, *Ireland, 1798–1998* (Oxford, 1999), pp. 254–5.

34. Macardle, *Republic*, pp. 339–40; J. H. Bright, 'What's Wrong with Ireland, No. 2', p. 16; J.Ward, 'The Army and Ireland', *The Nineteenth Century and After* (Jan. 1921), pp. dxvii, 7.

35. Mitchell, *Revolutionary Government*, pp. 279–81.

36. Kotsonouris, *Dáil Courts*, pp. 36–7, 45–50.

37. Mitchell, *Revolutionary Government*, p. 57.

38. Ibid., pp. 213–24; Lord Longford and T. P. O'Neill, *Eamon de Valera* (London, 1970), pp. 119–22.

39. Mitchell, *Revolutionary Government*, pp. 217–24, 291–5.

40. Townshend, *British Campaign*, pp. 182–6, 190–2; D. G. Boyce, *Englishmen and Irish Troubles* (London, 1972), pp. 43–141.

41. D. G. Boyce (ed.), *Revolution in Ireland, 1879–1923* (London, 1988), pp. 217–18.

42. 'The British Offer', London *Daily News*, 6 Sep. 1921; 'The Irish Crisis', *Manchester Guardian*, 27 Dec. 1921, in Shaw, *Matter*, pp. 244–5, 254. See also T. T. Turner, 'Bernard Shaw's "Eternal Irish Concerns', *Eire/Ireland*, XXI, 2 (Summer 1986), pp. 57–69.

43. C. Bay to State Department, 4 Oct. 1921, US Consular Reports, Weekly Summary, 800, National Archives, Washington, DC.

44. A. T. Q. Stewart, *Edward Carson* (Dublin, 1981), p. 124.

45. J. Lee, 'The Significance of the First Dáil', in Farrell (ed.), *Creation*, pp. 137–58.

46. Gregory, *Journals* (14 Jan. 1922), p. 168.

6

Propaganda II: Propaganda of Dáil Éireann, 1919–21

Keiko Inoue

Throughout the struggle for independence, the press played an important role in Irish nationalist propaganda. The period from the establishment of Dáil Éireann in January 1919 to the signing of the Anglo-Irish Treaty in December 1921 was no exception to this. There is, nevertheless, still no detailed analysis of the content of propaganda during these years. In Virginia E. Glandon's standard work on this topic an overview of the separatist press is provided, but she focuses on its operation in wartime circumstances and rarely discusses the actual contents of these papers.[1] In their recent works both Michael Laffan and Arthur Mitchell include sections on propaganda, but they do not focus on its content.[2] In this book, Ben Novick deals with aspects of advanced nationalist propaganda during the First World War (see Chapter 3), and recently I have analysed separatist propaganda during the Truce and the Northern Irish election campaign of May 1921,[3] but the Anglo-Irish War is still left virtually untouched.

The intention of this chapter is to fill this gap. First a survey is provided of the publicity campaign of Dáil Éireann between 1919 and 1921, and then the contents of the *Irish Bulletin*, the Dáil's chief medium, is scrutinised more closely. By doing so, I hope to assess the impact and achievements of republican propaganda in this period and to point out the problems it faced.

In contrast to the preceding years, there was a concentrated effort on foreign propaganda after 1918. This was a result of two developments.

Firstly, one of the main aims of Sinn Féin, formulated at its reconstitution in 1917, was to acquire international recognition for an independent Ireland at the post-war peace conference. Secondly, the triumph at the December 1918 general election marked the success of home propaganda. This election victory and the end of the First World War made international recognition an immediate priority.

This became clear with the foundation of the Department of Propaganda (later Publicity) as one of the earliest organs of the Dáil. Its first Director of Propaganda was Laurence Ginnell; however, much work was done by Desmond FitzGerald, who became substitute director after Ginnell's arrest in May 1919.[4] When FitzGerald was imprisoned from mid-February to July 1921, Erskine Childers replaced him. The department worked closely with the already existing Sinn Féin Department of Propaganda, which was maintained under Robert Brennan, and with Piaras Béaslaí, the IRA's Director of Publicity. The resources were limited both in finance and in personnel, and the department had to function in ever more difficult circumstances. In September 1919, Dáil Éireann and Sinn Féin were declared illegal, together with other separatist organisations and most of the separatist press, including *Nationality*, the principal organ of Sinn Féin.

To facilitate foreign propaganda a network of Dáil representatives was established abroad. Already in February 1919 Sean T. O'Kelly was sent to Paris to appeal to the Peace Conference to take up the case of Ireland. Later he was joined by George Gavan Duffy, and they were to stay there until long after the end of the conference. From there, the foreign network of the Dáil spread widely throughout Europe. In June 1921 the Dáil Department of Foreign Affairs reported that there were representatives in France, Italy, America, Britain, Germany, Russia, Argentina and Chile; that official press bureaus were working in Paris, Berlin, Rome, Madrid, Geneva and the United States; and that propaganda material had been circulated in Denmark, Canada, South Africa, Australia and South American republics.[5] Dáil supporters in other countries also provided valuable assistance.[6] The power of publicity abroad was demonstrated by Eamon de Valera's 18-month American mission, which started in June 1919 and received enormous attention. However, the Dáil's foreign mission was too ambitious as well as optimistic, and inevitable overlapping of personnel and functions caused some administrative confusion.[7]

When FitzGerald took over the directorship, the main medium of Dáil propaganda was pamphlets. The Foreign Relations Committee of Sinn Féin had prepared most of these pamphlets, and they were distributed through Sinn Féin and its supporters in foreign countries.[8]

FitzGerald introduced the *Weekly Summary*, a mimeographed sheet that was issued to the national and international press about once a fortnight from 7 July 1919, providing a simple but effective summary of British 'acts of aggression'. A full-blown paper, the *Irish Bulletin*, was started on 11 November 1919, six weeks after the wholesale suppression of the separatist press. It was launched as the official organ of the Dáil under Arthur Griffith, Brennan, and FitzGerald.[9] Soon Frank Gallagher, then assistant to the Director of Propaganda, joined the *Bulletin*'s staff and served as a main writer of the paper. Childers joined the team as soon as he replaced FitzGerald. Although the department concentrated on the *Irish Bulletin*, pamphlets continued to be printed and distributed. However, few were issued after mid-1920. This shift was probably due to the fact that the department found it more difficult to 'bring their contents to the notice of foreign readers'.[10]

The *Bulletin* targeted opinion makers as its readers, and thus was sent to pressmen, politicians, influential public figures, and heads of churches in Britain, Ireland and other countries. It was published five times a week, and for over two years the *Bulletin* never missed an issue despite raids, arrests of staff, and the capture of machinery. Prominent members of the *Bulletin*'s staff were arrested: FitzGerald was imprisoned for five months; Gallagher was jailed from 20 March to 14 April 1920; Childers, arrested on 9 May 1921, was, however, released on the same day. To avoid discovery, the office of the *Bulletin* was forced to change its address 13 times. The printing presses of the *Bulletin* were nevertheless confiscated on 26 March 1921, and subsequently a bogus *Irish Bulletin* was published by Dublin Castle.[11]

Unfortunately, it is uncertain how many copies of the *Bulletin* were published daily. At first the *Bulletin* had a circulation of about 50 to 70 copies, but it multiplied fast and by the end of October 1920 it reached about 600.[12] In August 1921 it was reported that the number had reached 900, and it was even claimed that, eventually, more than 2,000 copies were published daily.[13] As all these figures stem from the records of the Dáil propaganda department and its staff itself, they may well be exaggerated. Nevertheless, it is certain that the circulation of the *Bulletin* grew strongly, in spite of the practice of omitting from the list of recipients people who were not making use of the *Bulletin*. It circulated in India, Egypt, and other nations asserting their right to freedom,[14] and in 1921 special runs of the *Bulletin* were produced in small quantities in some other countries.[15]

The primary aim of the *Bulletin* was to contradict the official statements from Dublin Castle 'misrepresenting the situation in Ireland', and 'to acquaint persons resident outside of Ireland with the case for Irish Independence'.[16] Reflecting this, the most prominent topic was the misconduct of the British forces. Striking headlines such as 'War on women and children', 'Dying Irish prisoners beaten in English prisons' and 'Irish babies murdered by English militarism' appeared repeatedly in the paper. Ill-treatment of prisoners was exposed frequently; destruction of creameries by the British was called 'the economic war against the Irish people',[17] and the British forces in Ireland were equated to the German regime in Belgium during the war.[18]

Reflecting the low profile of the Irish Question in British governmental policy, the reaction of the British press to the situation in Ireland was by no means responsive. Despite the continuous violence in Ireland, only a major event such as the 'sacking' of Balbriggan in September 1920 was able to bring the Irish case to the forefront.[19] The frustration with the unsympathetic attitude of the British press frequently came to the fore in the *Bulletin*. It pointed out that British papers distorted the state of affairs in Ireland by carefully excluding reports on police terrorism.[20] By citing examples of alteration by omission of words, British news agencies were branded as 'the chief channels of British imperial propaganda' and as unreliable.[21] Dublin Castle was accused of forging the *Irish Bulletin*, Dáil proclamations, and Republican documents allegedly intercepted by the British, as well as inventing episodes of ambushes committed by the Volunteers that actually did not take place.[22] The readers were also reminded that the voice of the Irish people was heavily censored: British propaganda was 'in full swing in every country in the world',[23] and in Ireland any paper that dared to voice opinions sympathetic to Dáil Éireann 'could not ... exist twenty four hours'.[24] Nevertheless, tributes to the achievements of republicans appearing in the British press, especially from leading politicians known to be hostile to Sinn Féin, were reproduced to embarrass the British and impress readers in other countries more efficiently.

The legitimacy of Dáil Éireann, and that of the independent Irish Republic, was the main point being advocated consistently. Sinn Féin's victory at the general election of December 1918 was portrayed as an overwhelming statement of the Irish desire for national independence.[25] The results of two sets of local government elections held in 1920, and the general election in 1921, were useful to strengthen this claim. On Griffith's advice, the analysis and detailed results of the elections were publicised both in the *Irish Bulletin* and in the form of a pamphlet.[26] Accordingly it was boasted that '[the Dáil] Government ... now holds the allegiance of 83 per cent of the

Irish people'.[27] It was noted that these elections were fought in alliance with other organisations: with Labour and the Nationalist Party in Ulster, and with Labour in the three remaining provinces.[28] However, the fact that at the municipal elections 'even outside the four counties of north-east Ulster, Sinn Féin captured only 572 seats to the 872 won by other parties'[29] was deliberately ignored.[30]

The constructive side of the activities of the Dáil was another important aspect to publicise, since showing that the Dáil functioned as a *de facto* government was assumed to be helpful in impressing the outside world.[31] The republican courts proved to have the greatest propaganda value. By showing the Dáil's ability to keep law and order, it contradicted British propaganda portraying Ireland as a country overcome by anarchy. Publishing the lists of the sessions of the republican courts, the *Irish Bulletin* stressed their fair-mindedness, and pointed out that even unionists had recourse to these courts: 'having sought protection in vain from the British Courts and Police, these Unionists have requested protection from the Republic and have been generously accorded it'.[32] However, the coercion applied by the British Government after June 1920 curbed the courts' effectiveness, and particularly from August 1920 onwards military raids made public sittings impossible. When Lloyd George referred in the British House of Commons to the disappearance of the republican courts, the *Irish Bulletin* claimed that the courts still sat in frequent session, but that 'by arson and assassination the English Constabulary have terrorised the Irish Press into not reporting the business at these Courts'.[33]

Closely connected to the republican courts were the activities of the republican police. From mid-1919, owing to the situation caused by the escalation of the struggle, the Volunteers had become involved in local police work. The activities of the republican police, officially established in June 1920, were a valuable propaganda topic. From the beginning of 1920 the formation of police units was reported in the *Bulletin*. Contrasting the list of police activities carried out by the Volunteers with that of the crimes committed by the British police forces, the *Bulletin* claimed that the first essential step to preserve law and order in Ireland was the withdrawal of the British forces.[34]

Emphasising the achievement of the Dáil courts and the republican police on the one hand, and denouncing the increasing violence of the British forces on the other, it was asserted in July 1920 that:

there is seen in Ireland an English Military Government, detested by the Irish people, a Military Government whose decrees are ignored, … which is forced to rely for its continued presence in Ireland upon machine guns, tanks and innumerable armed camps; and that English Government by the admission of those directing it stands not for the material rehabilitation of Ireland but for its further suppression and impoverishment.[35]

In the first half of 1921, the scope of the *Bulletin* was further widened. Reports of the meetings of the Dáil and the text of interviews with De Valera were published, and a weekly supplement comprised of Dáil decrees, presidential statements, and important official news was attached.

In comparison with its effort in exposing British atrocities, the *Bulletin* was reticent in publicising Volunteers' activities, and its attitude towards violence was consistently defensive, making a sharp contrast with the belligerent *An tÓglách*, the organ of the IRA.[36] The Anglo-Irish War was portrayed as being provoked by the coercive policy of the Lloyd George government.[37] The *Bulletin* claimed that it did not hesitate to describe 'the acts of violence on the parts of the supporters of the Republican Movement', but apart from correcting mistakes it did not issue statements about them because 'sufficient publicity is given to them by Dublin Castle, by Members and Ministers of the English Parliament and by the English Press'.[38]

The defensive attitude to physical force was also seen in the perception of the IRA in the *Bulletin*, which differed from the IRA's self-image as the 'Army of Ireland' which had 'created the Irish Republic' and was acting with the backing of the nation.[39] In June 1921 the *Bulletin* wrote:

> Before the present reign of terror began there was no standing army in Ireland. Eighteen months ago the Irish Volunteers were a territorial reserve rather than an army in the field. But when a price was placed upon the heads of its more active members, these men went into permanent active service, determined to defend their liberty with their lives.[40]

However, under Childers the military side of the struggle came to receive more attention. Official reports of the IRA's activities were included from time to time with the cooperation of its officers in the field. Later the IRA's General Order on Reprisals was published.[41] It was claimed that the general body of the nation admired and assisted the Volunteers.[42] Asserting that between 1 January 1920 and 4 June 1921 the IRA had freed, unhurt, 807 British prisoners whom it had captured, the *Bulletin* described the Volunteers' chivalry as being 'difficult to equal in any war in history'.[43] Conversely the *Bulletin's* accusations of the British forces became fiercer.

Prior to his official appointment, contributing to both British and Irish newspapers, Childers had strongly attacked the governmental policy, and some of these articles were reproduced in the *Bulletin*.[44] He described the situation in Ireland as a war between an organised army and 'a civil population, physically well-nigh helpless, spiritually indomitable'.[45] This war in Ireland was, he argued, not a war in the ordinary sense of the word; for the British army operating in Ireland was neither defending Britain against a foreign enemy, nor sustaining British honour or interests.[46] He warned the people of Britain that if this seemingly small Irish war persisted, it would 'corrupt and eventually ruin not only your Army, but your nation and your Empire itself'.[47] It is not certain, however, whether this change in the *Bulletin* was solely a result of Childers' influence, since this period was the most violent as well as the most crucial of the struggle.

This growing publication and advocacy of IRA activities can also be assumed to be a result of the necessity to counter war weariness in Ireland. Although the Anglo–Irish War was coloured by brutal episodes, it was not widespread. Most of the fighting was carried out in Munster and Dublin City.[48] The people in these areas suffered severely from restrictions imposed under martial law. In March 1921 even Frank Gallagher confessed to fatigue caused by continuous strain: 'Even now the death-stillness of the street outside horrifies me and a strange step makes me physically weak. This has gone on for five months. It is all but unbearable.'[49] On the other hand, a large portion of the west remained quiet except for a period at the end of the war.[50]

Also, from the beginning the Volunteers' headquarters had suffered from considerable difficulties in building up a centralised structure and in animating the Volunteers in inactive areas. Most of the Volunteers' activities were planned locally, and were not under the direction of the headquarters. By publishing the official reports of the IRA's engagements the *Irish Bulletin* could give an impression that the guerrilla fighting was not restricted to any particular county but was carried out throughout the country.[51] Publication of the orders issued by headquarters also created the image that the IRA was acting under strong central control.

The escalation of violence in late 1920 came with a growing effort to find peace. As early as February 1921, some Irish newspapers started to express a strong desire for an early truce.[52] Such reactions of the Irish daily press were certainly damaging, and they were discussed at a meeting of the Dáil on 11 March 1921.[53] The increased attention to military matters in 1921 was therefore probably a reaction to a certain amount of war weariness among the Irish people, and to counter moderate opinion in the Irish press.

In comparison with the suppressed advanced nationalist press, the *Irish Bulletin's* scope was narrow. When it was launched, FitzGerald's intention was to make the *Bulletin* 'explanatory and educational as well as a channel for news items'.[54] Reflecting this the *Bulletin* initially also contained articles on topics such as industrial and economic disadvantages in Ireland caused by British rule. However, in 1920, when the conflict intensified with the arrival of the Black and Tans and the Auxiliaries, more and more articles were written on British atrocities. There was almost no information on De Valera's American tour, or other international items, which occupied columns in *Nationality* and *Young Ireland*.

Recurring topics in Sinn Féin propaganda during the previous years had been 'Ireland's right to be an independent nation', and 'British exploitation in Ireland,' which were backed up statistically. During the Anglo-Irish War period, these were still prominent in pamphlets,[55] but rarely dealt with in the *Bulletin*; this was probably due to the difference between pamphlets and a newspaper – the process of producing pamphlets is more time-consuming and less flexible – and by June 1920 the Propaganda Department had decided that pamphlets would contain matter of permanent or outstanding rather than news value.[56] Also, the *Bulletin* found no great need to assert Ireland's right to independence, because it was the organ of the Dáil, a parliament of the Republic, which was already 'in existence'.

Before its suppression, *Nationality* had also stressed the importance of educating the population. While the people were waiting for the departure of British administration, they were urged to de-anglicise their minds, for Irish minds would be required to reconstruct the country after the enemy's evacuation.[57] Columns were devoted to encouraging the economic and industrial revival of Ireland. In addition to that, since it was expected that the local government elections would be held in June 1919, *Nationality* urged the people, as early as March 1919, to start preparing, and gave practical advice concerning election work, encouraging Sinn Féin clubs to get to work early to increase the chances of success.[58]

These calls clearly reflected the anxiety of the leaders about the decline of the Sinn Féin organisation. Sean Milroy, Sinn Féin's Director of Organisation, found that the recruitment of the members had been too rapid for the education process. At the Extraordinary Ard-Fheis in April 1919, he pointed out that it was still desirable to aim at a better

understanding of the spirit of Sinn Féin.[59] However, this side of propaganda was rarely dealt with in the *Irish Bulletin*. Even the departmental report admitted that the earlier issues of the *Bulletin* dealt more with
'passing events than fundamental issues'.[60] This was mainly due to the
different character of the two papers: *Nationality* was an organ of Sinn
Féin, a political party, but the *Irish Bulletin* was an organ of Dáil Éireann
whose readers were sought mainly outside Ireland.

It is difficult to gauge the efficiency of the contents of Dáil propaganda
during this period. No doubt revelation of the misconduct of Crown
forces in Ireland shocked many British people, and as a consequence
various pressure groups were organised. It is true that the British
Liberal press such as the *Manchester Guardian* and the *Daily News*, which
were sympathetic to the Irish cause, contributed to formulating public
opposition to the Irish policy of the Lloyd George government, and
the contents of the *Bulletin* helped in this. The fact that many British
newspapers published stories from the *Bulletin*, and that it occasionally
became the source of questions in parliamentary debates, annoyed the
Chief Secretary of Ireland considerably.[61] The publication of the bogus
Irish Bulletin is another indication of the *Bulletin*'s effectiveness.

Not all Dáil propaganda, however, was equally effective. For
instance, the publication in France of a pamphlet called *The Freedom
of the Seas* was found to be of little use, because 'the French have given
up all hope of the freedom of the seas in the peace treaty and take
very little interest in the question'.[62] Patrick McCartan, who was sent
to Russia, found that the contents of the *Bulletin* were unsuitable for
the mission in Russia:

> They cannot consistently condemn the shooting of Irishmen by England
> while they themselves 'slice' their own 'bandits'. They cannot condemn impris-
> onment without trial in Ireland while their own jails are full of political pris-
> oners. They cannot advocate liberty in Ireland while the dictatorship of the
> proletariat is held up at the ideal to be aimed at in all countries ... Russian [*sic*]
> laughs at the Estonian language as the British are accustomed to laugh at the
> Irish language.... I am not so sure therefore that self-determination for
> Ireland would raise much enthusiasm in official circles.[63]

Surviving correspondence, on the other hand, indicates that Dáil propaganda was successful in impressing peoples who also demanded self-
determination. Irish propaganda was reported to have 'some effect' in
the Tyrol,[64] and the separatist papers in the Basque country and
Catalonia saw in the Irish case a mirror image of their own struggle

for autonomy.[65] As early as November 1919, Sinn Féin received a letter from staff of *La Veu de Catalunya* which stated that the Irish struggle gave them 'courage to pursue the fight … to recover the freedom and personality of Catalonia, politically as well as socially'. Later it was reported that 'the press of Barcelona is strongly pro-Irish'.[66] In August 1921, Sean T. O'Kelly even claimed that all the smaller countries supported Ireland, and pointed out that those countries were 'copying Irish methods and utilising Irish propaganda for inspiring their own men'.[67]

The consequences of the conflict provided the Dáil with excellent propaganda material. This is evident from the fact that during the Truce the *Bulletin* suffered from a lack of appropriate topics to publicise. By agreeing to the ceasefire and showing a wish for reconciliation, the British Government had succeeded in soothing public opinion. In such circumstances, a review of the brutality of the British or disclosure of ill-treatment of prisoners could not create the same impact as in the past. Once it lost its target for attack, and once the British Government restored its own reputation, the *Irish Bulletin* was unable to rouse public sympathy.[68]

The slow start of British counter-propaganda also helped the Irish. It was not until August 1920 that a British Propaganda Department was eventually established under Basil Clarke, but by this stage, Dublin Castle had, through its actions, already alienated the moderate element in Ireland.[69] And although Clarke was a skilled and able propagandist, the lack of interdepartmental cooperation inhibited his effectiveness.[70]

In this regard, the Irish side was fortunate, as its operations were by no means carried out smoothly either. In addition to the threat of arrests and raids, there were internal divisions. Michael Collins, Gavan Duffy and Art O'Brien criticised the work of FitzGerald,[71] while members of the Dáil did not always cooperate fully. When it was proposed that every TD 'should collect in his Constituency all the available accounts of burnings, outrages, shootings, and other crimes and transmit the evidence to the Propaganda Department', the result was disappointing: they received only a handful of contributions. One member stated that it was not the deputies' duty to go round the country taking out affidavits of information for the Propaganda Department.[72] Other Dáil departments were equally unenthusiastic in supplying reports or information.[73] When information was provided it frequently proved to be inaccurate. At a meeting of the Dáil, FitzGerald warned that 'Any information should be correct and should stand investigation afterwards. Information was no good unless detailed and accurate.'[74]

Although fairly successful abroad, the department's weakness lay in Ireland itself. Sinn Féin was not particularly interested in the Ulster question, and despite the party's weak position there, little effort was made in the north-east. It was only during the general election campaign in May 1921 that Sinn Féin engaged in systematic propaganda work in Ulster by sending speakers, posting Sinn Féin literature, and launching an ephemeral paper tactically named the *Unionist*. However, the methods used were inefficient and the results were even harmful to the party's own cause: the contents of the propaganda exposed Sinn Féin's inability to understand the area, and they could not impress the unionist inhabitants, but rather alarmed them.[75]

Propaganda work in the rest of Ireland also stagnated except during election time.[76] This was partly due to the practical difficulties caused by disorder, such as the suppression of the separatist papers, censorship, and the shortage of personnel. However, the papers that escaped the ban, *Young Ireland* and *An tÓglách*, were not utilised fully. Originally launched as an Irish-Ireland magazine, *Young Ireland* came to be issued from the Sinn Féin headquarters in November 1917, and later Griffith took over as its editor, but it only had a small readership.[77] *An tÓglách*, the army newspaper, on the other hand, failed to appear regularly, and was not published for a six-month period from March to September 1919, partly due to the arrest of Béaslaí, the editor of the paper. Its circulation was basically confined to the Volunteers, and utilising this paper for home propaganda was planned only in May 1921.[78]

Provincial newspapers, which had been an important medium for Sinn Féin, were not only under heavy censorship, but were also suppressed frequently.[79] The fear of suppression made the Irish press hesitant to give prominence to material provided by the Dáil and Sinn Féin. A comparison of provincial newspapers shows that, although the Sinn Féin propaganda department kept sending syndicated 'Sinn Féin News' to about 40 sympathetic local newspapers,[80] it was not always utilised.[81] In April 1921 De Valera wrote that both he and Collins thought there had so far been very little evidence in the Irish press that they had been influenced by the work of the propaganda department.[82] Later, the Director of Propaganda of Cumann na mBan reported that although they collected a great quantity of information on the conditions of prisoners and supplied it to the press, it was very difficult to get the Irish daily press to give proper prominence to these matters.[83]

Along with such pressure from outside, difficulties came from inside the Dáil and Sinn Féin. Once the Dáil and its cabinet were established,

and even before that, prominent Sinn Féin leaders began to be preoccupied with their new governmental tasks, neglecting propaganda.
Most of Sinn Féin's work was taken over by the Dáil, and the Sinn Féin
Party became virtually a subordinate body of the Dáil.[84] Brennan's
appointment as the Dáil Government's under-secretary for foreign
affairs on 6 February 1921 was a further blow.

Minutes of the Dáil from January 1921 report that in response to a
demand for improvement in home propaganda, the department
claimed it had no machinery to pursue it.[85] At the same time its attitude towards home propaganda was negative. In September 1920,
FitzGerald expressed the opinion that 'the Republican propaganda
campaign would continue to carry more and more weight outside
Ireland'.[86] The *Bulletin* had no significant domestic circulation even
after the Truce, despite request for it. It is almost certain that Sinn Féin
clubs never received copies,[87] and around July 1921 the IRA suggested
that it was: 'desirable to increase the Irish circulation of the "Bulletin",
because its articles are just the sort of material required to improve the
morale of large sections of the people – and those not the least influential sections'.[88] However, the Department of Propaganda frequently
refused this kind of application, insisting that the capacity of the
department did not admit extensive Irish circulation of the *Bulletin*,[89]
and moreover, the *Bulletin* was designed for use 'principally not in
Ireland but among the publicists in England and on the continent'.[90]

It cannot be said that the people of the propaganda department
entirely neglected home propaganda, but they were quite lukewarm
in carrying out this task. It is true that some general newspapers, most
notably the *Irish Independent*, helped Sinn Féin and the Dáil by giving
them sympathetic coverage.[91] However, their support was not always
available, since the Dáil had neither authority nor control over them.
Thus, without their own newspaper, republican propagandists must
have found it extremely hard, or almost impossible, to maintain the
morale of the Irish public.

The Dáil's propaganda campaign between 1919 and the end of
1921 was successful in supporting the war effort. It presented the Irish
case to the world, and received some favourable coverage in return. Its
effects were most obvious in Britain, where the *Irish Bulletin* made a
considerable impact and put pressure on the government. However, its
success was generally limited. Not surprisingly, Ireland's case was not
heard at the Versailles Peace Conference, and representatives of the Dáil
were neither recognised as the ambassadors of Ireland, nor able to
influence foreign governments. Their shock tactics were efficient only
during the conflict, and could not have the same effect in peacetime.

In contrast to the attention that was given to foreign opinion, little effort was made in the area of home propaganda. This was partly due to circumstances beyond the control of republican propagandists, such as censorship and intimidation, as well as to the limited resources that were available. At the same time it cannot be denied that Dáil propaganda failed to utilise available material, and played only a minor role in mobilising Irish opinion.

Notes

1. V. E. Glandon, *Arthur Griffith and the Advanced Nationalist Press: Ireland, 1900–1922* (New York, 1985).
2. M. Laffan, *The Resurrection of Ireland* (Cambridge, 1999); A. Mitchell, *Revolutionary Government in Ireland: Dáil Éireann, 1919–22* (Dublin, 1995).
3. K. Inoue, 'Propaganda of Dáil Éireann, from Truce to Treaty', *Éire/Ireland*, XXXII, 2 and 3 (Summer/Fall 1997); K. Inoue, 'Sinn Féin Propaganda and the "Partition Election", 1921', *Studia Hibernica*, no. 30 (1998–99).
4. Dáil Éireann, *Proceedings* (2 Apr. 1919), p. 36; (17 June 1919), p. 115.
5. Department of Foreign Affairs Report, 6 June 1921, NLI, ms. 11 404.
6. For more details, K. Inoue, 'Sinn Féin and Dáil Propaganda, 1919–21', M.Phil thesis (University College, Dublin, 1995), ch. 2; D. Keogh, 'The Origins of the Irish Foreign Service in Europe (1919–1922)', in *Études Irlandaises*, VII (1982); D. Keogh, *Ireland and Europe, 1919–1948* (Dublin, 1988); Mitchell, *Revolutionary Government*; and M. Kennedy, 'Civil Servants Cannot be Politicians: the Professionalisation of the Irish Foreign Service, 1919–22', *Irish Studies in International Affairs*, VIII (1997).
7. Inoue, 'Sinn Féin and Dáil', pp. 10–11.
8. Department of Publicity, History and Progress, Aug. 1921, UCDAD, P80/14; Report on Propaganda Department, June 1920, ibid.
9. Although Griffith was involved in the establishment of the *Irish Bulletin*, he rarely worked for the paper even before his arrest on 26 Nov. 1920, because of his responsibility as acting-president during De Valera's absence.
10. Report on Propaganda Department, June 1920, UCDAD, P80/14.
11. Since no complete set of the fake *Irish Bulletin* is available, it is uncertain how long it was published. Copies of some issues are available at NLI and the Bodleian Library, Oxford.
12. Claim of Kathleen Napoli, 17 Oct. 1936, NLI, ms. 18 346; K. McKenna, 'Irish Bulletin', *Capuchin Annual*, 1970, p. 513.
13. Department of Publicity, History and Progress, Aug. 1921, UCDAD, P80/14; Claim of Kathleen Napoli, 17 Oct. 1936, NLI, ms. 18 346; F. Gallagher, 'Literature of the Conflict', *Irish Book Lover*, XVIII, 3 (May–June 1930), p. 70.
14. D. Hogan, *The Four Glorious Years* (Dublin, 1953), p. 86.
15. For instance, the Madrid *Bulletin* started its publication on 25 May 1921 (Report for May and June from Spain, 1 Jul. 1921, UCDAD, P80/23);

the press bureau in Berlin took charge of the publication of the *Bulletin* in German (Department of Foreign Affairs Report, 6 June 1921, NLI, ms. 11 202); and in Switzerland the *Bulletin* was issued and circulated from the press bureau in Freibourg (Report on Foreign Affairs, [23?] May 1921, NA, DE 2/269). On 23 May 1921, the *Bulletin* was launched in Rome on a twice-weekly basis, Gavan Duffy to Dublin, 28 May 1921, NA, 1125/5; *Irish Independent*, 31 May 1921, p. 4.

16. *Irish Bulletin*, 29 Nov. 1920, p. 2.
17. Ibid., 5 Oct. 1920, p. 2.
18. Ibid., 5 Jan. 1921, p. 1.
19. On British public opinion during this period, see D. G. Boyce, *Englishmen and Irish Troubles: British Public Opinion and the Making of Irish Policy, 1918–1922* (London, 1972); and B. Norling, 'The Irish Disorders, 1919–1925, and the English Press', in *Cithara*, III, 2 (1964).
20. For instance, *Irish Bulletin*, 23 Apr. 1920, p. 2.
21. Ibid., 1 Jan. 1920, p. 1; 7 June 1920, p. 1.
22. Ibid., 5 Nov. 1920, p. 1; 7 Apr. 1921, pp. 1–2; 16 June 1921, p. 1.
23. *Nationality*, 1 Mar. 1919, p. 2.
24. *Irish Bulletin*, 1 Dec. 1919, p. 1.
25. For instance, Dáil Éireann, *The Authority of Dáil Éireann* (Dublin, 1919), pp. 4, 8; *The Voice of Ireland* (Dublin, 1919), pp. 3, 12.
26. D. O'Hegarty to Gallagher, 30 Mar. 1920, NA, DE 2/81; O'Hegarty to Gallagher, 28 Apr. 1920, ibid.; *Irish Bulletin*, 17 May 1920, pp. 1–4; 11 June 1920, pp. 1–3. See also [Sinn Féin], *Irish Councils for Irish Freedom* (Dublin, 1920).
27. *Irish Bulletin*, 1 July 1920, p. 4.
28. Ibid., 11 June 1920, p. 1; [Sinn Féin], *Irish Councils*, p. 9.
29. R. F. Foster, *Modern Ireland, 1600–1972* (London, 1988), p. 497.
30. There is a sharp gap between the treatment of the results of the elections in January and those in June. The analysis of the latter, which showed a greater Sinn Féin hegemony, included the detailed information on the seats won by respective parties. That of the former only stated the number of councils where each party secured a majority; see [Sinn Féin], *Irish Councils*, pp. 7–24.
31. Report of Department of Foreign Affairs, June 1920, NA, DE 2/269.
32. *Irish Bulletin*, 13 July 1920, p. 1.
33. Ibid., 3 Mar. 1921, p. 1.
34. Ibid., 21 May 1920, p. 1. For establishing the republican police, see Mitchell, *Revolutionary Government*, pp. 150–4; J. Augusteijn, *From Public Defiance to Guerrilla Warfare* (Dublin, 1996), pp. 285–9.
35. *Irish Bulletin*, 1 July 1920, p. 4.
36. See, for instance, *An tÓglách*, 31 Jan. 1919, p. 2; Feb. 1919, p. 1.
37. See, for instance, *Irish Bulletin*, 29 Nov. 1920, p. 3; 20 Dec. 1920, p. 1.
38. Ibid., 29 Nov. 1920, p. 3.

39. *An tÓglách*, 27 Mar. 1919, p. 1; 31 Jan. 1919, p. 2.
40. *Irish Bulletin*, 2 June 1921, p. 2.
41. Ibid., 28 June 1921, pp. 1–2.
42. Ibid., 7 Mar. 1921, p. 1.
43. Ibid., 8 June 1921, p. 1.
44. Ibid., 4 Mar. 1920, p. 1; 30 Apr. 1920, p. 1.
45. E. Childers, *Military Rule in Ireland* (Dublin, 1920), p. 3.
46. E. Childers, *A Strike-Breaking Army at Work* (n.p., 1919), p. 1.
47. Childers, *Military Rule*, p. 7.
48. P. Hart, 'The Geography of Revolution in Ireland, 1917–1923', *Past and Present*, no. 155 (May 1997).
49. Gallagher to Cecilia Saunders, [14?] Mar. 1921, TCD, ms. 10 050.
50. In March 1921, praising the war effort in Munster, *An tÓglách* deplored the inactivity in other areas, see *An tÓglách*, 1 Mar. 1921, p. 1.
51. *Irish Bulletin*, 7 Mar. 1921, p. 1; 24 Mar. 1921, p. 1.
52. For instance, see the leader article of the *Cork Examiner*, 21 Feb. 1921, p. 4; 4 Mar. 1921, p. 4; and *Freeman's Journal*, 8 Mar. 1921, p. 4.
53. Dáil Éireann, *Proceedings* (11 Mar. 1921), p. 274.
54. FitzGerald to Gavan Duffy, 18 May 1920, NA, 1125/7.
55. See for instance, [Sinn Féin], *The First of the Small Nations* (Dublin, 1919); *Can Ireland Pay Her Way?* (n.p., 1919); *The Cost of Slavery* (n.p., [1920?]).
56. Report on Propaganda Department, June 1920, UCDAD, P80/14.
57. *Nationality*, 21 June 1919, p. 3.
58. Ibid., 22 Mar. 1919, p. 2., see also, ibid., 3 May 1919, p. 1.
59. Ibid., 19 Apr. 1919, p. 1.
60. Department of Publicity, History and Progress, Aug. 1921, UCDAD, P80/14.
61. For instance, see *Hansard's Parliamentary Debate, House of Commons*, 24 Nov. 1920, col. 497.
62. Paris to Dublin, between 22 June and 15 July 1919, NA, 1125/1.
63. Conditions in Russia, Feb.–June 1921, E. de Valera Papers, UCDAD.
64. O'Brien to Collins, 25 Aug. 1920, NA, DE 2/402.
65. Keogh, 'The Origins', p. 158.
66. Joan Estelrich to Sinn Féin Press Bureau, 20 Nov. 1919, NLI, ms. 8427; Report on Foreign Affairs, Jan. 1921, E. de Valera Papers, UCDAD.
67. T. P. O'Neill (ed.), *Dáil Éireann, Private Sessions of Second Dáil* (Dublin, 1972), 18 Aug. 1921, p. 12.
68. For the details of the Dáil propaganda during the Truce, see Inoue, 'Propaganda of Dáil Éireann'.
69. Mark Sturgis Diary, 14 July 1920, PRO 30/59 (1).
70. See, Boyce, *Englishmen*, ch. 4; G. T. Downes, 'A Consideration and Evaluation of the Anglo-Irish War, with Particular Reference to the Performance and Effectiveness of the British Publicity Department,

1912–21', MA thesis (University of Keele, 1985); and Francis J. Costello, 'The Role of Propaganda in the Anglo-Irish War, 1919–1921', *Canadian Journal of Irish Studies*, XIV, 2 (Jan. 1989).

71. Mitchell, *Revolutionary Government*, p. 104.
72. Report on Propaganda Department, n.d., NA, DE 2/10; Dáil Éireann, *Proceedings* (17 Sep. 1920), p. 233; (25 Jan. 1921), p. 259; Report on Propaganda, 18 Jan. 1921, UCDAD, P80/14.
73. Dáil Éireann, *Proceedings* (10 May 1921), p. 290.
74. O'Neill (ed.), *Private Sessions*, 23 Aug. 1921, p. 54
75. See Inoue, 'Sinn Féin Propaganda'.
76. See Inoue, ibid.; Laffan, *Resurrection*, pp. 323–9.
77. It is uncertain how many copies of this paper were circulated. However, a report of a British County Inspector shows a trend. In Jan. 1919 the circulation of seditious papers was reported from County Down as follows: *Nationality*, 237; *Irishman*, 109; *New Ireland*, 36; *Irish Nation*, 30; *Irish Opinion*, 19; *The Harp*, 18; *Labour Leader*, 12; *Young Ireland*, 10. The County Inspector in West Galway reported the number of seditious papers circulated in his area almost every month, but nothing was mentioned of *Young Ireland* (PRO, CO 904/108).
78. Dáil Éireann, *Proceedings* (10 May 1921), p. 283.
79. The number of the papers suppressed was as follows: 1917, 3; 1918, 12; Jan. to Sep. 1919, 23, see *Irish Bulletin Weekly Summary*, 30 Sep. 1919.
80. Annual Ard Comhairle of Sinn Féin, 21 Aug. 1919, NLI, ms. 8786 (i).
81. For instance, while papers such as the *Sligo Champion*, and the *Meath Chronicle* published it almost every week, it appeared only occasionally in papers such as the *Tipperary Star* and the *Mayo News*, and did not appear at all in the *Leinster Leader*. After mid-October 1919, even the *Sligo Champion* stopped publishing it.
82. De Valera to Childers, 11 Apr. 1921, E. de Valera Papers, UCDAD.
83. Cumann na mBan, *Annual Convention, Oct. 22nd and 23rd 1921, Report* (1921), p. 6.
84. For further details of the process of the relegation of Sinn Féin, see Laffan, *Resurrection*, ch. 8.
85. Dáil Éireann, *Proceedings* (25 Jan. 1921), p. 258.
86. Ibid. (17 Sep. 1920), p. 226.
87. Memo to Director, 7 Nov. 1921, UCDAD, P80/15; from Gallagher, 14 Oct. 1921, UCDAD, P80/31.
88. Assistant Chief of Staff to Béaslaí, July 1921, UCDAD, P80/22.
89. Childers to O'Keeffe, 5 July 1921, UCDAD, P80/31.
90. *Irish Bulletin*, 11 Nov. 1921, p. 2; O'Neill (ed.), *Private Sessions*, 23 Aug. 1921, p. 52; Gallagher to De Valera, 29 Oct. 1921, UCDAD, P80/17.
91. Laffan, *Resurrection*, p. 264.

7

Motivation: Why did they Fight for Ireland? The Motivation of Volunteers in the Revolution

Joost Augusteijn

In recent historiography it has been shown that the reasons why people joined the Volunteers and became involved in violence during the revolutionary period in Ireland had often more to do with social context and coincidence than with an exceptional ideological commitment.[1] There were many what we can call 'recruiting agents' at work in the period before and after 1916, which drew in relatively a-political members. The GAA and the Gaelic League in particular supplied many new Volunteers. The popularity of militarism in the early twentieth century not only induced young men to join armies and volunteer organisations in great numbers throughout the western world, but also affected young women. Some of them set up or joined their own organisation, while many others showed their admiration for those who did in such a way that it constituted another motivating force for unattached young men. Peter Hart has also asserted that the mobilisation and activities of the Volunteers in the early period showed many similarities with traditional youth culture.[2] In general one could argue that a lot of young men took their lead from the local opinion makers and joined because they did so.

As I have pointed out elsewhere, Volunteers who joined in this manner very seldom expressed an ideological motivation that went beyond the desire to obtain an Irish republic.[3] It has also long been established that, as cross-class organisations, Sinn Féin and the Volunteers did not involve themselves or allow their members to involve themselves in socio-economic questions, and merely defended the existing status quo (see Chapter 13).[4] Although more sophisticated ideas were occasionally voiced, as a whole the shared objective for most Volunteers was merely the take-over of political power. Why this was necessary and what they would do differently once this was achieved were questions rarely raised.

If we accept this lack of ideological sophistication, which is certainly not unusual among volunteers in all kinds of conflicts, the question remains, how Irish Volunteers justified the use of physical force to themselves and to the wider community. What did they think made it right to kill in order to replace the union with Britain with native Irish rule? This question is all the more poignant as it was quite clear at this stage that Britain was committed to granting Ireland some form of autonomy. Also, the fact that Ireland had one of the lowest murder rates of the western world indicates that the use of physical force was not something easily engaged in. To answer the above question, this chapter will try to discern trends in the diverse experience of individual Volunteers.

One of the issues most frequently mentioned by Volunteers to explain their actions is the behaviour of the government and the Crown forces during the revolutionary period. The depth of feeling engendered in the general population by the official response to Volunteer violence is well encapsulated by the reaction to the arrest, trial and execution on 1 November 1920 of Kevin Barry, the first death-sentence since the 1916 Rising. A female student at UCD, where Barry studied, wrote in her diary:

> There were terrible stories current of how the poor fellow was being tortured in Mountjoy to make him reveal the names of his companions. I never experienced anything like the surging fury which the news produced in everyone. ... I shall never forget my feelings when the poster 'He Must Die' met my gaze, we lost all our humanitarian feelings & actually rejoiced when later we heard three English Officers would be shot for every Irishman hanged.[5]

In her description of these events there is no recognition of the fact that Barry had been arrested following his participation in a raid on a bread van, which had left one soldier dead and two seriously wounded. This student displayed a similar response to the events after

Bloody Sunday and the circumstances surrounding the death of three Volunteers in custody, which were probably accurately portrayed as wilful killing.[6]

The treatment of prisoners on hunger strike was another hot issue in the public's mind. A young woman from Cork, sympathetic to the republicans, wrote about this in her diary:

> The cabinet have determined not to release them because of their strike, and so they are slowly dying through English brutality. ... Four of the hunger-strikers ... were deported to England. ... The brutality of bringing them on a sea-voyage in their weak state is typical of England's methods! There are very few Unionists left in Ireland now, but I am afraid some sad things will happen yet before we get our independence.[7]

She added: 'The country is in a dreadful state at present, owing to the frightful conduct of the military and the Black and Tans.' Although clearly feeling the government and Crown forces were responsible for the violent events, she displayed a strong ambivalence between a desire for revenge and the pity she felt when alleged informers were actually shot.

The raids and searches of private residences, which, as the authorities acknowledged, involved 'cases of ill-discipline, looting and drinking on the part of the troops engaged',[8] and which were reported in the press, were another important contributor to the poor image of the police with the general population. This was such a persuasive image that when a loyal businessman developed a dispute with other civilians he informed the authorities of his fear that false information about him was passed on to the Crown forces, which would inevitably lead to a raid and consequently to 'the total destruction of his premises'. To avoid this he assured them that his premises were open day or night and that he was willing to facilitate any search that might be made. In reply the General Staff assured him that there was no reason for his fear: 'it is a well-known fact moreover that the Military do not wantonly destroy property'.[9] Although this was clearly not a generally accepted view, the actual experience of raids was, much to the surprise of the people involved, indeed often quite different from their expectation.[10] In a letter to General Boyd, the commander of the Auxiliaries, a woman wrote:

> I am tending you a line to tell you how very courteous and well behaved all the men of the Auxiliary police were during the raid they carried out in this street last Saturday as well as one before. ... I know you will think that is only

quite natural from English ex-soldiers, but as they get such a lot of abuse, I wanted to just say a word in their favour.[11]

The poor image of the Crown forces and in particularly the Black and Tans and Auxiliaries was of course partly created by effective Sinn Féin propaganda (see Chapter 6), but also dictated the response of Volunteers themselves. In Westport, Co. Mayo, the announcement of the arrival of some Auxiliaries, sent on to the IRA by a friendly policeman, made some flee their homes instantly in anticipation of what would follow. Several Westport Volunteers gathered on a nearby hilltop waiting in vain for instructions from their brigade officers. These anxious hours spent in extremely poor weather was a disheartening experience, and although it eventually led to the formation of an active service unit, most men returned home dejected the next morning. When the Auxiliaries finally arrived they did not live up to expectations:

> This murder gang consisted of 3 plain's clothed [*sic*] men, for we had expected armoured cars and lorries, but actually only the 3 men came then. It was a kind of a bombastic show-off around the town. They were swinging guns. They brought the military from the Quay. The 3 of them raided with the military then: and there were quite a number of raids. Their attitude in Westport was to kind of make us look foolish. But these 3 were not violent. It was really a bit of swash-buckling more than anything else.[12]

That in many areas the police and especially the Black and Tans and Auxiliaries were not behaving according to the image portrayed of them confused the local IRA, as is brought to light in a report of the North Mayo Brigade to IRA headquarters:

> The Auxiliaries are in town since 16th. Those seem different to the famous 'Gentlemen' of motto-making-flag-waving memory. They laugh at the police and seem to prefer an easy time to anything else. They told some people they should walk about and not have curfew! They had a 'tiff' with the police one night ... on the street. I wonder what's their game?[13]

Despite this discrepancy between perception and reality, the portrayal of the auxiliary police forces did not convince only Volunteers, their sympathisers and many in the general population, but also some British army officers:

> They [the Auxiliaries] seemed to make a habit of breaking out of their barracks at night, illicitly; and killing men they thought were suspect rebels, and in this way the habit spread surreptitiously even to a few army officers and men. Whenever some of them accompanied me, on any search, patrol or foray in

which I was in command, my first action was always to detail 2 or 3 of my own jocks [soldiers] simply to watch over them, and see that they did not commit any atrocities such as unlawful looting or burning houses, when they were acting under my command, or even shooting prisoners, on the grounds they were attempting to escape![14]

The wide acceptance of this image led to some interesting mix-ups: 'In the Tan War MacGrath and [Michael] Collins broke up a pub in Mount St. by shooting it up. Garry reported the matter to the IRB but the people thought the two of them were Tans.'[15] A more puzzling one concerns a British soldier who apparently describes being sent down from Northern Ireland to aid in the attack on the Four Courts, the headquarters of the anti-Treaty republican side at the start of the Civil War:

> I do not remember how long it took us to reach Dublin we marched by night and were told to speak to no civilians and to keep as quiet as possible. ... So the two guns went into the battle of the four courts; ... it appeared that some Black and Tans had stormed and captured some buildings of the courts and were using rifles to hold their position.[16]

The actual and alleged bad behaviour of the Crown forces was thus an extremely persuasive force, which caused and justified a violent response by the IRA in the eyes of men and women on all sides. However, this alone does not explain why some men became willing to use force to attain political objectives, neither does it answer the even more fundamental question of why it was that this image of the government and the Crown forces as mindless oppressors was so readily accepted. Why was it that the violent activities of the Volunteers, which generally initiated the response from the Crown forces, did not engender the same response, and why was the death of the, often Irish, members of the Crown forces not seen to be as unjustified as that of those men who had originally targeted them?

The most likely explanation for this is that the legitimacy of the government was already widely questioned before the revolutionary period started and that the violent response to IRA activity merely confirmed an already existing image of Britain as an alien oppressor, an image carefully created by the nationalist press in the decades before (see Chapter 3). Once such a fundamental perception had been established, every subsequent action of the government would be fitted into this existing framework and the violence of the IRA would become a justified response to the actions of a tyrannical government even if it pre-dated state violence. It is clear that by 1920 the government's monopoly on the use of force, a good indicator of popular acceptance of a government, was no longer acknowledged by wide sections of Irish society.

Considering the majority support for the IPP's demand for home rule since the 1880s this perception of Britain may not be so surprising. However, apart from a conviction that local control over government decisions was important, this does not necessarily imply a total rejection of ties with Britain in line with the image of Britain as an alien oppressor. Although there was at least a widely accepted view that Ireland was different from Britain and needed a separate government, it does not explain where this negative image of Britain came from nor why it became so persuasive in the second decade of the twentieth century that the use of physical force became widely acceptable.

For the leaders of the Volunteers in the revolutionary period, not only did Ireland need home government, but it was a separate nation and was held by force against the wishes of the people. This was made very clear in the 1916 Proclamation and again in the pledge taken by thousands of people during the Conscription Crisis of April 1918:

> We join with our fellow country men at home and in foreign lands in proclaiming once more that Ireland is a distinct nation with a just right to Sovereign Independence. This right has been asserted in every generation, has never been condemned and never allowed to lapse. We call the Nations to witness that today as in the past it is by force alone that England holds Ireland in her Empire and not by the consent of the Irish people.[17]

In their eyes this right to independence was thus based on an unbroken history of resistance to British rule. In the 1918 Sinn Féin election manifesto another element is added to Ireland's claim to independence:

> It is based on our unbroken tradition of nationhood, on a unity in a national name which has never been challenged, on our possession of a distinctive national culture and social order, on the moral courage and dignity of our people in the face of alien aggression.[18]

This provides a very clear argument for Ireland's right to independence. It was a separate nation with a different culture and social order and had asserted a desire for independence ever since the first presence of the English in Ireland. If the population accepted this image, and preferably the international community as well (see Chapter 6), it would give the Irish the right to resist British rule even with physical force; particularly, now that Britain had apparently refused to accept the democratically expressed wish of the Irish people for the past 30 years. During the First World War the principle of government based on consent of the governed had, of course, gained a strong international appeal as the ideological justification for fighting the war. However, the fact that republicans felt it necessary to actually argue their case for the existence of a separate Irish nation indicates that its existence was not as widely accepted as may be assumed. In reality Volunteers themselves rarely claimed that it was its distinct culture and social order that gave Ireland its right to independence. One can assume that they did not find it necessary to make such a claim as it was something too obvious to be mentioned. However, the 1918 manifesto, which was, after all, intended to induce the Irish people to vote for Sinn Féin, puts doubt on this as it states that (contrary to what people may think) Ireland's claim 'is not based on any accidental situation arising from the [First World] war'. Thus acknowledging that even in nationalist Ireland the right to independence was questioned.

Nevertheless, the emphasis on a revival of supposed ancient Gaelic traditions by the Irish-Ireland movement at the end of the nineteenth century did develop the sense of distinctiveness: 'The Irish classes were a great help towards the development of a genuine national outlook, and an encouragement to the young men who were asking why should our country be subject to any outside power.'[19] The decline of distinct Gaelic expressions such as language, sport, music and dance, in the nineteenth century, also strengthened the image of Ireland as an oppressed nation.

For most Volunteers, however, the history of resistance to British rule was the main argument underlying Ireland's right to independence. In their mind this resistance was directly related to the way Ireland had been treated in the past – a view fostered by the growing body of historical writing, which painted a very romantic image of an unscrupulous Britain violently repressing an independent people. Much of this was initiated by the Young Irelanders in the 1840s and had been taken up at the end of the century by members of the Irish-Ireland movement. This particular view of Irish history, emphasising the separateness and historic unity of the Irish nation, which gallantly defended itself against the overwhelming strength of the British Empire, was ultimately accepted by a majority of the Irish people, and contributed to the changed political objective in the revolutionary period, from home rule within the UK to total rejection of any ties between the two countries.

Most activists in the 1916–23 period date their conversion to the need for total independence to 1916. They justify the use of force by pointing to the Easter Rising and the government's response to it:

> These few months following the rebellion had an effect on me and many of my contemporaries which determined our future way of life. The executions imprinted on my young mind an abiding hatred of British domination of Ireland. Ireland and its destiny became an obsession which was to remain with me for the rest of my life.[20]

To those who supported their actions during the revolutionary years the fighting men of 1916 become the saviours of the nation in a strongly religious sense:

> What did they do?
> What did they do, Oh Irishmen whose souls are dead ...
> And walk the way that saints have led ...
> You ask of me what did they do?
> I ask of you – What did Christ do?[21]

In a great number of households pictures of Pearse were hung next to that of Christ (later joined by JFK).[22] Grass from the grave of the executed leaders, and locks of Terence MacSwiney's hair, were examples of particularly revered items.[23]

In the period following the revolt of 1916, popular opinion did indeed change much more rapidly than it had done before. The overwhelming support for a constitutional and peaceful struggle for Irish autonomy within the United Kingdom gave way to support for total independence gained by more radical methods, which for some included violence.[24] A number of issues affected this change. Apart from the British response to the Rising and the ever-existing threat of the introduction of conscription,[25] this included a general disillusion with the First World War and what it was fought for as well as with the continued inability of the IPP to get even a limited measure of home rule introduced (see Chapter 4).

Few of these issues directly motivated those who actually fought in 1916. For them, and to an extent also for those who joined after 1916, dissatisfaction with the concept of constitutional nationalism adhered to by the previous generation was strong. Younger radicals contrasted their approach with the violent rebellions earlier: 'I think it was Joe, my brother, who pointed out to me that we should be ashamed of our father's generation. They were the first generation of Irishmen who had not struck a blow for Ireland.'[26] On one level the radical stance was thus an expression of a generational switch, of a younger generation, possibly frustrated in their political aspirations by the older generation, which wanted to take control.

The inability of the British Government to introduce home rule in the face of opposition from Ulster Protestants and Conservatives had turned many nationalists, including Patrick Pearse, away from constitutional methods before the First World War:

> Some of the younger members of the UIL, who had grown up in the atmosphere created by the Gaelic League; and were falling under the influence of such papers as 'Sinn Féin' and 'Irish Freedom' began gradually to doubt the efficacy of constitutionalism and to turn their thoughts to physical force.[27]

The events during the Home Rule crisis generated a distrust of the British that became a strong mobilising factor for some. A priest in Thurles who was involved in the IPP described the attitude of the Irish Volunteers in 1913: 'The views about Home Rule were optimistic in some quarters but in there [among Volunteers] it was thought that the Government were insincere and that they would finally give us such a Home Rule measure as would be of no use to us.'[28] The disillusion with the parliamentary constitutional approach of the IPP is nicely reflected in the following poem about Pearse:

> Yours not with abject mien to scrape and bow
> And face assembled ministers with civil smile
> And beg, if weightier matters will allow
> They'll cast some small crumb to the 'Sister Isle'.[29]

The British disdain for the Irish and particularly for the kind of people involved in the republican movement had a further radicalising effect: 'What probably drove a peacefully inclined man like myself into rebellion was the British attitude towards us: the assumption that the whole lot of us were a pack of murdering corner-boys.'[30] In the early reports on the republican movement in the years before and after 1916 the police indeed tended to underestimate the gravity of what was taking place as they continuously stressed that 'nobody of any importance' was involved.[31]

This attitude of the authorities and the distrust it engendered had much to do with the generally negative perception of the Irish in Britain. The prejudice against the Irish in England had a long history, and although it has been shown that the relationship was much more complicated than it appeared on the surface, many Irish, particularly in Britain, would have experienced discrimination at first hand, while st Irish people would sense they were not fully accepted by many in Britain.[32] The supposed savagery and lesser ability of the Irish were often used as a political argument against granting Ireland home rule. This contempt for the Irish probably contributed to the rejection by many Irish people of membership of the British nation. The growing acceptance that England was another country justified to Volunteers the use of force, even if it was aimed at other Irishmen in the service of the government. When Michael Kilroy and some other Volunteers were challenged by four RIC men they felt free to use their weapons: 'Those men represented a foreign power in our country and we were out to end their domination as quickly as possible.'[33] Other Volunteers expressed this attitude in much stronger terms: 'It is no use damning your body if I don't damn your soul also, said a Clare man as he shot a peeler, who was crying for a priest.'[34]

In the years before 1916 there was thus a growing dissatisfaction with the ineffectiveness of the methods of previous generations and an increasing distrust of the intentions of the British Government. In a general sense one could argue that although the accepted political objective between 1880 and 1916 remained home rule, to be achieved peacefully through and within the UK system, the dominance of the nationalist canon resulted in a generation of people growing up in an environment where breaking ties with Britain was the generally accepted ideal. For this generation home rule was the starting point of their political aspirations. They had internalised Ireland's right to a separate state and were far more susceptible to an ideology that advocated total independence obtained by force, particularly when the constitutional methods of their parents' generation appeared ineffective.

If this was the case, when did this realisation among pre-1916 activists that physical force was an acceptable option take place? Many mention the centenary of the 1798 rising as a defining moment in their turn to violence. These celebrations generated many leaflets and booklets about that period, informing people about 'the deeds and noble stand made by the many leaders'.[35] Schoolchildren were particularly strongly influenced by this:

> [We] vied with each other as to who knew most about any one, or all of the '98 leaders. ... In 1898 children insisted on keeping the step when two or more walked together, whether business or pleasure. Those ideas persisted for years after the centenary celebrations of 1898. Then the Boer War created a fresh wave of enthusiasm.[36]

Commemorations of this kind, starting with the 1798 centenary and continued with the yearly one for the Manchester Martyrs, had a strong influence on young people of all backgrounds who identified with the heroes of previous rebellions.[37] 'Inspiration was sought from those Gaelic heroes of the past – Tone, Mitchell and O'Donovan Rossa. We were refreshed and exhilarated by our contact with those great leaders of the past.'[38] The Boer War also showed that, contrary to their parents' assessment, resistance to the British Empire could be successful. Some activists remember re-enacting the battles of that war as a child, preferably taking on the role of one of the Boer generals.

The Boer War also provided an opportunity to express latent anti-British feelings: 'I recall their [the neighbours'] exultation over the victories gained by the Boer generals, and how thrilled they were by the British defeat at Spion Kop.'[39] During the Great War this anti-British sentiment resulted in pro-German and even pro-Bolshevist feelings among some Volunteers.[40] This grew even stronger during the Anglo-Irish War:

> God curse the British Empire.
> May he wither the flag that flies
> May he shatter the strength that still remains
> Of that father of sins and lies
> May he strengthen the hands of its enemies
> May he hasten its dying gasp
> May Satan rise from the depth of hell
> That [?] of earth to grasp.[41]

The impact of these commemorations and of the Boer War is probably explained by the influence of the kind of Irish history taught by parents and, from 1908, in schools as well. The effect of this could be fairly innocent: 'My father taught me Irish history … [he] forbid me to take my hat off, or call any Englishman Sir.'[42] Occasionally a more threatening note was struck:

> Our schoolteacher would remind us of our ancestors and what they suffered. Talks like this would cause us to dream and wonder if there was any chance of something of a nationalist military nature likely to happen in our time.[43]

The treatment of past rebels mobilised resistance, and some prepared themselves for every eventuality: 'I remember I used to exercise to harden my neck against the Hangman's rope.'[44]

The perceived historical misdeeds of the British thus gained a great relevance to the existing situation in the early twentieth century. This historical awareness surprised and bewildered a newly arrived British army officer on a train journey from Waterford:

> With me was a relatively well-educated man. Not knowing how delicate were religion and politics as a subject for conversation, I allowed myself to be engaged in a discussion of them. Suddenly he pointed at a tower, obviously of great age, and said 'When King John came here to receive the allegiance of the Irish Kings, he made them kiss his foot and laughed at their clothes.' 'This', he said, 'was an example of the behaviour of the hated English.' He went on from there to Cromwell.[45]

Apart from ridicule and the military exploits of the British the issue of land held a great significance for many rural people. This becomes clear from the response of a small farmer from Wexford to the question of where his republicanism came from:

> All that came from the generations before, the way they carried on of course. The British carried on, it was shocking sure. They take over the land, British Army officers, big kind of people they had big mansions, the local people had mud cabins.[46]

This sense of injustice associated with the century-old practice to reward soldiers with land was paired with an image of abuse of feudal rights, which still engendered strong feelings.[47] That this still had a bearing in the revolutionary period is shown by the reaction of Tom Barry, the famous Cork IRA leader, to the suggestion that Protestant landowners wanted to sell their estates and leave: 'We put a ban on all sales of the property because we were not going to have them leave Ireland with money in their pockets from land they had stolen from the people.'[48]

The commemorations and the growing awareness of a nationalist interpretation of history slowly changed some people's outlook upon the link with Britain: 'We began to look at the soldiers in the streets differently – to think of them as Englishmen rather than Irishmen. The Union Jack and portraits of the King and Queen were no longer accepted as ours.'[49] The dangers associated with the teaching of Irish history were realised by some. In December 1916, objections were raised to the teaching of Irish history, which was seen as the source of the 1916 Rising. The Christian Brothers' Irish history reader and Stephen Gwynn's 'Stories from Irish History' were singled out: 'Why do our Protestant Commissioners allow these books? Would it not be possible to eliminate Irish history books from the curriculum?'[50]

This perception that Britain had raped and pillaged Ireland in the past and would again do so given half a chance, instilled a total distrust

of the British Government in some and made it irrelevant wha
did. As Pierce McCan – a well educated large Catholic landowner and
Sinn Féin parliamentary candidate – put it in 1918: 'Sinn Féin stands
for the right of Irishmen to live as freemen in their own country
exactly as they willed. It does not matter one bit whether England's
government of Ireland is good or bad. They want their government
and they must get it.'[51] Peter Wall, a small farmer and member of the
Volunteers from Wexford, simply stated: 'They [the English] were here
and they shouldn't be here and they were ruling us and they shouldn't,
they had no right to rule here.'[52]

It is clear from the above that the rejection of the British right to
rule Ireland was primarily build on a negative image of the British.
Irish nationalism was, above all, based on the geographical unity
of Ireland and on the development of a shared conception of a separate
Irish nation among the majority of its people. To a large extent this
was a negative nationalism in that what united Irishmen was their
opposition to English rule, not any thought-out notion of what
Ireland should be like. The tradition of resistance, no matter how
widespread it had been among Irishmen in past times, was the basis
for the notion that Ireland was held against its will. For most
Volunteers it was enough to call upon the old litany of dates of rebellions and of its heroes to justify the use of physical force. Their willingness to fight for Ireland was therefore not rooted in a highly
developed nationalism divergent from that of most people. In an environment in which separatism was the rule, there was apparently no
need to develop an elaborate ideology to justify their stance.

Very few Volunteers actually expressed a clear idea of what
Irishness exactly entailed beyond speaking Irish and playing Gaelic
games, or what should be done differently once independence was
achieved. Most had a naive notion that all things wrong in Irish society would be righted as soon as the British left. A select few had a
more developed image of how a prosperous, self-confident Ireland
could be created through the education system and the development
of its economic resources.[53] There were also a few social radicals and
members of the lower classes who believed that the revolution should
make a real change in the social system (see Chapter 13). These people sometimes actively engaged in attempts to transfer land and occasionally entire industries into the hands of the poor, but republican
organisations were against any change in the existing social relations,
afraid to cause disunity within their own ranks. Maintaining the status
quo always remained their official policy.

This lack of a positive self-image and simplistic analysis of Ireland's problems can at least partly be held responsible for the shape of Irish society after independence. As a result of the absence of a clear Irish alternative and owing to the demands of the Civil War, the new rulers generally copied government institutions and policies from Britain.[54] Within the political rivalry between pro- and anti-Treaty factions of Sinn Féin, which followed the Civil War, the Irish language and Catholicism became the two defining issues which received increasing emphasis in a desperate attempt by them to distinguish themselves from their former rulers and appeal to the Irish electorate.

In the decades leading up to the Irish revolution a growing acceptance of the existence of a separate Irish nation, held against its democratically expressed will, can thus be detected. The popularity of a nationalist interpretation of the history of Anglo-Irish relations was largely responsible for this. Events in the past were often given as reasons for opposition to England's rule in general and for the necessity of a free and independent Ireland. They formed the basis on which the legitimacy of England's rule was challenged. Once this was done, a framework was created in which some people could justify violent action.

The past and present behaviour of the government and of those seen as its representatives, Crown forces, landlords, and so on, were a recurrent image in the validation of Volunteer violence. While Ireland's nationhood was safeguarded by the sporadic resistance to British rule in the past, these rebellions and the election results since the 1880s convinced Volunteers that the Irish wanted independence and that this desire gave Ireland the right to it on the basis of the contemporary notion of government by consent of the governed. Nevertheless, it is questionable whether this view represented the ideas of the majority of the people before 1916. Even the drafters of the 1916 Proclamation felt it necessary to convince the people that there was such a thing as an Irish nation with a right to independence.

In the lives of those involved in the fighting between 1916 and 1923 the perception of Britain as an alien oppressor was confirmed by commemorations of historic acts of resistance and by the contemporary actions of the British Government. In the period before 1914 the distrust of the government's intentions was exacerbated by a government report showing that Ireland had been overtaxed in the nineteenth century,[55] and by the apparent lack of willingness by the government to push through home rule against opposition from Irish unionists and

British Conservatives. The demands of the First World War and the British response to the 1916 Rising further confirmed the image of Britain as an alien oppressor unwilling to give Ireland its 'rightful freedom'. This made the use of political violence acceptable and allowed the lowering of a normally high threshold to the use of force, by providing an external justification for the rights of the Irish nation.

Once this perception of the British Government had become widely accepted, the reports on the conflict during the revolutionary period caused a further backlash against the government. The feelings of anger and revenge that accompanied specific events convinced more and more people of the correctness of the republican position. For many people it justified the violence of the IRA against the police and other representative institutions of the British Government in Ireland and to some it worked as an encouragement to get (deeper) involved in the IRA. The real and imagined maltreatment of people throughout Ireland continually proved the illegality of British rule in the minds of many nationalists. Increasingly it was the legitimacy, not the merit, of British rule that was challenged. In this atmosphere it had become almost impossible to justify British rule even to the large group of people in Ireland who were opposed to political vio-lence and had no strong sense of Irish nationality. Although the behaviour of the government forces was generally a reaction to IRA activity, it became widely felt that the government fought the people and therefore had no right to rule. Its use of force therefore only rein-forced the idea that complete independence offered the sole solution to Ireland's problems.

Notes

1. P. Hart, *The IRA and its Enemies* (Oxford, 1998); J. Augusteijn, *From Public Defiance to Guerrilla Warfare* (Dublin, 1996).
2. P. Hart, 'Youth Culture and the Cork IRA', in D. Fitzpatrick (ed.), *Revolution? Ireland, 1917–1923* (Dublin, 1990).
3. J. Augusteijn, 'The Importance of Being Irish', in Fitzpatrick (ed.), *Revolution?*
4. This was highlighted again in the recent discovery that republicans planned to poison Jim Larkin to prevent him from turning Irish work-ers towards socialism, *Irish Times*, 3 August 1999.
5. Diary of Celia Shaw, Oct. 1920, NLI, ms. 23 409. Whether he was actu-ally maltreated is in doubt. Contrast, 'Sworn Statement by Kevin Barry', NLI, ms. 8412; S. Cronin, 'Kevin Barry', *Capuchin Annual*, 1970, p. 537.
6. Diary of Celia Shaw, 21 Nov. 1921, NLI, ms. 23 409.

7. Diary II of Cecilia Saunders, 29 Aug. 1920, TCD, ms. 10 055.

8. PRO, WO35/180/3. Many other raid reports and reports on meetings show a similar acknowledgement.

9. PRO, WO35/71/8/117.

10. A positive experience with a raid, contrary to her expectation, was reported by Bridie Quirke, Interview 26 Apr. 1990. Similar experiences were reported by Willy Parle, Interview 6 May 1990; also Jimmy Murry (The Turk), UCDAD, P17/b/106.

11. Helen Fowle, PRO, WO35/71/8/117.

12. Quoted from Tommy Heavey, UCDAD, P17/b/120; for the experiences of one of the men on the hill who did return home, see Charlie Hughes, Interview. The police observed known Volunteers leaving home, CIR Mayo, Nov. 1920, PRO, CO904. Similar discrepancy between experience and expectation can be found in Ned Colfer, Interview 8 May 1990; Martin Kennnedy, Interview 7 May 1990; John Quinn, Interview 9 May 1990.

13. UCDAD, P7/A/18 (13).

14. Major-General D. Wimberley, 'Scottish Soldier', IWM, PP/MCR/182, 153. See also W. G. Roberts, 'Recollections and Conclusions', IWM, PP/MCR/98.

15. Alfie White, UCDAD, P17/b/110.

16. This is the only unsuspected reference I have found that appears to prove actual involvement of British troops in the attack on the Four Courts, which has been alleged by republicans but which has always been denied by the Free State as well as the British Government, Memoir of Creek, IWM, 64.

17. L. A. Brady, *Derry Journal*, 8 May 1953. Similar examples are: in Dublin, C. S. Andrews, *Dublin Made Me* (Dublin and Cork, 1979), p. 114; and Donegal, NLI, ms. 10 916.

18. D. Macardle, *The Irish Republic* (London, 1968), appendix 6, pp. 842–3.

19. M. Kilroy, 'The Awakening', Clew Bay Heritage Centre.

20. Andrews, *Dublin*, p. 91. Similar statements by: E. Lysaght, 'Master of None', ch. VIII, p. 1, NLI, ms. 4750; Brighid Lyons Thornton, in K. Griffith and T. O'Grady, *Curious Journey* (London, Melbourne, 1982), p. 85; Andy Roe, Interview 6 June 1990. One Wexford Volunteer claimed that he and his brothers joined the Volunteers as a direct result of the British reaction to the Rising (see Willy Parle, Interview 6 June 1990).

21. NLI, P4548.

22. Diary of Celia Shaw, Jan. 1921, NLI, ms. 23 409.

23. D. Roche, *Here's Their Memory* (1966), p. 57; Hart, *The IRA*, p. 207.

24. Revd M. Maher, 'Annals, 1910–1926', 1914, St Patrick's College, Thurles, Co. Tipperary.

25. Maher, 'Annals', 1918.

26. Seamus Robinson, UCDAD, P61/13, fol. 2.

27. M. Moran, 'With Michael Kilroy during Easter Week and the Years Before', Clew Bay Heritage Centre.
28. Maher, 'Annals', 1914.
29. NLI, ms. 18 533(6).
30. Lysaght, 'Master of None', ch.VIII, p. 17. The same feeling was expressed by Andrews, *Dublin*, p. 134.
31. CIRs, PRO, CO904.
32. R. F. Foster, *Paddy and Mr. Punch* (London, 1993), pp. 171–94; S. Gilley, 'English Attitudes to the Irish in England, 1789–1900', in C. Holmes (ed.), *Immigrants and Minorities in British Society* (London, 1978), pp. 81–110.
33. Kilroy, 'Awakening'.
34. Diarmuid MacManus, UCDAD, P17/b/94.
35. Kilroy, 'Awakening'.
36. Ibid.
37. Mentioned by R. Brennan, *Allegiance* (Dublin, 1950), p. 1; S. Robinson, 'Statement by Mr. Seamus Robinson', NLI, ms. 21 265, p. 58; John Duffy, Archdiocese of Armagh, Records Centre, Fr O'Kane Papers, Interview on tape, A20; Paddy Larkin, Interview 4 May 1990; Sean Moylan, NLI, ms. 27 731, p. 8; Griffith, *Curious Journey*, p. 11.
38. Commandant P. Casey, 'Idle Thoughts of an Officer of the Irish Volunteers', p. 2, Archdiocese of Armagh, Records Centre, Fr O'Kane Papers. Also expressed by J. Mathews, 'Statement', NLI, ms. 9873, pp. 1–2.
39. D. Breen, *My Fight for Irish Freedom* (Dublin, 1981), p. 21.
40. Among many others: Andrews, *Dublin*, pp. 81, 133; and Lysaght, 'Master of None', ch.VI, p. 11.
41. Wimberley, 'Scottish Soldier', p. 148.
42. Thomas Heavey, 'Statement', p. 2. Also Charlie Hughes, Interview.
43. Kilroy, 'Awakening'. See also Griffith, *Curious Journey*, pp. 11–12; Ned Brough, UCDAD, P17/b/98.
44. Griffith, *Curious Journey*, pp. 11–12.
45. Major-General L. A. Hawes, IWM, 87/41/1.
46. Andy Roe, Interview 6 June 1990. See also Patrick Owen Mugan, Interview 19 Feb. 1990.
47. Andy Roe, Interview 6 June 1990.
48. Griffith, *Curious Journey*, pp. 221–2.
49. Andrews, *Dublin*, p. 61.
50. Quoted by Rt Revd Mons. Michael Curran, NLI, ms. 27 728(1), p. 179. The teaching by the Christian Brothers has indeed been shown to have had some impact on the willingness to use physical force; see P. Hart, 'The Geography of Revolution in Ireland, 1917–1923', *Past and Present*, no. 155 (May 1997).
51. Deaglan O Bric, 'Pierce McCan, MP. (1882–1919)', *Tipperary Historical Journal* (1989), p. 109.

52. Peter Wall, Interview 27 Apr. 1990.
53. In particular among leaders such as Pearse and Griffith, but occasionally this can also be found among provincial Volunteers, see Moran, 'With Michael Kilroy'.
54. See, for example, J. J. Lee, *Ireland, 1912–1995* (Cambridge, 1989), pp. 562–643; J. Regan, *The Irish Counter-revolution, 1921–1936* (Dublin, 1999).
55. Examples of the public debate on overtaxation, in NLI, ILB 300, p. 4, no. 78 and 86.

8

Negotiation: The Anglo-Irish War and the Revolution

Michael Hopkinson

Historical interest in the Anglo-Irish War has been enormous but historiographical debate minimal. Roy Foster has also observed how little effect debates amongst historians have had on popular attitudes to the Irish past.[1] Nowhere is this more true than with regard to the final stages of the Irish revolution.

Until the 1970s there was little writing of a scholarly nature on the subject. Traditional narrative accounts dominated and biographies and memoirs were hugely popular. The story told was of a heroic victory against the odds, of dramatic ambushes and raids, of hunger strikes and prison resistance. One need only cite the best-selling accounts by Tom Barry, Dan Breen and Ernie O'Malley, and the various local studies put together by veterans of the conflict, with titles like *Kerry's Fighting Story* or *Dublin's Fighting Story*.[2] Such work was vital to the Irish state's perception of its origins. Academic history did little to challenge this picture – witness Dorothy Macardle's *The Irish Republic*, written in a cottage in Glenmalure in homage to the republican ideal.[3] The traditional nationalist, stereotypical views created by this have proved extremely difficult to alter, which has been exacerbated by the revisionist debate.

Black and Tan reprisals rival the culpability of the British Government for the Great Famine as the most emotive subject in modern Irish history. By contrast, the massive advance in scholarly approach to the conflict – beginning in the 1970s with Charles Townshend's and David Fitzpatrick's brilliant books[4] – has resulted in comparatively little debate about the key issues relating to it. Both the Anglo-Irish and Civil Wars were surprisingly neglected in George Boyce's collection of essays entitled *The Revolution in Ireland* and more recently there is nothing on the subject in Boyce and Alan O'Day's volume on issues central to the revisionist debate.[5] Some argument has been generated on particular aspects of the Anglo-Irish War, for instance, on how far the IRA's GHQ directed the guerrilla warfare and on whether there was any democratic accountability for the IRA's actions.[6] More interesting has been the discussion of why areas were or were not active during the fighting – beginning with Erhard Rumpf's work and including massively researched articles by Fitzpatrick and Peter Hart on the geography of Irish Nationalism, and Joost Augusteijn's and Hart's recent books.[7] Conclusions on this are bound to remain problematic and the debate is somewhat marginal to the most important elements of the conflict. Enormous gains have been made from the study of localities, most lately in Marie Coleman's and Michael Farry's research,[8] and this has added greatly to knowledge of who made up the IRA as well as to an understanding of the nature of the conflict.

Thanks to this wave of scholarly activity and the opening-up on a considerable scale of archive sources, a whole series of tired orthodoxies have been effectively challenged. It is no longer unquestionably accepted that there was a symbiotic relationship between the IRA and the people. No IRA veteran's account of the war is complete without acknowledgement of the population's heroic support and the constant availability of room and shelter. Criticism of compulsory levies, however, was not limited to the Truce period and the lack of fighting in some areas may be partly explained by the dread of reprisals[9] – blame for tit-for-tat violence was often targeted at the local IRA as well as the British forces. Tom Garvin has pointed out how relatively small a proportion of the young male population were Volunteers, and GHQ opposition to emigration was a demonstration of this.[10] It is now widely accepted that the fighting was extremely patchy and heavily localised, that large areas saw virtually no military activity, and that most action was confined to Dublin and some parts of Munster. Even in active areas, for every successful ambush there were dozens of examples of flying columns unavailingly waiting for days for enemy forces to arrive, as well as frequent testimony of faulty mines and inaccurate information. It is also broadly agreed that the IRA's achievements were more in the intelligence and publicity spheres than in the purely military.

Advances in the understanding of the period have gone far beyond military aspects. Eunan O'Halpin and John McColgan in two undervalued books have laid bare the chaos and confusion of the last years of Dublin Castle rule.[11] Broader approaches to the 1919–21 period have been reflected by changes in historical writing – the role of women in the Revolution has at last been credited and Richard English's biography of Ernie O'Malley uses an interesting, innovative method.[12] Fitzpatrick and his many outstanding research students have done much to integrate the social and economic with the political, in contrast to the traditional Irish preoccupation with high politics alone.

For all this, popular attention remains focused on personalities. Whole shelves in bookshops are devoted to biographies of Michael Collins with blurbs telling us about 'the man who won the War'. There is still something of an obsession with attaching blame and responsibility for the divisions that succeeded the conflict, but the drive to demonise Eamon de Valera has hopefully reached its apogee in Neil Jordan's film and Tim Pat Coogan's biography.[13] The reasons for this are readily apparent: colourful biographies sell well, all nations, and especially young ones, feel the need to romanticise their founding fathers. The short, dramatic life and tragic death of the photogenic Collins is a case in point. To re-evaluate the subject is not an easy task in contemporary Ireland. We are constantly told that Civil War politics are dead: to judge by much recent literature, Civil War history is very much alive. In this self-confident period in the southern state's history, many historians are taking an unsympathetic view of the republicans in the Treaty and Civil War times. Present-minded approaches continue to influence Irish historical writing. Tom Garvin's *1922: The Birth of Irish Democracy* celebrates the Free State's founding fathers in reaction against the long-dominant, ultra-nationalist, de Valera orthodoxy. Moreover, despite Garvin's and Joe Lee's[14] wide use of international examples and perspectives, there is often still too narrow a focus.

The central questions posed by the Anglo-Irish War have often been neglected: they relate to how and why a large measure of independence for the 26 counties was won and whether that achievement was at the expense of partition. There should be a consideration of how necessary the use of violence was and whether something akin to dominion status could have been won without it. It is therefore the most sensitive and difficult of subjects, not easily adapted to the professional historian's techniques and language and involving consideration, often disliked, of hypothetical issues.

Why was the British Government willing in July 1921 to offer what amounted to unconditional truce terms and a settlement far in advance of anything offered before? Ronan Fanning has recently argued that it was the effectiveness of guerrilla warfare, and particularly Collins' ruthless intelligence methods, which was crucial in causing the British Government's volte-face.[15] Nicholas Mansergh, in his last book, asserted that it was inconceivable that dominion status could have been conceded before the summer of 1921.[16] By contrast, Roy Foster writes: 'whether the bloody catalogue of assassinations and war from 1919–21 was necessary to negotiate thus far may be fairly questioned'.[17]

Fanning pours scorn on the suggestion that any settlement along dominion status lines could have been achieved without the militarisation of advanced nationalism. He writes: 'there is not a shred of evidence that Lloyd George's Tory-dominated Government would have moved from the 1914-style niggardliness of the Government of Ireland Act of 1920 to the larger, if imperfect, generosity of the Treaty if they had not been impelled to do so by Michael Collins and his assassins'.[18] He claims that Bloody Sunday caused an abrupt change in Lloyd George's outlook. While the railings went up at the end of Downing Street and bodies were brought back to London for ceremonial burial following the Kilmichael ambush, it is claimed that fear and pessimism brought about a search for a negotiated settlement.

To argue this is to underplay the extent of the collapse of British Government authority in large areas of south and west Ireland following on the evacuation of police barracks from late 1919, and the partial establishment of the Republican counter-state (see Chapter 5). Peace feelers were extended long before Bloody Sunday: since the spring of 1920 there had been a belated realisation that British authority had collapsed. In the short term, the grisly events of the end of November 1920 resulted in the implementation of martial law for Munster, large-scale internment and a tightening of the military screw. Very probably, Bloody Sunday and Kilmichael had a profoundly negative effect on the peace moves in progress at that time. Any public readiness to compromise with Sinn Féin and the IRA would have appeared totally objectionable to military and public alike. The eventual decision to negotiate with Sinn Féin was determined by the logic of events after the elections of May 1921 and not by reaction to Bloody Sunday. Additionally, the British Government realised that no end was in sight to the wretched guerrilla warfare and perceived that domestic opinion would not tolerate an escalation in the conflict.

The possibility of a negotiated peace in the second half of 1920 on early 1921 has been generally underestimated. Terms discussed in various peace moves were similar to those eventually agreed in the early hours of 6 December 1921 – safeguards on defence and Ulster, fiscal autonomy for the 26 counties and a form of dominion status. Concentration on the immediate context of the Treaty's signing detracts from the predictability of the terms. Both at the time and since, it suited all sides to the conflict to devalue the significance of the earlier peace moves. Republicans were unwilling to admit any talk of compromise with the enemy and British politicians were averse to accusations of talking with gunmen and of compromising imperial principles. Collins was always quick to deny negotiating with Andy Cope before the Truce[19] and the British Government keen to insist that a consistent line had been followed. None the less, from the autumn of 1920 the Sinn Féin leadership, including Collins, indicated through intermediaries a clear interest in a truce prior to negotiations. Collins commented on 2 December in terms anticipating his future defence of the Treaty: 'It is too much to expect that Irish physical force could combat successfully English physical force for any length of time if the directors of the latter could get a free hand for ruthlessness'.[20] Lloyd George, the Foreign Office and General Macready encouraged sundry peace efforts. The Prime Minister, for instance, was directly responsible for Archbishop Clune's undercover visits to Dublin in December 1920 and the safe conduct that gave him access to Sinn Féin and the IRA leaders. At various times in early 1921, Lloyd George appeared flexible on fiscal autonomy and backed attempts to bring Carson and de Valera together.[21] Both British and Irish leaders, however, refused to make a first public move and exhibited mutual distrust – while the Irish pointed to Lloyd George's undoubted deviousness, the British were unsure with whom they should be negotiating. This resulted in the continued use of a variety of middlemen and the meeting, brought about by British pressure, of Craig and de Valera in early May. In agreeing to confer at a particularly sensitive time, the northern and southern leaders showed a flexibility they could never afford to demonstrate in public.[22]

Mark Sturgis, a leading civil servant in Dublin Castle, felt that Lloyd George should have made the opening move[23] and that, throughout, Lloyd George displayed a lack of consistency and commitment. Shortly after the signing of the Anglo-Irish Treaty, Sir Warren Fisher, Permanent Under-Secretary of the Treasury and Head of the British Civil Service, wrote: 'Better late than never, but I can't get out of mind the unnecessary number of graves'.[24] The implication is that over 12 months had elapsed between the arrival of Fisher's team of seconded civil servants and the signing of the Truce – a period in which several leading British officials in Ireland had consistently impressed upon the government the need for negotiation rather than coercion. Those last 12 months were the most violent of the war, the memory of which has ever since embittered Anglo-Irish relations. By torpedoing any hope of success for Clune's initiative, in suddenly insisting on arms surrender in December 1920, Lloyd George put prospects for peace back by several months; under military and Tory pressure, the Prime Minister effectively ruined his own initiative. Asquith told Sturgis that this was the 'big missed opportunity' and Tim Healy, veteran maverick constitutional nationalist, commented: 'The silly Cabinet turned him (Clune) down, believing they can crush the Shinns, and that their acceptance of a Truce spelled weakness. No worse incident has occurred for 100 years'.[25]

In defence of the Prime Minister, it is frequently argued that his freedom for manoeuvre was greatly limited by the Tory-dominated coalition and by military advice. However, leading Conservatives, notably Lord Curzon and Austen Chamberlain, were supportive of conciliation.[26] In contrast to his skilful handling of the Treaty negotiations, Lloyd George made no attempt to isolate diehard opinion and indeed frequently encouraged it. Lloyd George's failure to act on the advice offered by his own senior officials in Dublin Castle from the summer of 1920 represented a failure of political nerve and will. While dominion status may not have been discussed publicly until the Truce,[27] it is clear it was being widely considered for many months before it. When a direct approach was made to De Valera in June, it was brought about by political reality. Following the May elections the government was faced with a choice between martial law and Crown Colony government on the one hand or negotiations with Sinn Féin on the other; by that time, the establishment of the Northern Government made Lloyd George's decision easier. Personally, he had little sympathy for the Irish and, apart from consideration of his own political future, was chiefly concerned about the international, and especially American, repercussions. In late January 1921, Sir John Anderson affirmed that it was Lloyd George himself who was the key apologist for reprisals:[28] the Prime Minister was not the prisoner of his Cabinet.

Lloyd George does not merit the favourable historical press he has generally received on the Irish Question, which was almost entirely based on the Anglo-Irish Treaty. It was he who, in 1919, allowed Lord French and Ian Macpherson, the Chief Secretary, a free rein to pursue their reactionary and counter-productive policies; he appointed Hamar Greenwood as Chief Secretary while realising that this man knew nothing about Ireland.[29] Having agreed to the administrative reform of Dublin Castle and the secondment of leading civil servants in the summer of 1920, the Prime Minister failed to give a clear lead on policy in the following year. Blame for the reprisals should be applied less to the Black and Tans and the Auxiliaries themselves than to the politicians who set them up without a disciplinary code and a clear definition of their purpose.

Tom Garvin has argued that the achievement of Irish independence owed much to British governmental ineptitude.[30] Charles Townshend's *The British Campaign in Ireland* is a damning chronicle of government and security force incompetence. There was a complete failure to establish any unity of command (even under martial law). The militarisation of the police, the tolerance and probably tacit encouragement of reprisals and the policy of drift had appalling consequences. Up to the spring of 1920 remarkably little attention was paid to Irish affairs in Downing Street; thereafter a confused mix of conciliatory and coercive policies was pursued.

The fundamental weaknesses of the military campaign were well summed up by Macready and Anderson at the end of the conflict. Macready wrote to Frances Stevenson, Lloyd George's secretary and mistress, in June 1921: 'There are, of course, one or two wild people about who still hold the absurd idea that if you go on killing long enough peace will ensue. I do not believe it for one moment, but I do believe that the more people that are killed, the more difficult will be the final solution'.[31] In addressing the problem of the tactics and strategy to be used if the Truce broke down, Anderson criticised the methods followed in the previous two years:

> Our dispositions hitherto have all been based on the assumption that we had to deal with a minority of extremists engaged in a murder conspiracy for so called political ends. We have accordingly relied in the main on police action enforced by processes of law, the military acting in the name of the civil power except in a limited area ... we have at the same time endeavoured everywhere to discharge the ordinary functions of civil government.
>
> This fundamental assumption – long known to be unfounded – has now proved to be utterly untenable. It would seem to follow that if the conflict unhappily has to be resumed our methods must be completely changed.
>
> A civil police force cannot operate effectively as such in a hostile country. ... The processes of judicial enquiry and trial are far too slow and cumbersome to serve as a useful adjunct to military operations.

> We have been fighting on a hopelessly extended front … hitherto we have presented a front of almost infinite extension with our local Post Offices, Income Tax Offices and individual members of every branch of the civil administration scattered all over the country and easy prey to the enemy who has taken toll of them at will. The results have only been what might have been expected: the surprising thing is that they have not been more serious.[32]

The machinery of government based in Dublin Castle and its relationship to Westminster was a barrier to any effective decision-making. It is easy also to criticise the individuals at the head of the administration – French proved a disastrous appointment as Lord Lieutenant; Macpherson showed no relish for the Chief Secretaryship, was anti-Catholic and spent little time in Ireland; Greenwood was pompous and absurdly over-optimistic, being described by Macready as 'a double-distilled ass';[33] while an able political general, Macready had a contempt for the Irish and his refusal to accept a joint military/police command had calamitous results. To attach too much blame to individuals, however, is to confuse effect with cause. Nonentities were appointed as Chief Secretary because major figures turned down the poisoned chalice – Lloyd George in 1916, H. A. L. Fisher in 1920, for instance. Responsibility should rather be attached to those that appointed them.

The events in the north-east during the War of Independence have too often been neglected. Some of the most important consequences of the conflict related to the six counties. Ulster unionist resistance, by preventing a settlement along home-rule lines and by radicalising opinion in the south and west, was the most significant cause of the war. The Truce terminating the conflict followed soon on the establishment of Partition: hence the Northern Question had been the key factor in dictating the fighting's duration.

Partitionist attitudes have inspired much of the writing on the North in this period. On the one hand, southern historians have by-passed the subject or shown, as in Joe Lee's case,[34] contempt for Northern unionism. On the other hand, accounts written from a unionist perspective have sought to defend, and even justify, the intransigent policies of the Northern Government. Patrick Buckland and A. T. Q. Stewart argue that nationalist refusal to recognise it, together with IRA aggression, made it all but inevitable that Craig's regime would adopt a siege-like mentality.[35] Beneath both approaches is the assumption that Partition was virtually inevitable and irreversible at least in the short term. There was, however, no inevitability about the precise form of the Government of Ireland Bill nor about the laissez-faire attitude taken by the British Government to the situation in the north-east between June 1920 and the Truce. Stances taken at the time were frequently less hard-line than they appeared superficially and retrospective accounts by contemporaries tend to emphasise consistency and dogmatism as opposed to flexibility. There is a need for someone to write the northern equivalent of John Bowman's *De Valera and the Ulster Question, 1917–1973*. Until Eamon Phoenix's recent book, the Catholic minority in the North was largely ignored by historians.[36]

The Government of Ireland Act of 1920 was drawn up and amended with the need to palliate Ulster unionist opinion as the priority. There was no expectation that it would be implemented in the 26 counties. Even before the formation of Craig's government the British Government gave way to virtually all the loyalists' demands. By failing to act over the shipyard expulsions of July 1921 and by agreeing to the establishment of the Special Constabulary, they alienated themselves completely from the Catholic minority in the North. These policies were even less defensible than the establishment of the Black and Tans had been a few months before. Both Macready and Anderson warned the government in the strongest possible terms of the consequences of their actions. Macready stressed:

> It is well to analyse the expression 'Loyalist' as applied to Ulster. The Force it is now proposed to mobilise is the same force who, for their own opinions, armed against the government of the day in the early part of 1914, and I am firmly convinced that they would take up arms again tomorrow if they thought that they could gain their own ends, even against the Constitution of the Empire, by so doing.[37]

Anderson told Bonar Law:

> 'We have ... tried the experiment of setting up an unarmed body of Special Constabulary in Belfast and even that has not been an unqualified success. On the first night three of the Special Constables were arrested for looting ... you cannot in the middle of a faction fight recognise one of the contending parties and expect it to deal with disorder in the spirit of impartiality and fairness essential in those who have to carry out the Orders of the Government.[38]

Nothing could have been more absurd than Churchill's suggestion that Ulster Specials be used to augment British Forces in the south.[39]

These developments defined the long-term character of loyalist government of the six counties even before the Government of Ireland Bill was passed. A memorandum laying down the essential points for the new administration can leave no one in any doubt as to what was to be expected. The Northern Government, it promised:

> will undoubtedly be formed from the Protestant majority. Consequently the steps now taken should be in accordance with that majority. It should not be a government in which both sides are treated as being equally entitled to a voice in whatever measures are taken … the essential point to remember is that the Unionists hold that no rebel who wishes to set up a Republic can be regarded merely as a 'political opponent' but must be repressed.[40]

No attempt was made to divide nationalist moderates from hardliners. Inflexible attitudes towards the Catholic minority long preceded any widespread or effective IRA activity in the six counties.

The Ulster unionist position was aided not only by British neglect but also by the absence of a coherent southern nationalist northern policy. The northern Sinn Féiner Louis J. Walsh 'perceived … that, whilst the Sinn Féin movement had made great play with "the naked deformity of Partition" in its campaign to displace the Irish Party, it had tended to rank the Ulster Question as a poor second to "Independence" in its scale of priorities'.[41] The Belfast Boycott only served to reinforce Partition.

For all the debate during and after the Paris Peace Conference about self-determination and the rights of minorities there had been no coherent plan setting out any rational concept behind the partition of Ireland. In a tortuous, often confused way, the British Government implemented it in an ad hoc fashion with a view to preventing the Ulster Question from blocking home rule. They seemed unaware of the acute irony that the only part of Ireland that accepted a devolved government was the north-east. The early stages of Northern Irish self-government assumed a kind of appalling inevitability.

Keith Jeffery has observed how problematic it is to find an appropriate title for the confused fighting between January 1919 and July 1921.[42] To use the terms 'War of Independence' or 'Anglo-Irish War' is to pose many questions; whatever nomenclature is employed, events should be placed in a wider chronological framework. It was the Ulster Crisis of 1912–14 and the First World War which represented the point of no return for the British Government in Ireland: from then on, a home rule settlement was not viable as southern Irish opinion had moved on from support for constitutional nationalism. The British Government chose not to acknowledge that fact. The years 1919–21 were the crucial final stages of the Revolution: the coincidence of the Dáil's first meeting and the Soloheadbeg ambush was a significant turning point.

Doubt has also been expressed over the extent of the Revolution. Left-wing republicanism has laid emphasis on its conservatism and on the continuity in many respects between British and Free State rule (see Chapter 13). Pro-Treaty sources unsurprisingly played down the extent of any revolutionary change. The Civil War and its legacy of long-term bitterness and mistrust divorced the new state from an objective evaluation of its revolutionary past.

A mixture of long- and short-term considerations should also apply to Irish nationalist aspects of the War of Independence. Collins' famous intelligence work needs to be seen from a broader perspective than it is generally. Collins' success was based on the willingness of large numbers of the Catholic middle class in public-service appointments to provide valuable information. Peter Hart has pointed out that in the late nineteenth century, RIC men were valued members of the community and employment in the police was regarded as a sound career objective.[43] By 1919, with the successful boycott of the force, they had become pariahs in their own land. Collins and the IRA's chief-of-staff, Richard Mulcahy, had both been Post Office employees. Collins was the first leader to realise the potential of this. Ned Broy, one of Collins' key agents inside Dublin Castle, had been striving for over a year to find a contact within Sinn Féin before he met Collins.[44] The qualified success of IRA arms and intelligence was based on the widespread feeling that the British Government had shown a treacherous reluctance to implement home rule for the whole of Ireland.

The 'Irish Revolution' is not an easy term to define: the revolutionaries themselves could not agree on what it achieved. Any social revolution long preceded the political one and Kevin O'Higgins could proudly assert that they were the most conservative revolutionaries that ever succeeded.[45] The Irish equivalent of Bastille Day is Easter Monday 1916: it has been easier for later Irish nationalists to associate themselves with failed uprisings rather than the successful guerrilla warfare following the First World War. The explanation for this lies in the guilt and bitterness caused by the Treaty and Civil War divisions, and by the failure to prevent Partition and its consequences.

The final stages of the Revolution therefore had many negative consequences. The fact that success was achieved by means of physical force made establishing democratically accountable government difficult. Frank Aiken commented: 'We were great believers then in the power of the gun alone to cure all our evils'.[46] There has been a striking unwillingness to acknowledge that similar tensions within the revolutionary elite occurred in other colonial struggles for independence, and at least the Irish avoided military dictatorship, albeit narrowly.

As a result of the war, the social and economic elements of republicanism took a back seat; the emphasis was on preserving the Republic. The problem came, of course, as in so many independence movements, in reconciling the claim to be an independent nation with the necessity for pragmatic compromise. The influence of the methods used to win independence was considerable. The guerrilla warfare tactics and what Townshend has called 'armed propaganda'[47] have become the pattern for armies of liberation from South America to Vietnam. Though the relationship between the political and military sides of advanced nationalism caused many problems, the formation of the Dáil and the republican counter-state gave respectability and coherence to the armed rebellion. For the first time the Irish were efficient and successful revolutionaries. All this, however, was dependent on the virtual collapse of British Government in Ireland by 1920.

Notes

1. R. F. Foster, *Paddy and Mr Punch* (London, 1993), pp. 18–20.
2. T. Barry, *Guerilla Days in Ireland* (Dublin, 1949); D. Breen, *My Fight for Irish Freedom* (Dublin, 1924); E. O'Malley, *On Another Man's Wound* (London, 1936); *Kerry's Fighting Story, 1916–1921* (Tralee, 1949); *Dublin's Fighting Story, 1916–21* (Tralee, 1949).
3. D. Macardle, *The Irish Republic, 1911–1925* (London, 1937).
4. C. Townshend, *The British Campaign in Ireland* (Oxford, 1975); D. Fitzpatrick, *Politics and Irish Life, 1913–1921* (Dublin, 1977).
5. D. G. Boyce (ed.), *The Revolution in Ireland, 1879–1923* (London, 1988); D. G. Boyce and A. O'Day (eds), *The Making of Modern Irish History* (London, 1996).
6. For debate on GHQ control, see M. G. Valiulis, *Portrait of a Revolutionary* (Dublin, 1992); C. Townshend, *Political Violence in Ireland* (Oxford, 1983). For analysis of democratic accountability, see A. Mitchell, *Revolutionary Government in Ireland* (Dublin, 1995), pp. 65–8.
7. E. Rumpf and A. C. Hepburn, *Nationalism and Socialism in Twentieth-Century Ireland* (Liverpool, 1977); D. Fitzpatrick, 'The Geography of Irish Nationalism, 1910–1921', *Past and Present*, no. 78 (Feb. 1978); P. Hart, 'The Geography of Revolution in Ireland, 1917–1923', *Past and Present*, no. 155 (May 1997); J. Augusteijn, *From Public Defiance to Guerrilla Warfare* (Dublin, 1996); P. Hart, *The I. R. A. and its Enemies* (Oxford, 1998).
8. M. Coleman, *County Longford and the Irish Revolution, 1910–1923* (Dublin, 2002); M. Farry, *The Aftermath of Revolution: Sligo, 1921–23* (Dublin, 2000).
9. The IRA's defence of Ballinalee, Co. Longford, in the autumn of 1920 was a rare instance.

10. T. Garvin, *The Evolution of Irish Nationalist Politics* (Dublin, 1981), p. 122.

11. E. O'Halpin, *The Decline of the Union* (Dublin, 1987); J. McColgan, *British Policy and the Irish Administration, 1920–22* (London, 1987).

12. M. Ward, *Unmanageable Revolutionaries* (London, 1983); R. English, *Ernie O'Malley: IRA Intellectual* (Oxford, 1998).

13. T. P. Coogan, *De Valera: Long Fellow, Long Shadow* (London, 1993).

14. T. Garvin, *1922: The Birth of Irish Democracy* (Dublin, 1996); J. J. Lee, *Ireland, 1912–1985* (Cambridge, 1989).

15. R. Fanning, 'Michael Collins: an Overview', in G. Doherty and D. Keogh (eds), *Michael Collins and the Making of the Irish State* (Cork, 1998), pp. 204–7.

16. N. Mansergh, *The Unresolved Question* (New Haven, 1991), pp. 152–3.

17. R. F. Foster, *Modern Ireland, 1600–1972* (London, 1988), p. 506.

18. Fanning, 'Michael Collins', p. 204.

19. Collins to S. T. O'Kelly, 2 May 1922, NA, DE2/514.

20. Collins to J. McDonagh, 2 Dec. 1920, NA, DE 234A.

21. For Clune and later peace negotiations see M. Hopkinson (ed.), *The Last Days of Dublin Castle* (Dublin, 1999), pp. 86–188; Mitchell, *Revolutionary*, pp. 217–24, 291–9.

22. Hopkinson, *Last Days*, pp. 69–186.

23. Ibid., pp. 109, 102.

24. Warren Fisher to Mark Sturgis, 17 Dec. 1921, in Grant–Sturgis Papers. Private.

25. Healy to Lord Beaverbrook, NLI, ms. 23 628.

26. See Cabinet Conference, 23 Jul. 1920, PRO, CP 1693, CAB 24/109.

27. This is strongly argued in Mansergh, *Unresolved Question*.

28. T. Jones, *Whitehall Diary*, vol. III: *Ireland, 1918–25*, ed. K. Middlemas (London, 1971), p. 53.

29. O'Halpin, *Decline*, pp. 157–213.

30. T. Garvin, 'The Rising and Irish Democracy', in M. ni Dhonnchadha and T. Dorgan (eds), *Revising the Rising* (Dublin, 1991), pp. 21–8.

31. 20 Jun. 1921: Lloyd George Papers, House of Lords Record Office, F/36/2/19.

32. Anderson to Chief Secretary, 17 Aug. 1921, PRO, CO 904/232.

33. Macready to Lord French, 17 Dec. 1921, French Papers, Imperial War Museum, 75/46/13.

34. Lee, *Ireland*, pp. 1–18.

35. P. Buckland, *The Factory of Grievances* (Dublin, 1979); A. T. Q. Stewart, *The Narrow Ground* (London, 1977).

36. J. Bowman, *De Valera and the Ulster Question, 1917–1973* (Oxford, 1982); E. Phoenix, *Northern Nationalism* (Belfast, 1994).

37. Macready Memorandum, Sep. 1920, Bonar Law Papers, House of Lords Record Office, 102/10/6.

38. 2 Sep. 1920, ibid., 102/9/1.

39. Cabinet Conference, 23 July 1920, PRO, CAB 24/108.

40. Undated, PRONI, CAB 5/1.
41. Phoenix, *Northern Nationalism*, p. 99.
42. K. Jeffery, 'British Security Policy in Ireland, 1919–21', in P. Collins (ed.), *Nationalism and Unionism* (Belfast, 1994), pp. 163–75.
43. Hart, *The I. R. A.*, pp. 1–2.
44. UCDAD, P17/b/98.
45. Dáil Éireann, *Proceedings* (1 Mar. 1923).
46. Aiken to Director of Publicity, 18 Apr. 1924, TCD, 7847.
47. Townshend, *Political Violence*, pp. 337–8; C. Townshend, 'The Irish Republican Army and the Development of Guerrilla Warfare, 1916–21', *English Historical Review*, Apr. 1979.

9

Nationalism: The Framing of the Constitution of the Irish Free State, 1922 – the Defining Battle for the Irish Republic

Brian P. Murphy

The ideals of the Irish Republic proclaimed in arms by Patrick Pearse at Easter 1916, received more specific enunciation in the declarations of Dáil Éireann in January 1919, notably in the Declaration of Independence, the Message to the Free Nations of the World, and in the Democratic Programme. Members and officials of the Dáil, and soldiers in the IRA, were called upon to take an oath to the Republic. These proclamations of Dáil Éireann and the attempt to establish an alternative government (see Chapter 5) marked the highpoint of the advanced nationalist position.

However, failure to secure recognition for that government, either in the negotiating chambers of the Peace Conference in Paris or in the armed struggle with England in the War of Independence, led, ultimately, to the Truce of 11 July 1921 and the Anglo-Irish Treaty of 6 December 1921. The split in Sinn Féin, following the acceptance of the Treaty on 7 January 1922 by 64 votes to 57, left a divided party to tackle the task of implementing the terms of the Treaty. Fundamental to this task was the drafting of a constitution for the new Irish Free State. It was in this context that the final battle took place to preserve as much as possible of the ideals of Dáil Éireann, the Government of the

Republic. That clash marked a defining stage in the evolution of the nationalist Sinn Féin movement.

The ground rules for settling the constitutional relationship between Great Britain and Ireland were laid down in the Articles of Agreement of 6 December 1921, and the same document decreed that a time span of exactly one year was allowed to provide for a solution. During that year the British coalition government (and the new Tory government of October 1922) remained firmly united in its purposes, as it had been during the Treaty negotiations; the Sinn Féin Party, which had entered the Treaty negotiations united, gradually became more sharply and bitterly divided. The differences in Irish ranks manifested by the small majority in favour of the Treaty were never reconciled. Of the various national organisations only Cumann na mBan remained almost solidly anti-Treaty, voting in February to reject it by 419 votes to 63; all the six women deputies were also opposed to the Treaty.

However, in the immediate aftermath of the Treaty vote, it was still possible for all Sinn Féiners to dream of a Republic. Their hopes centred on the possibility of drafting the Free State constitution in a manner that was acceptable to republicans. They were encouraged in this by Richard Mulcahy, Minister of Defence, who gave his pledge on 10 January, in the very last words of the debate on the Treaty, that 'the Army will remain the Army of the Irish Republic'.[1] Furthermore, on 25 January, Gavan Duffy, the Dáil Minister for Foreign Affairs, declared that 'this Government has undertaken the duty of maintaining the existing Republic'.[2] Coming from one of the signatories of the Treaty, these words fostered the belief that the Republic had not, as yet, been irretrievably lost.

The British immediately challenged the existence of the Republic by insisting that, in conformity with clauses 17 and 18 of the Articles of Agreement, the Treaty had to be approved by the assembly of the Southern Ireland Parliament set up under the 1920 Government of Ireland Act. This meeting took place on 14 January. The pro-Treaty supporters had to swallow their pride, their principles and their oath to the Republic in order to legitimise their approval of the Treaty in a British assembly. Although it was claimed that the assembly was not the Parliament of Southern Ireland, the event highlighted the constitutional issue at stake: the British demanded that the Treaty should be fully implemented in accord with English law, and not, as they saw it, by the illegal authority of Dáil Éireann; the Irish attempted to preserve the Republic by preserving the Dáil and by securing a republican dimension in the new Free State constitution. Michael Collins was just as prepared to carry out this policy as Eamon de Valera.

Michael Collins and the Constitution

Collins, as Chairman of the Provisional Government and chairman of the Constitutional Committee, had the major responsibility for drafting the Free State constitution. He appointed a committee under Darrell Figgis. Many of the members were experienced lawyers, and they considered the values of a number of constitutions, among them those of Switzerland, the United States, and Weimar Germany. Collins advised the committee, which began meeting in the Shelbourne Hotel on 24 January 1922, that the Free State Constitution should rest solely upon the authority derived from the Irish people. On the advice of Hugh Kennedy, Collins informed the committee that 'clauses dealing with the governor general and the oath should be left out altogether. They are unnecessary as part of our constitution and should not form part of it.'[3]

The republic was to be preserved by a clever process of omission: on the one hand, reference to the King was not to be made; on the other hand, emphasis was to be placed upon the sovereignty of the Irish people. Akenson has called it 'a radically independent constitution'.[4] De Valera was made aware of these developments and, as a result, both he and more militant republicans were prepared to give the Constitution a chance.

Faced by the fear that republicans might influence the Constitution in meetings of the Dáil, Churchill declared on 27 February that the Treaty would be upheld and that 'the Constitution will be submitted by and with the authority of the Provisional Government and not by and with the authority of Dáil Éireann'.[5] Despite this warning, the three drafts of the Constitution presented to Collins on 8 March reflected his instructions and limited the British dimension of the Treaty. They contained, for example, no oath to the King. Signs of serious division in the pro-Treaty ranks became apparent, however. Arthur Griffith, President of Dáil Éireann, commented on 11 March that for a constitution to be acceptable it would have to recognise 'this Nation's solemn contractual obligations in the Treaty'.[6] While this potentially damaging difference in Irish ranks was emerging, the British remained united in their insistence on the Constitution conforming to the terms of the Treaty.

The British Parliament approved the Irish Free State Agreement Act on 31 March. In legislating for an election within four months, it declared that 'the Parliament of Southern Ireland shall be dissolved'.[7]

It deliberately refrained from referring to the assembly as Dáil Éireann. The British, in the words of one commentator, scored 'in forcing
the Dáil to keep the application of that Constitution restricted to 26
counties and to hold future elections to the Dáil for the 26-county
area alone'.[8] Republicans were conscious of the implications of this.
Cathal Brugha immediately noted that 'an election … means partition'; and Harry Boland appealed for them all to realise that 'from the
point of view of the Republic', the election 'recognises Partition'.[9]
Despite the gravity of the situation, they still retained some hope that
their position might be ameliorated by the new Constitution.

Wading 'through Irish blood', a prospect presented by de Valera to
the Volunteers in Killarney on 18 March (words subsequently denied
by him), was far removed from the constitutional path, but it did not
effectively determine republican policy.[10] De Valera, it should be
remembered, had also taken political initiatives in January 1922 with
the foundation of Cumann na Poblachta, and by securing his own
election as President of the Irish Race Congress in Paris at the end
of the month. Even after Rory O'Connor's break with the Dáil on
22 March and the occupation of the Four Courts on 13–14 April, leading IRA officers such as Liam Lynch and Frank Aiken encouraged the
IRA to await the publication of the Free State Constitution. Another
sign that sections of the IRA were slow to reject the constitutional
authority of the Dáil was provided by a six-point statement of the
Army Council issued on 25 April, which called upon all Dáil deputies
to act together to save the Republic. This action was one of the factors that led both parties in the Dáil to engage in a concerted effort
for peace from 26 April onwards. Another factor was the armed confrontation that had occurred between anti-Treaty and Provisional
Government forces at Kilkenny City in the first week of May.

Cathal Brugha gave articulate expression of the aims and fears of
republicans in these Dáil debates. On 17 May he proposed a free vote,
based on adult suffrage in Ireland, on the issue of 'the Republic or
the Free State'.[11] It was when that proposal was rejected, that he and
others, notably Harry Boland, focused on the issue of partition. Aware of
the pogroms in the North and fearing Civil War, Brugha declared that
'I for one would prefer to die by an English or an Orange bullet rather
than by a bullet fired by one of the men with whom we have been
fighting together during the last six years.'[12] Brugha was so concerned
with the issue of partition that he suggested that both he and Michael
Collins should withdraw from politics, and engage in the armed struggle in the North. There was no response to that suggestion.

On the very day that Brugha made his appeal, 17 May, the delegates representing both sides of the political divide presented their own accounts of their failure to reach an agreement. The pro-Treaty delegates were S. MacEoin, S. Hales, P. O'Malley, J. McGuinness and J. O'Dwyer; the anti-Treaty delegates were Kathleen Clarke, S. Moylan, P. Ruttledge, L. Mellows and H. Boland. Despite their failure to come to terms, both sides submitted appendices, which were designed to serve as the basis for future discussion. Finally, at the last hour and to the surprise of most, an agreement was reached which culminated in the pact between Collins and de Valera on 20 May, and was approved of by Dáil Éireann.[13] The main aim of the Pact was to prevent rivalry during the coming election and to provide for a shared Cabinet after the election – five members were to be pro-Treaty, and four anti-Treaty. It was also presumed that the constitution that would be presented to the country would limit the role of the English King in Ireland.

Harry Boland and the Constitution

Within 24 hours, on 21 May, Lionel Curtis, the secretary of the British Committee of the Provisional Government, was in possession not only of the terms of the Pact, but also of the contrasting appendices submitted by the opposing sides in their quest to secure agreement. This was possible thanks to the efforts of Andy Cope, the principal British official in Ireland, who was the influential liaison contact between Collins and Churchill. Curtis compared appendices 'C' and 'D', which were submitted by Harry Boland, with the final terms of the Pact, and concluded that 'Boland is clearly the real architect of the agreement.'[14] He informed Churchill that Collins has 'clearly capitulated to the Republican Party, but it must not be assumed that Griffith will follow his example'.[15] Significantly, the British had accurately detected that Griffith and Collins were not at one with each other over the Constitution. Curtis added that the Pact, which had been ratified by both Sinn Féin and Dáil Éireann, was inspired by Boland's suggestion in the Dáil that 'if the constitution were made Republican enough to be considered outside the Bounds of the Treaty (in England) there might instantly be formed a Coalition Government'.[16]

Other advice came to Churchill that the draft Constitution 'appears not so much a departure from the Treaty, as a direct negation of it ... a republican constitution almost without disguise and adapted for an independent state'.[17] Determined to uphold the Treaty,

Churchill advised rejection of the Pact, and urged the British Cabinet on 23 May that, 'if a Republic were proclaimed "before or after" the election then "that is war".'[18] He had already made provisional plans for the renewal of war, in a British military directive of 10 April which he had personally annotated in red ink and which suggested a realignment of British troops, if civil war broke out in Ireland.[19]

Collins and Griffith were summoned to London at the end of May. Although there was acute conflict over the Constitution, both sides had an agreed plan of campaign for an election. On Saturday 27 May, as Collins and Griffith were engaged in private and group meetings with British officials, the *Dublin Gazette* announced that the Provisional Government had summoned a new Parliament for 1 July. On the same day Viscount FitzAlan, the Lord Lieutenant of Ireland, also issued a summons for a new Parliament, and in preparation for it he decreed that 'the Parliament of Southern Ireland shall be, and is hereby, dissolved'.[20] The British promulgation, which stressed that the Parliament was for a 26-county southern Ireland and not an all-Ireland Dáil, was not published in the *Dublin Gazette* until 30 May 1922. The delayed publication gave the impression that the primacy in calling the Parliament lay with Griffith and Collins, and concealed the fact that the Dáil was confined to 26 counties.

From the very first it was made clear that the Constitution proposed by Collins would not be countenanced by the British, and, on becoming aware of that, Collins stated on 30 May that 'the gulf is unbridgeable'.[21] He talked of going back to armed resistance in the face of a British Government which seemed 'bent on war'. The return of Collins to Dublin the next day, 1 June, was tantamount to an admission that he had lost the battle for his own views on the Constitution – views that were acceptable to most republicans. Lloyd George then addressed six specific questions relating to the Constitution, which stressed Irish acceptance of the role of the King and Empire, to Griffith on 1 June 1922.[22]

An element of mystery surrounds the final signing of the Constitution. Although it was Collins, Chairman of the Provisional Government, who was designated to draft a constitution, it was Griffith, President of Dáil Éireann, who took over that role. Why Collins did not go to London for the final constitutional talks is, in many ways, just as intriguing a question as why de Valera did not go to London for the Treaty negotiations. Griffith, accompanied by Cosgrave, O'Higgins and Kennedy, was made aware that a breakdown might lead to the British seizure of ports and the imposition of economic and financial sanctions. When Lloyd George insisted that the Constitution must 'conform with the Treaty', Griffith conceded that 'in so far as it can be shown that the draft Constitution is in conflict with the Treaty, we are prepared to insert such amendments as will reconcile its terms with those of the Treaty'.[23] The capitulation could not have been more complete. It was in this humiliating concession by Griffith – a 'surrender', Akenson called it – that the last vestige of the Irish Republic was finally lost.[24]

Subsequently, authorities on the Constitution have argued with some justification that the Free State Constitution of Griffith did confer far more sovereignty upon the Irish people than was enjoyed by other British dominions at that time. Leo Kohn, for example, maintained that 'the monarchical forms paled into insignificance in the light of the formal enunciation and the consistent application of the principle of the sovereignty of the people as the fundamental and exclusive source of all political authority'.[25] Arguing on the same grounds, 'some astute British observers', it was noted, 'perceived that the Irish were the real victors in the struggle over the Constitution',[26] an opinion based, in large part, on the views of Berridale Keith.

Following Kohn there has been an attempt to claim a republican dimension in the Free State Constitution, and to portray the anti-Treaty republicans as undemocratic. However, the view that the republicans were undemocratic fails to give due recognition, first, to their wish for a free vote on an all-Ireland basis, a vote that was rejected by the British Government; and secondly, to their contention that the sovereignty of the people could only be expressed in accord with the territorial unity of the Irish nation, and free from any association with the King of England.

In the first six months of 1922, moreover, the constitutional issue was measured not by looking forward, in theoretical terms, to the evolving status of Ireland within the British Commonwealth, but by looking back to the republican ideals of Dáil Éireann, which had been formally accepted by many individuals under oath. It was this touchstone that, in republican eyes, marked the success or failure of the struggle, and this reality was recognised by both English and Irish protagonists. They both described the conflict over the Constitution and the June election as a contest for a republic. It was that battle that was won by the British, when Griffith yielded to Lloyd George's demands.

Griffith's words acknowledging the primacy of the Treaty were enshrined in the Constitution along with 11 other specific references to the King, including the oath. It was this constitution that Collins received from Churchill on 12 June, on his final visit to London, and which he presented to the Irish people on the morning of the election on 16 June, advising them to vote without regard to the panel of candidates agreed by the Pact. The election resulted in a victory for the pro-Treaty party: 58 pro-Treaty candidates were returned; 36 anti-Treaty; 17 Labour; 7 Farmer's Party; 6 Independents; and 4 from Dublin University.

The Republican response to the Constitution

Even after the electoral defeat and the breaking of the Pact over the election, Harry Boland still hoped that Collins would observe that part of the agreement that had recommended shared Cabinet responsibility, but it was not to be. On the military side, Cathal Brugha and Liam Lynch still persuaded the IRA Army Convention on 18 June not to initiate action against British troops, and the formal start of the Civil War on 28 June was occasioned by the Provisional Government's attack on the Four Courts.[27] This was carried out by Free State troops using British weapons at the instigation of Lloyd George, after the assassination of Sir Henry Wilson. The time for talking about the Constitution was over: the drift to war was inevitable. De Valera gave his view on the situation on the day war started, declaring that 'the soldiers of the Republic have been attacked by the forces of the Provisional Government at the instigation of English politicians'.[28]

On that day, de Valera, Brugha, Boland and others returned to the ranks of the IRA. Harry Boland made clear his views on the new situation to an American supporter on 13 July, when he wrote, 'England has again waged war on us, this time she has employed Irishmen to do her dirty work ... the black and tans have given way to the green and tans. Hamar Greenwood is outdone by Mick Collins.'[29] The American dimension to the Civil War came to have a paramount importance. Collins, for his part, returned to the ranks on 12 July when he resigned his civilian position as Chairman of the Provisional Government and became Commander-in-Chief of the Army.[30] It was evident that Collins, whatever his doubts about the Constitution, was prepared to fight to defend the ideals of the Free State. Any hope of resolving divisions by means of an agreed Constitution had ended.

As a result of the commitment of Collins, the war in general was pursued more vigorously. For example, on 29 July Collins was handed some letters from Harry Boland to Sean T. O'Kelly, which had been captured by the Intelligence Service based at Oriel House. One of the letters reported that Joe McGarrity was 'solidly with us in this fight', which would be long and drawn out; that Thompson sub-machine guns, revolvers and ammunition would be needed; and that someone must go on a mission to the States.[31] Collins informed Cosgrave immediately and urged that the Provisional Government should publicise the letter to show that Boland, in cooperation with McGarrity, was committed to waging civil war.[32] This would justify taking drastic action against these leading opponents of the Treaty.

On the same day the Provisional Government acted on the advice of Collins, and directed Desmond FitzGerald to get the letters published. They appeared in the *Irish Independent* on the very same day, Tuesday 1 August, that news was carried of the fatal wounding of Harry Boland. Harry Boland's killing serves as a reminder of the personal emotions that coloured these tragic events, as close friendship gave way to bitter rivalry. Cathal Brugha had died before Boland on 7 July, and Collins was to die after him on 22 August; all three killed by fellow Irishmen in terrible circumstances. Despite these killings, and the death of Griffith, some republicans still hoped for a constitutional resolution to the conflict. Their hopes rested on the fact that the Second Dáil had not yet met to dissolve itself.

Republicans hoped that, as long as the all-Ireland Second Dáil existed, then a meeting of that body might ensure a return to unity. However, despite a ruling of the Supreme Court of Dáil Éireann on 11 August that the Chairman of the Dáil should explain why the Second Dáil had not been summoned to meet, it was not recalled.[33] It did not meet to dissolve itself, but instead, on 9 September an assembly summoned by the Provisional Government met. It was variously described in the press as 'An Dáil', 'The Parliament of Southern Ireland', and 'The Provisional Parliament of Southern Ireland'. When Laurence Ginnell, an anti-Treaty deputy, inquired 'was the assembly Dáil Éireann, or only a partition Parliament destroying Eirinn's integrity?', he received no answer, and was expelled from the hall.[34]

De Valera had no constitutional platform from which to operate, unless he conceded that the Provisional Government had won the battle, and entered the new Dáil. His immediate reaction was to resign from political life. Encouraged, however, by messages of support from Joe McGarrity in America, de Valera resolved to continue the struggle for the republican pre-Treaty ideals. On 12 October he wrote to Liam Lynch, Chief-of-Staff of the IRA, and gave three reasons for restoring a government for the Republic: first to provide a rallying point for republicans; secondly, to preserve the continuity of the Republic; and thirdly, to establish a claim to the funds of the Republic, in particular to the $2,500,000 (*c*. £500,000) deposited in American banks.[35] Lynch had been reluctant to bring the army under civilian authority, but the messages emanating from McGarrity induced him to change his mind. A meeting of the IRA Executive Council on 16–17 October called upon 'the former President of Dáil Éireann to form a government which will preserve the continuity of the Republic'.[36]

This action by the IRA was the necessary prelude to de Valera's reconvening of the Second Dáil as the Government of the Republic on 25 October. The timing was no mere coincidence. It was a direct challenge to the Provisional Government, which, on that very day, finalised the drafting of the Free State Constitution. The Second Dáil declared that it was the lawful government of the country; that de Valera was President of the Republic; and that a Council of State and a Cabinet were to be formed.[37] On 17 November, the Second Dáil effectively denied the legitimacy of the Free State Constitution by declaring that the resolution passed by Dáil Éireann on 7 January 1922 purporting to approve of the Treaty 'be hereby rescinded and revoked … and that any act purporting to be done thereunder is void and of no effect'.[38]

When, therefore, on 6 December 1922 the final ritual passages took place to establish the Irish Free State, there was a pretended rival Republican government already in existence. Moreover, to republican eyes, the legislation which signalled the inauguration of the state served as a reminder that the expression 'Free' was coloured by a marked dependence on Great Britain. On 5 December, the British Parliament and King of England approved the Constitution of the state, and on the morning of 6 December, the King signed that approval. On 7 December, the Northern Ireland Parliament voted itself out of the Irish Free State, and the next day four men (Liam Mellows, Dick Barrett, Rory O'Connor and Joe McKelvey), who opposed the Treaty, were executed as a reprisal for the assassination of Sean Hales.

Conclusion

The Free State Government justified its position and its actions by arguing that it was guided by democratic principles, as embodied in the majority support it had obtained in the June election; and that the

Constitution, while recognising the King of England, also derived its sovereignty from the Irish people. Cosgrave made the Free State position very clear, when he defended the executions on 8 December. He declared that 'the people who have challenged the very existence of society have put themselves outside the Constitution ... [and] there is only one way to meet it, and that is to crush it and show them that terror will be struck into them'.[39] Tactically Cosgrave was correct: terror would win the day. His reference to the Constitution, however, was instructive; and demonstrated both the significance and the importance of the Free State Constitution in defining the differences between those who supported the Republic and supporters of the Free State.

The republicans based their opposition to the Free State on the grounds that the all-Ireland Republic had been lost without a free vote of all the people of Ireland. This opinion, it should be noted, was the decision of the American courts dealing with the Dáil Bonds Case in 1927 when, after taking affidavits from a vast number of those engaged in the events of 1922, the judge decreed that the Free State was not the successor of Dáil Éireann.[40] The evidence of Gerald Horan, 'Clerk of the Crown and Hanaper', was found to be of special value. As an official of the Crown in Dublin, he had published the Lord Lieutenant's notification of the June election, and he acknowledged that the election was for a Provisional Parliament of a 26-county Ireland.[41] The final verdict of the judge was that the Free State, while being the lawful government of the country, did not preserve continuity with the all-Ireland republican Second Dáil.

The policy of the Labour Party throughout 1922 provides an independent commentary on the events surrounding the formulation of the Free State Constitution and the creation of the Free State. Most of the Labour Party's efforts were concentrated on social issues, but it also made several precise interventions on constitutional matters: for example, on 21 February it was proposed that a special plebiscite be held on the issue of the Treaty, because 'it cannot ... be said with any truth that in an election for a Parliament the only duty of the electors is to say "Yea" or "Nay" to the Treaty'.[42] The Labour Party criticised the publication of the Constitution on the morning of the election with the result, it claimed, that 'not one out of ten thousand of the voters was able to read it before voting, much less give it any consideration'; and it commented that 'every sign on the face of the Constitution ... shows that the Provisional Government has compiled this document in such a way as to harmonise it with the strictest English interpretation of the Treaty'.[43]

After the June election the Labour Party denied that the government had a mandate to govern, pointing to the majority of deputies who were in opposition; it protested that the attack on the Four Courts had been made without regard for civilian life; and it criticised the continual postponement of the new Dáil meeting after the June election with the same intensity as anti-Treaty republicans.[44] Aware that many of its criticisms were directed against the government, the Labour Party issued a statement attributing blame to both parties. 'We have condemned the political policy of the Government Party in many respects', it said, 'as being dangerous to democracy and freedom. At the same time we denounce the Republican Party both for its political tactics and military policy as quite indefensible, inevitably leading to disaster.'[45]

The Labour Party's verdict on the Free State Constitution, however, had far greater accord with that of the republicans. This was confirmed in the speech that the Labour leader, Thomas Johnson, made in the Dáil on 6 December, which prefigured, in many ways, the policy of de Valera some five years later. Concerning the oath, he said 'we recognise the act of taking the "Oath of Allegiance" as a formality, a condition of Membership of the Legislature'. He said that the Treaty and the clauses of the Constitution conditioned by that Treaty were accepted 'under protest, having been imposed upon Ireland by the threat of superior force, and were not freely determined by the people of Ireland'.[46]

The final implementation of the Irish Free State Act confirmed the worst fears that anti-Treaty republicans had expressed in relation not only to the role of the King of England, but also to the partition of Ireland. This final denouement also confounded the best hopes of Cosgrave and his supporters for some form of a united Ireland. Some had hoped that unionists would actually vote to join the Free State on 7 December. Certainly Cosgrave, in recommending the Free State Act on 6 December 1922, had fully expected the Boundary Commission's recommendations to be implemented. While denying any intention of coercing Ulster, he identified himself with the sentiments and the very words of Lloyd George, made during the Treaty negotiations, that 'although I am against the coercion of Ulster, I do not believe in Ulster coercing other units'.[47]

Both Cosgrave and Lloyd George had in mind the counties of Tyrone and Fermanagh. Cosgrave maintained that to ignore them 'would be to acquiesce in a great injustice, more so now than ever, after the result of the recent Election in the great constituency of

Tyrone–Fermanagh ... the result was a vast and unmistakeable majori-
ity of over 6,000 for remaining within the Free State – a verdict
which it is impossible to ignore'.[48] The verdict, however, was ignored
in the final report of the Boundary Commission (leaked in November
1925), which acted on the assumption that 'the wishes of the inhabitants are made the primary but not the paramount consideration'.[49]
The ratification of a six-county Ulster in the subsequent Boundary
Agreement of December 1925 was not only an integral element of
the Free State settlement, but also marked the culmination of the
Home Rule crisis that had begun in 1911.

A valuable overview of these events, in the wider context of the
evolving political situation in Ireland since 1911, was provided by
John Dillon in March 1924, when paying tribute to John Redmond.
Dillon maintained that, from the origins of the Home Rule crisis,

> Mr Redmond never agreed to the principle of partition. It is now a well
> known fact that if he and I had agreed to give up Tyrone, Fermanagh and
> Derry City, at the Buckingham Palace Conference, we could there and then,
> in June 1914, have settled the question with the goodwill of Ulster. We
> refused.[50]

He argued, in much the same language as Harry Boland, that following the Treaty, Lloyd George's Machiavellian policy of using the Treaty
men to crush republicans 'has been successful so far as to make it possible for him to carry out his partition policy and to set up an Orange
Parliament in Ulster with the apparent consent of the Irish people'.[51]
Dillon then asserted that 'there ought to be no boundary in Ireland',
and was critical of the Boundary Commission because it 'would be a
fresh endorsement of the principle of Partition, and an official declaration to the whole world that the government of the Irish Free State
solemnly recognised that Ireland is not one country, and that in it are
two separate nations'.[52]

Dillon's reflections alert one to the unionist influence in the shaping of the Irish Free State, and serve as a reminder that the evolution
of Irish nationalism was inextricably linked with that of unionism.
This may be briefly illustrated by a consideration of two leading conservatives, Arthur Balfour and Andrew Bonar Law. Balfour, who since
his appointment as Chief Secretary for Ireland in 1887, had acted res-
olutely to preserve the Union, notably in the framing of the 1920
Government of Ireland Act, was asked late in life what was left of his
Irish policy since the foundation of the Irish Free State. He replied:
'Everything, Everything. What was the Ireland the Free State took

over? It was the Ireland that we made.'[53] In like manner Bonar Law was happy to associate himself with the Irish Free State. Law, who had supported Ulster resistance to Home Rule in 1912 and who, like Balfour, had played a vital role in the 1920 Government of Ireland Act, became Prime Minister of England in October 1922. By a strange irony he presided over the final implementation of the Irish Free State Act, thus effectively symbolising the centrality of unionist interests at the heart of the British Government.

The role of unionists and the theme of partition, so clearly delineated in the recollections of John Dillon, serve as a forcible reminder that the most important development to take place in Ireland during the revolutionary years of 1911 and 1925 was not the division among the political parties, but rather the division of Ireland itself. Irish nationalism, be it the constitutional nationalism of Parnell, Redmond and Dillon, or the separatist nationalism of Clarke, Pearse and Brugha, was given expression in a divided country after the foundation of the Irish Free State. For that reason the framing of the Constitution of the Free State, which copper-fastened a six-county Northern Ireland, was a defining moment not only in the evolution of Irish republicanism, but also in the history of Irish nationalism.

Notes

1. Dáil Éireann, *Official Report: Debate on the Treaty between Great Britain and Ireland* (Dublin, 1922), 10 Jan. 1922, p. 424.
2. Foreign Office Memo, 25 Jan. 1922, NA, DE 4/11/51.
3. Notes by Collins to the Constitutional Committee, in J. A. Gaughan (ed.), *Memoirs of Senator James G. Douglas, Concerned Citizen* (Dublin, 1998), pp. 85–6; see also D. H. Akenson and J. F. Fallin, 'The Irish Civil War and the Drafting of the Free State Constitution', *Eire/Ireland*, v, 1 (Spring 1970), p. 24, and v, 2 (Summer 1970). These series of articles make reference to the memoir of James Douglas before its publication.
4. Akenson and Fallin, 'Irish Civil War' (Spring 1970), p. 20.
5. V. J. DeLacy Ryan, *Ireland Restored: The New Self-Determination* (New York, 1991), p. 75.
6. Griffith to Thomas Johnson, 11 Mar. 1922, in *Report of the Twenty-Eighth Annual Meeting of the Irish Labour Party and TUC* (Dublin, 1922), pp. 42–3.
7. Ryan, *Ireland Restored*, p. 77
8. Ibid., pp. 78–9.
9. Dáil Éireann, *Official Report*, 19 May 1922, p. 467, for Brugha and p. 473 for Boland.
10. J. M. Curran, *The Birth of the Irish Free State, 1921–1923* (Alabama, 1980), pp. 174, 200–18.

11. Dáil Éireann, *Official Report*, 17 May 1922, p. 429.
12. Ibid.
13. Ibid., 20 May 1922, p. 479. See also M. Gallagher, 'The Pact General Election of 1922', in *IHS*, XXI (Sep. 1979); and T. Towey, 'The Reaction of the British Government to the 1922 Collins–de Valera Pact', *IHS*, XXII (Mar. 1980).
14. Note by Lionel Curtis on the Collins/de Valera Agreement, 21 May 1922, PRO, CO 739/5, p. 9. See also M. Laffan, *The Resurrection of Ireland* (Cambridge, 1999), p. 386f.; and B. Maye, *Arthur Griffith* (Dublin, 1997), pp. 261–6.
15. Ibid., p. 10.
16. Ibid., p. 9; Dáil Éireann, *Official Report*, 19 May 1922, pp. 472–3, conveys Boland's sentiments, but I could not find these exact words.
17. Note on 'the origin of Article 2 of the Irish Free State Constituent Act', PRO, DO 35/397/10, p. 32.
18. 'Note of Meeting of British Representatives, 23 May 1922', PRO, CAB 43/1. See also S. Lawlor, *Britain and Ireland* (Dublin, 1983).
19. DC of IGS to CIGS, 10 Apr. 1922, PRO, WO 35/182, part 1, pp. 1–3 with additions in red ink by Churchill.
20. *Dublin Gazette*, 27 and 30 May 1922.
21. T. Jones, *Whitehall Diary*, vol. III: *Ireland, 1918–1925*, ed. K. Middlemas (London, 1971), p. 203.
22. Ibid., p. 205.
23. Note on 'the Origin of Article 2', PRO, DO 35/397/10, p. 33.
24. Akenson, 'Irish Civil War' (Summer 1970), p. 59.
25. L. Kohn, *The Constitution of the Irish Free State* (London, 1932), p. 81; Curran, *Birth of the Irish Free State*, p. 217; see also D. W. Harkness, *The Restless Dominion* (London, 1969), pp. 21–9; and J. McColgan, *British Policy and the Irish Administration, 1920–22* (London, 1983), pp. 91–6.
26. Curran, *Birth of the Irish Free State*, p. 218; and T. Garvin, *1922: The Birth of Irish Democracy* (Dublin, 1996), pp. 16–18.
27. *Cathal Brugha Anniversary Brochure, 1922–1972* (Dublin, 1972), p. 13; M. Ryan, *The Real Chief: The Story of Liam Lynch* (Cork and Dublin, 1986), p. 114. See also J. M. Regan, *The Irish Counter-Revolution, 1921–1936* (Dublin, 1999), pp. 65–74.
28. Statement by De Valera to the People of America, 4 July 1922, NLI, ms. 8425.
29. Boland to 'Sally', 13 July 1922, NLI, ms. 15 991.
30. Meeting of Provisional Government, 12 July 1922, NA, G 1/2, which noted that Kevin O'Higgins, Joe McGrath and Fionan Lynch were also appointed to military posts.
31. Boland to McGarrity, 13 and 25 July 1922, in S. Cronin, *The McGarrity Papers* (Kerry 1972), pp. 120–1.
32. C. in C. (Collins) to Government, 29 July 1922, UCDAD, P7/B/29/159.
33. Ryan, *Ireland Restored*, p. 69.

34. Irish Legation Circular, public letter of Ginnell, 1 Jan. 1923, NLI, ms. 17 655(3).

35. De Valera to C. of S. (Lynch), 12 Oct. 1922, in, M. V. Tarpey, 'The Role of Joseph McGarrity in the Struggle for Irish Independence', thesis (Ann Arbor University, MI, 1970), p. 187.

36. Proclamation of Army Executive, 16/17 Oct. 1922, in J. A. Gaughan, *Austin Stack: Portrait of a Separatist* (Dublin, 1977), p. 220. See B. P. Murphy, *Patrick Pearse and the Lost Republican Ideal* (Dublin, 1991), p. 139f.; B. P. Murphy, *John Chartres: Mystery Man of the Treaty* (Dublin, 1995), p. 141f.; and E. O'Halpin, *Defending Ireland* (Oxford, 1999), pp. 27–9.

37. For the names of those appointed, see Ryan, *Ireland Restored*, pp. 90–2; and D. Macardle, *The Irish Republic* (Dublin, 1937), pp. 807–8.

38. Gaughan, *Stack*, p. 221; Murphy, *Pearse*, p. 141.

39. Dáil Éireann, *Official Report*, 8 Dec. 1922, cols 93 and 95.

40. NLI, ms. 18 111, for *New York Evening Post* of 11 May 1927; F. P. Walsh to de Valera, 11 May 1927, UCDAD, de Valera Papers, 1753/2.

41. NA, D/T S 9569/3 (Horan evidence), in which questions 30 to 98 are relevant.

42. Johnson to Griffith, 24 Feb. 1922, in *Report of the Twenty-Eighth Annual Meeting of the Irish Labour Party*, p. 41.

43. Ibid., pp. 52–3 under the heading 'Proposed Constitution for Saorstat Éireann'.

44. Ibid., p. 36 under the heading 'The Government's Mandate'; p. 31 for Johnson to the Lord Mayor, 29 June 1922; and pp. 34–6 under the heading 'Postponement of Dáil Éireann'.

45. Ibid., p. 39 under the heading 'Labour and Republican War Policy'.

46. Dáil Éireann, *Official Report*, 6 Dec. 1922, col. 3.

47. Ibid., 6 Dec. 1922, col. 17.

48. Ibid.

49. E. Phoenix, *Northern Nationalism* (Belfast, 1994), p. 327.

50. *Belfast Newsletter*, 11 Mar. 1924; and Dillon, Family Papers, Tribute to Redmond (1924), p. 8.

51. Ibid., p. 9.

52. Ibid., p. 2.

53. C. B. Shannon, *Arthur J. Balfour and Ireland, 1874–1922* (Washington, 1988), p. 281.

10

Unionism: The Irish Nobility and Revolution, 1919–23

Peter Martin

After the establishment of a dominant Nationalist Party in Ireland in the 1870s, the House of Lords became an important parliamentary base for Irish unionism. There were a few peers who were Liberals (Lord Granard, for example) and others, like Dunraven or Killanin, whose constructive approach to unionism allowed them to cooperate with nationalists at local level. The majority of peers who either maintained Irish residences or had a strong economic or family connection with Ireland were, however, emphatically unionist. For a long time, they were represented by the Irish Unionist Alliance (IUA), which was led by mainly southern peers and was headed by Lord Midleton.[1] Midleton's authority came from the fact that he had the support of 'all the peers and men of the greatest commercial strength like Lord Iveagh'.[2] The prospect of partition, however, split the IUA between southern and northern unionists. In a letter to IUA members, Midleton claimed that 'our representatives in Parliament feel that they cannot represent Southern Unionist interests under the control of Ulster'.[3] The numerically stronger Ulster Unionists took control of the IUA in January 1919 and the Midletonites formed the Anti-Partition League (APL), which included most of the southern unionist peers and their wealthy supporters.[4] As the country moved towards open conflict, therefore, the nobility were disunited and politically weak.

The purpose of this chapter is to examine how Irish nobles experienced the conflict. The term 'Irish peers' in this context is problematic. Peers were among those for whom the Union was a daily reality.

151

Usually they were born in England, maintained property and business interests in both countries, were educated in English schools and universities but would frequently pronounce themselves 'Irish'. As Lady Sybil Lubbock described it they felt 'profoundly Irish and intensely English, both at once, and could not for a moment contemplate the surrender of either allegiance'.[5] Therefore I am defining as 'Irish' any peer who maintained an Irish residence or had a large economic interest in the country.[6] This is the story of a political and economic elite, not of ordinary Protestants or unionists. It therefore focuses on the issues that mattered most to peers; agrarian disturbances, raids on houses, house burnings, and the political and constitutional situation.

Agrarian agitation

In April 1919, Lord Oranmore & Browne proposed an amendment to the Criminal Injuries (Ireland) Bill to include property.[7] This showed that the agrarian side of the conflict was beginning to concern nobles. That month, five of the Earl of Kenmare's cattle were poisoned at Killarney because he had set up a butcher's shop and was underselling local traders.[8] In May 1920, an unoccupied house owned by Lord Ashtown was destroyed so that the lands around it could be divided.[9] Few peers however, were personally targeted. This may be explained by the fact that, as so many of them spent a great deal of time out of Ireland, they were hard to intimidate directly, and that many nobles had already sold land in the areas of greatest controversy.

Nevertheless, leading peers became increasingly concerned about the situation. On 9 April 1920, Lords Midleton, Desart, and Oranmore & Browne, who were all significant members of the APL, lunched with the Lord Lieutenant, Viscount French. They informed him of 'the terrible state of the country', and especially of the land agitation in the west 'which is virtually a form of Bolshevism'. Lord French offered them little solace, except to say that if he were only allowed to 'intern 10,000 men he could restore order'.[10] A few weeks later, in a debate in the House of Lords, they developed their analysis. Though unsympathetic to both the republicans and the rural population, it raised some relevant issues. Midleton claimed that the agrarian situation had been caused by a combination of the end of emigration during the Great War and consequent high levels of youth unemployment. He also distinguished between ideological republicans, with 'an academic hatred of British rule who are not directly associated with [agrarian] outrages', and those men who had simply banded together to commit crimes.[11]

The military campaign

The growing military conflict also affected peers. Men seeking arms raided several peers' homes. Nobles were traditionally associated with the army, and as a result they were a logical target. However, few peers had useful weapons, and raiders came away with an array of arms including some Russian muskets from the Crimean War from the Earl of Arran's house,[12] an old rifle from Lord Killanin's chauffeur, sporting guns from Lord Granard's residence[13] and a shotgun from Lord Castletown taken while he was motoring in Cork.[14] Only in the last case was the peer himself in Ireland at the time of the incident. IRA attacks, or those mounted by people who used the name to cover up vendettas, were often directed at servants who had offended the republicans rather than against peers themselves. In February 1919, the Earl of Kenmare's gamekeeper was shot in the thigh;[15] the attack was probably linked to the fact that he had shot a poacher with Sinn Féin connections.[16] In another incident, a herdsman who worked for Lord Inchiquin was fired on. The incident was put down to a local row over meadowing.[17]

None of the attacks could be described as part of a military campaign against peers as a class. The attack on a tennis party held at Roslevan, the home of Lord Inchiquin's brother, was significant, however. The raiders' commander commented later that 'the party would be composed of the county aristocracy who are certainly associates of the enemy. In short, all this class must be made to realise that the country is at war'.[18] Similar rhetoric was used when Sinn Féin launched a systematic campaign against hunting. One of the resolutions passed in February 1919 forbade 'fishing by alien and resident gentlemen holding anti-Irish ideas'.[19] In March, W. Milling, the RM in Westport, was killed, probably because of his attitude towards the Volunteers.[20] As it was common for peers to hold local offices, this would have brought home to them the seriousness of the situation. The Marquis of Sligo's naive call to the people of Westport to help the police was typical of their response.[21]

As the conflict intensified in 1920, peers began to doubt the ability of the British Government to protect their families and interests. Lords de Vesci and Inchiquin left a House of Lords debate early, saying they wanted to avoid leaving their wives at home alone.[22] In June, Monteagle warned an associate that the government could not impose law and order – even by 'Amritzer [*sic*] methods' – because of its failure to bring 'the machinery of justice into harmony with the

moral sense of the community'.[23] Lord Sligo told fellow peers that
Sinn Féin had issued permits for flour, held court sittings and struck
rates. Desart was concerned that the government make it clear
whether loyalists could expect Sinn Féin to be defeated or whether
they should make terms.[24] Speaking in the House of Lords several
weeks later, Midleton complained: 'there are two [governments of
Ireland] now – a legal government which talks and an illegal one
which acts'.[25] In late 1921, Oranmore & Browne was told that Lord
French's ideal solution to the crisis was the mass internment of all
rebel sympathisers. Oranmore & Browne protested that 'Sinn Féin
[*sic*]' would burn 'all our houses'. '*À la guerre comme à la guerre*', an
unsympathetic French replied.[26]

A small number of nobles were not completely hostile to the
republicans. A very few even helped the IRA while others campaigned
against British reprisals and excesses. The most famous noble rebels
were two women: Albinia Brodrick, the sister of Lord Midleton, and
Mary Spring-Rice, the daughter of Lord Monteagle. His sister's politics and active campaigning for Sinn Féin were a source of embarrassment to Midleton; in 1921, for example, he received a note from
'GHQ Ireland, Parkgate', apologising for 'a slight altercation with
Miss Broderick, but I'm afraid her sympathies are not altogether on
our side'.[27] In 1923 she went on hunger strike but her brother's meagre response was to write to the Governor-General that 'I earnestly
hope she will receive any consideration shown to female prisoners
similarly situated'.[28] Mary Spring-Rice had republican friends such as
the Childers family and Alice Stopford Green, a nationalist historian
and future senator. Her involvement in republicanism was a long one;
she had provided funds to buy arms for the *Asgard* shipment and had
been present on Childers' yacht bringing them in. During the War of
Independence, she ran missions for the IRA's GHQ in Dublin, shel-
tered men on the run at Mount Trenchard and used the house for
Cumann na mBan lectures. She also brought British people to
Limerick to show them the outrages committed by British forces.
At her funeral in 1924, she was buried in a coffin wrapped in the
Irish flag.[29]

There were other nobles who voiced their objections to the tactics
used by the Crown forces. Lady Fingall forced an official inquiry, which
resulted in the commanding officer being rebuked, when she heard that
several young men had been 'indecently treated' by the military in July
1921.[30] Lord Monteagle was heavily involved in the causes of several
prisoners who faced execution.[31] He wrote directly to the authorities

and tried to get questions asked in the House of Commons. He was also active in opposing British reprisals. When the Auxiliaries burned shops and a creamery in Shanagolden, he wrote to Sir John Anderson, the Under-Secretary at Dublin Castle, seeking that the system of organised reprisals be stopped.[32] He also organised legal representation for some of those involved.[33] When Lord Curzon declared that he did not know of any cases of British forces destroying creameries, Monteagle sent him a file of correspondence on the subject.[34] In November he published an article on government reprisals in *Foreign Affairs* in which he accused British forces of destroying 26 creameries in six months.[35] He was careful about what causes he championed, however, and warned one correspondent that he could 'take no notice of anonymous complaints against the police'.[36] His attempts to recruit allies among his class were unsuccessful. Oranmore & Browne informed him that he would not oppose 'acts of violence directed openly by the military authorities' if that was what it took to restore order.[37] His views pushed Monteagle into a kind of affinity with Sinn Féin. In 1921 he decided that to run candidates against them in the next election 'would be almost tantamount to supporting Black and Tan militarism'.[38]

Monteagle's analysis was sometimes naive; in 1920 he declared that he did not believe Sinn Féin leaders were responsible for murders, as the killings were costing them the support of the British public.[39] It should be emphasised, however, that nobles who had any sympathy with the republicans were rare. During a House of Lords debate on British reprisals, no Irish peer spoke.[40] This may imply distaste for the issue as well as a fear of coming to the attention of the belligerents.

The 'Big House' novel has created many people's image of how the aristocracy experienced the revolutionary period. Inevitably such tales end with the great old pile going up in highly symbolic flames. This has produced some fine literature but little historical analysis. Recently Terence Dooley has compiled an exhaustive survey of the extent and timing of house burning in both the War of Independence and Civil War periods. He argues that the burning of houses began in February 1920 but did not become widespread until April that year. This corresponds with the arrival of the Black and Tans.[41] Between April 1920 and July 1921, he found 72 cases of big houses burned by the IRA.[42] These houses were mostly burned for military reasons. In one-third of these cases the house had been used by the army as a billet. This led to a British decision, in September 1920, that houses owned by loyalists were not to be used by the army.[43]

During 1921, the IRA began to burn loyalists' houses in response to British reprisals. Lord Listowel's residence, Convamore, was destroyed in April 1921 in retaliation for the destruction of the houses of six republicans and because he was, the attackers alleged, 'aggressively anti-Irish'.[44] In June 1921, an order to burn loyalist houses in retaliation for British reprisals was issued by IRA GHQ, making such actions official policy.[45] Most contemporary accounts and fiction written by those who lived through this period ascribed the motive for the attacks to the desire to avenge British actions. It was also believed, however, that the choice of targets was political. The *Irish Times* complained that 'many houses were destroyed because their owners or occupiers showed themselves on too friendly terms with the forces of the crown'.[46] This view is endorsed by Ernie O'Malley who recalled how, in April 1921, Liam Lynch, enraged by the destruction of several houses in reprisal for an IRA ambush, declared 'six big houses and castles of their friends, the Imperialists, will go up for this'.[47] The IRA's own order permitted retaliation against the property of 'the most active enemies of Ireland'.[48]

Republicans were not the only ones to destroy property owned by the aristocracy. General Sir Nevil Macready was warned that 'the houses officially burned [by the British] were likely to be in any case the property of landlords'; and that Crown forces had destroyed two houses belonging to Lord Midleton in January 1921.[49] The crucial difference was that aristocratic residences – 'big houses' – were targeted by the IRA whereas when a property was destroyed by British forces it was a coincidence if the landlord was a loyalist. Desart and Midleton both raised the matter of house burnings with the deputy lord mayor of Cork in June 1921 and warned him that the victims were 'the men who had been most favourable to the Irish cause'.[50] In a later meeting with Midleton, de Valera tried to evade the issue by noting that 'in war-like operations such things were bound to occur'.[51] In the Civil War period, most houses were burned between the end of January and March 1923. This was a time when the republicans were incapable of doing much of strategic value. Houses were destroyed as reprisals for government executions, to deprive Free State troops of barracks and as part of a campaign of intimidation against Free State senators, that destroyed 37 houses.[52]

In Table 10.1 the total number of houses that were burned and those owned by Irish peers are indicated for each year. The proportions of burned houses owned by peers remain at roughly one in five for the period up to 1923. For that year, however, the number of

Table 10.1 House burnings in
Ireland, 1919–23

	All houses	*Peers' houses*
1919	0	0
1920	30	6
1921	46	6
1922	82	16
1923	117	8

Table 10.2 Peers' residences burned per county

	Peers' houses	*War of Independence*	*Civil War*		*Peers' houses*	*War of Independence*	*Civil War*
ULSTER				**LEINSTER**			
Antrim	6	0	2	Carlow	1	0	0
Armagh	3	0	1	Dublin	11	0	1
Cavan	3	0	0	Kildare	6	0	0
Londonderry	1	0	0	Kilkenny	7	0	2
Donegal	2	0	0	Queen's	5	0	0
Down	10	0	1	Longford	1	0	0
Fermanagh	4	0	0	Louth	4	1	0
Monaghan	3	0	0	Meath	9	1	2
Tyrone	5	0	1	King's	3	0	1
				Westmeath	4	3	0
				Wexford	6	0	2
				Wicklow	7	1	0
MUNSTER				**CONNACHT**			
Clare	2	0	0	Galway	9	0	1
Cork	10	5	2	Leitrim	1	0	0
Kerry	4	0	3	Mayo	5	0	1
Limerick	9	1	0	Roscommon	3	0	0
Tipperary	4	0	3	Sligo	0	0	0
Waterford	2	0	0				

peers' houses destroyed declined while the figure for all houses
increased. There were only 152 peers' residences in total and by 1923,
the obvious targets may have already been destroyed. Table 10.2 com-
pares the number of peers' residences in each county with the number
destroyed in both the War of Independence and Civil War periods.[53]
The 152 houses, divided over 31 counties, were owned by 124 peers.
There were 37 peers' houses in Ulster, 18 in Connacht, 64 in Leinster

and 31 in Munster. The figures show that peers suffered a similar inci-
dence of arson on a province-by-province basis to non-peers. In the
War of Independence period, there were 11 burnings in Ulster of
which none were peers' houses. The ratio in Connacht was 4:0, in
Leinster 20:6 and in Munster it was 42:6. During the Civil War, the
ratio in Ulster was 17:5, in Connacht it was 39:2, in Leinster 74:8,
and 69:8 for Munster. It is clear that nobles in Munster and Leinster
were worst affected.[54] Over the entire period, 14 of 31 peers' residences in Munster were burned (45%) and 14 of 64 in Leinster (22%).
By contrast, only 2 of 18 peers' houses were destroyed in Connacht
(11%) and 5 of 36 in Ulster (14%).

It appears that the IRA during both the War of Independence and
the Civil War treated peers in the same way as other big house owners. This is further borne out by anecdotal evidence of actual incidents
of incendiarism. The attackers usually gave some warning, although
families and servants were often given only a few minutes to evacuate.
In many cases, the peers and their families were not in residence at
the time of the attack.

As the Civil War began, it soon became clear that nobles were now
dependent on the Free State forces. Donoughmore warned one distressed unionist that 'there is no hope in the [British] coalition government'.[55] Likewise, Captain Belton advised Lord Midleton that he
should approach the Provisional Government for help rather than
Dublin Castle.[56] At the same time nobles' houses were used as billets
by pro-Treaty forces.[57]

The closest contact nobles had with the republican side in the conflict came when their houses were occupied. Occupations often led
to the destruction of the property as the republicans wished to make
it useless to the pro-Treaty forces. Edith Somerville described how
carpets were ruined and on one occasion, soldiers 'used a Rembrandt
as a dartboard'.[58] The most vivid description of a house under occupation came from the Earl of Ossory. Throughout it, he portrayed
himself as cool and collected, in keeping with his class's self-image.[59]
He stayed in the castle to prevent republicans destroying it and saw it
retaken by the pro-Treaty forces. Considerable damage was done to
the castle in the ensuing battle; paintings were damaged, antiques were
destroyed and windows were smashed.[60] Lord Donoughmore was
advised not to remove valuables from his house for fear that it would
look empty and be more likely to be occupied.[61] In the case of Lord
Lansdowne's house, Derreen, the house was looted and when the
raiders broached the wine cellars, 36 hours of chaos ensued. Even the

local parish priest was unable to recover the stolen items. The house was burned in September 1922.[62] When Lord Granard's house was badly damaged in 1923, Cosgrave wrote to the senator personally to offer his regrets, sent him a copy of the official report, and offered his car and personal guard to help him to visit the site.[63]

Lawlessness and the new state

In many ways the anti-Treaty IRA campaign was a lesser threat for peers than the increase in agrarian disturbances after 1921. The non-payment of rent had become a serious problem for landowners. Having begun in late 1920, it spread rapidly – aided by the general breakdown of the legal system and expectations of a swift completion of land purchase.[64] In June 1922, Midleton warned Michael Collins that 'rents have been withheld in most counties' in anticipation of a new land act.[65] The subsequent financial problems caused Lord Courtown to claim that he did not attend the House of Lords because he could no longer afford to travel.[66]

Peers were soon sending pleas to the new administration. Sometimes the problem was simple: in March 1922, Lord Castletown had a dispute with local officials over the use of two of his buildings, which was resolved by Griffith's secretary.[67] The problems on Lord Lansdowne's estates, however, were far more serious. Lansdowne's difficulties began in June 1922, when timber stolen from his land was used to improve a local house.[68] Several days later, a farm named Inchinlough was seized. The incident was reported to the local authorities but no action was taken.[69] Further incidents occurred; salmon were dynamited, animals were poisoned, cattle drives occurred and buildings were destroyed.[70] Most seriously, the tenants were refusing to pay rent.[71] The Department of Home Affairs wrote in December, after waiting a month in the hope that the situation 'would have improved before now', that Civic Guards had been stationed at Listowel and Tralee.[72] There was no improvement as trouble continued until December 1924.[73]

Lord Lansdowne was not the only peer to suffer. Lord Leitrim's estate office was burned in January 1922.[74] A month later, 20 of Lord Donoughmore's cattle were stolen and a man claiming to be from the IRA demanded a £200 levy.[75] The 'levy' was, of course, unauthorised.[76] In late 1922, Lord Leitrim's agent was shot during a confrontation with about 50 men over rents and land sales. Afterwards notices were put up ordering people not to work for Lord Leitrim or to participate in purchasing land from him.[77] In January 1923, cattle drives occurred on the estate of Lord Langford. The incidents were related to an ITGWU strike on the estate caused by the dismissal of three men.[78] Lord Leitrim's estate suffered further disturbances, particularly the theft of trees. The officials in Dublin were of the view that these acts were intended 'to keep Lord Leitrim away by any means in their power'.[79] Timber was also stolen from Lord Clarina's estate.[80] As late as December 1923, graziers on Lord Castlemaine's estate were intimidated by men who mutilated their cattle.[81] Other cases of agitation were reported by Lords Castletown, Powerscourt, and Kingston.[82]

There was also evidence that some crimes were motivated by sectarianism. Lansdowne claimed that the minority was being persecuted 'because it is regarded as of alien origin'.[83] A government report concluded 'there is some evidence that the [agrarian] movement is, to a certain extent at any rate, influenced by sectarian feelings'.[84] These feelings were also present among some officials. In the case of Lord Leitrim's agent, referred to above, the Garda Commissioner downplayed the victim's right to complain, since 'as a Scotsman his interest in Ireland is probably confined to its possibility as a source of revenue'.[85] He was sternly rebuked but his view was probably not unique. Even in 1921, Bandon, whose residences were in Cork, had written to Midleton that 'the Sinn Féiners [*sic*] are trying to drive all the Protestant farmers out of the country … a great many of them are selling their farms and leaving … they are warned not to sell their farms to other Protestants'.[86] In 1922 Midleton wrote to the King to warn of 'the selection of Protestant victims for murder in retribution … for the treatment of Catholics in Belfast'.[87] Lord Ashtown received a notice ordering 'the unionists and *freemasons* of the south and west [my emphasis]' to supply the needs of refugees from Belfast, and confiscation of his house.[88] In Queen's County, agitators evicted four large farmers who had purchased their land from Lansdowne in the 1880s. All were Protestant and were told to make way for 'local landless Catholics'.[89] Likewise, Lord Castletown drew the government's attention to the fact that local people had evicted several Protestants, who were his leaseholders.[90] This sort of action against Protestants is consistent with that detailed by Peter Hart in his study of Cork.[91] Peers were rarely well informed enough about the republicans to accurately determine whether sectarian persecution of their tenants was directed by the IRA or motivated by local issues. It is clear from the cases above, however, that several nobles did believe that a campaign against their co-religionists existed, and took it upon themselves, as landlords and traditional leaders of the Protestant community, to act on behalf of those affected.

The nobility and Irish politics

Peers still retained enough influence on public affairs to play a part in some of the attempts to settle the conflict in Ireland. Monteagle had the idea of a constitutional assembly but failed to convince Sinn Féin.[92] He also campaigned for dominion home rule,[93] and was involved with the Peace With Ireland Council, a group formed in October 1920 with a large number of other nobles among its members, including Lord ffrench (not to be confused with the Lord Lieutenant), and Ladies Aberdeen, MacDonnell and Clare Annesley – the daughter of the Earl of Annesley.[94] Lord Midleton actually assisted the government in its negotiations with Sinn Féin in the later months of 1921 in cooperation with a Captain Belton, who dealt with the rebel leadership. Sinn Féin gave Belton information 'with the full knowledge that I would transmit it to you [Midleton] as other communications had been transmitted and that you would in all probability pass it on to the Prime Minister'.[95] Part of this 'back door' diplomacy involved Lord Bandon, who had been kidnapped by the IRA in June 1921[96] and was released on 12 July.[97]

When, under the Government of Ireland Act 1920, the southern Irish Senate was nominated by the Lord Lieutenant, 19 of the senators refused to meet as they could not accept 'any body nominated by the Lord Lieutenant to replace an elected Lower House'.[98] Of these, 15 were peers including several Midletonites as well as the Lords Granard and Dunraven. For most, the desire to keep their options open was probably a more genuine reason. On 4 July 1921, Midleton and other southern unionists met de Valera, who made it clear to them that he was willing to meet Lloyd George but only as head of the Irish nation, not to sue for peace. They duly delivered the message.[99] The meeting was controversial and generated a debate in the newspapers.[100] Midleton was used again in August when he was asked by Belton to ensure the release of Sean MacEoin, the Longford IRA leader.[101] During September he acted as a conduit for different wordings of possible agreements.[102]

As Buckland has pointed out, however, the government did not take Midleton's work into account when negotiating the position of the minority population and few of the safeguards in the 1920 Act were included in the treaty.[103] This, in part, led to Midleton's subsequent condemnation of it as conceding 'terms which America had fought the greatest civil war in history to avoid'.[104] His concerns were echoed by Oranmore & Browne, who was also worried about the weakness of the oath of allegiance.[105] Lansdowne and several other unionist peers were shocked that the Treaty contained so few concrete safeguards.[106] The former was even more concerned by the Sinn Féin split, however, and feared that the anti-Treaty forces would eventually gain a majority.[107] Dunraven, on the other hand, was delighted with the Treaty as 'it gave to Ireland all I had long laboured for'.[108] He was disappointed, however, by the small majority supporting it in the Dáil,[109] and feared that Ireland would 'once again destroy herself'.[110]

Despite these misgivings, many peers were willing to work with the Provisional Government. The Earl of Mayo wrote to Midleton to inform him that he was calling a meeting to endorse the new regime.[111] The meeting was attended by Powerscourt, Headfort, Dunraven and Cloncurry and received the support of Dunsany, Kenmare and Courtown.[112] It is significant that Mayo neither asked Midleton's permission nor offered him the chair.[113] This may imply that the divisions in the southern unionist ranks, which opened up later that year over the Irish Free State Constitution, had already begun. Soon afterwards Castletown wrote to Griffith to assure him of his loyalty.[114] Meanwhile, Midleton and his allies were negotiating directly with representatives of the new government, particularly Darrell Figgis. They wanted a powerful senate elected on a very limited franchise and a prime minister selected by the Governor-General rather than 'a chance election'. Figgis, for his part, seemed to think that promising to include 'the Irish peers' in the senate would help the situation. In fact, as Midleton pointed out, the southern unionists did not see their inclusion as a concession to 'moderate opinion'.[115]

His allies suspected that Midleton was not being fully open with them about his discussions. At a meeting on 9 May, Midleton had asked for wide powers to negotiate on behalf of his colleagues.[116] Lansdowne warned Midleton that he could not 'commit your friends to the approval of a scheme which has never been submitted to them'.[117] In fact, Midleton was arguing for a strong senate with the power to delay bills for a year, and protection for the southern minority: by which he meant 'Commerce, the Universities, Education, or the Landed Interest'.[118] Midleton believed full adult suffrage would be a mistake as 'there is great intimidation. The Irish are mostly moral cowards.' He also feared that an Irish government would be spendthrift.[119] It is significant that Midleton wanted some sort of direct representation for commerce as well as for property.[120] This demonstrates the importance of unionist businessmen, who had to come to an accommodation with the new state.

The British Government accepted the Irish Free State Constitution in June 1922, putting the southern unionists in a poor negotiating position. Cosgrave told a delegation of southern peers that he, Patrick Hogan and Kevin O'Higgins had gained limited concessions on the senate only 'by frequently threatening their own resignation and by appeals to Mr Griffith's memory'.[121] Ironically, it was Midleton who opposed the proposed constitution because he deemed the senate provisions to be too weak. At a meeting of peers he advocated amending it in the House of Lords. Lansdowne and Oranmore & Browne were willing but the meeting as a whole feared alienating their new government and being accused of 'having broken up the Treaty'. Midleton watched as his old allies, Desart, Iveagh and Jameson, deserted him.[122] He resigned as head of the Anti-Partition League soon after.[123] Nothing his old allies said could persuade him to stay until the Constitution was passed.[124]

When the occasion arose for a new senate to be elected by the Dáil, many of those who had refused the Lord Lieutenant's nominations in 1921 were elected, which suggests that they were still seen as politically important. Midleton, however, ruled himself out of contention. He was joined in exile by Desart, Donoughmore and Iveagh.[125] Cosgrave told Desart that he was 'most anxious that the Landed Gentry should be represented, as he desired eagerly to keep them in the country'.[126] He saw Lord Granard, a Catholic and former Home Ruler, as a bridge between the traditions. The peers selected were not, however, notable for their ability as leaders. Dunraven was too old, and Lord Granard's politics were wrong. Several of the new senators continued to live in London. Almost by default, the Earl of Mayo took up the role. Though he was 'an amateur in politics', he had a detailed knowledge of parliamentary procedure, and treated the chairman Lord Glenavy with considerable condescension.[127] Of the other peers, Wicklow was quite active, the Countess of Desart voted but rarely spoke, and Lords Headfort and Kerry rarely even attended. The peers made some contributions however, most notably on the controversial subjects of land reform,[128] and compensation for damages during the conflict.[129]

Conclusion

In 1942, Lord Powerscourt told Harold Nicolson that he was 'marooned – the last of the Irish aristocracy, with no-one to speak to'.[130] While he was exaggerating, it is true that most of the nobility left southern Ireland after independence. Peers as a class were not disproportionately persecuted during the revolutionary period, especially when compared with other Protestant groups. However, they did suffer harassment and violence unlike anything they had seen since the

days of the Land War. This led many of them to live in Britain for the
duration of the conflict. The burning of their big houses, while not as
extensive as is often assumed, was a traumatic experience and made it
very difficult for them to trust the good intentions of the Free State.
At least as important was the psychological impact that independence
had on a class which had economic, social, cultural and landed roots in
both Ireland and Britain. It forced them to choose to be Irish or
British and it is not surprising that many of them found the New
Ireland insufficiently attractive to keep them.

Notes

1. For a detailed examination of the role of southern peers in the IUA, see
   P. Martin, 'Irish Peers, 1909–24', MA thesis (University College, Dublin,
   1998), ch. 7.
2. Midleton to the Prime Minister, 6 Dec. [1918], PRO, 39/2351.
3. Midleton, general letter to IUA members, 24 Oct. 1918, ibid., 39/2340.
4. Martin, 'Irish Peers', p. 169.
5. Earl of Desart and Lady S. Lubbock, *A Page from the Past* (London, 1936),
   p. 218.
6. See Martin, 'Irish Peers', ch. 6.
7. Lords Debates, 34 HL Deb., 5s, 15 Apr. 1919, 328.
8. RIC Inspector General's Confidential Report, Apr. 1919, PRO, CO
   904/108.
9. T. Dooley, *The Decline of the Big House in Ireland: A Study of Irish Landed
   Families, 1860–1960* (Dublin, 2001), p. 128.
10. Oranmore & Browne (John Butler) (ed.), 'Lord Oranmore's Journal,
    1913–27', in *IHS*, XXIX (Nov. 1995), p. 580.
11. Lords Debates, 40 HL Deb. 5s, 6 May 1920, 201–5.
12. *Irish Times*, 5 Feb. 1919.
13. Ibid., 21 Sep. 1920.
14. Ibid., 30 Aug. 1920.
15. *Roscommon Messenger*, 1 Mar. 1919.
16. Inspector General's Confidential Report, Feb. 1919, PRO, CO904/108.
17. *Irish Times*, 24 Aug. 1921.
18. D. Fitzpatrick, *Politics and Irish Life, 1913–21* (Dublin, 1977), p. 78.
19. *Irish Times*, 10 Feb. 1919.
20. J. Augusteijn, *From Public Defiance to Guerrilla Warfare* (Dublin, 1996), p. 88.
21. *Irish Times*, 4 Apr. 1919.
22. De Vesci to Midleton, 23 Dec. 1920; Inchiquin to Midleton, 29 Dec.
    1920, PRO, 30/67, 43/2540 and 2545.
23. Monteagle to M. B. Jellet, 26 June 1920, NLI, ms. 13 417.
24. Memorandum of meeting, 15 July [1920], PRO, 30/67, 43/2456–62.
25. Lords Debates, 41 HL Deb., 5s, 9 Aug. 1920, 1038.
26. Oranmore & Browne, 'Lord Oranmore's Journal', 30 Oct. 1921, p. 584.

27. [?] to Midleton, 19 Feb. 1921, PRO, 30/67, 44/2558.
28. Midleton to Governor-General, Irish Free State, n.d. [10 May 1923], PRO, 30/67, 53/3145.
29. *Limerick's Fighting Story* (Tralee, 1947), p. 170.
30. Lady A. Gregory, *Lady Gregory's Journal, 1916–1930*, ed. L. Robinson. (New York, 1937), p. 156.
31. Monteagle to Edie, 7 Apr. 1921; Monteagle to Chief Secretary's office, 16 Feb. 1921; Monteagle to Lord Lieutenant, n.d.; NLI, ms. 13 416.
32. Monteagle to Anderson, 10 Sep. 1920, ibid.
33. Monteagle to Mr Swayne, solicitor, 10 Oct. 1920, ibid.
34. Monteagle to Curzon, 27 Oct. 1920, ibid.
35. Ibid.
36. Monteagle to C. Wilkenson Esq., 28 June 1920, ibid.
37. Oranmore & Browne to Midleton, 30 Nov. 1920, ibid.
38. Monteagle to K. Walter, 31 June 1921, NLI, ms. 13 417.
39. Lords Debates, 40 HL Deb., 5s, 1 July 1920, 1116.
40. Lords Debates, 43 HL Deb., 5s, 26 Apr. 1921, 16–28.
41. Dooley, *The Decline*, p. 171.
42. Ibid., p. 182.
43. Ibid., p. 183.
44. Ibid., p. 184.
45. Augusteijn, *Public Defiance*, p. 298.
46. *Irish Times*, 22 Oct. 1921.
47. E. O'Malley, *On Another Man's Wound* (Dublin, 1936), p. 306.
48. Augusteijn, *Public Defiance*, p. 298; quoting, NLI, ms. 739, 21 June 1921.
49. C. Townshend, *Political Violence in Ireland* (Oxford, 1984), p. 352.
50. Memorandum of meeting, 16 June [1921], PRO, 30/67, 45/2634.
51. Memorandum of meeting, 8 July 1921, ibid., 45/2651.
52. Dooley, *The Decline*, p. 190.
53. Based on *Thom's Directory* (1919).
54. Figures for burnings of all houses are from Dooley, *The Decline*, pp. 286–7.
55. Donoughmore to Mr Saunders, 18 Apr. 1922, TCD, K/28/4.
56. Belton to Midleton, 3 May 1922, PRO, 30/67, 50/2956.
57. J. T. Seigne & Sons to Minister of Defence, 1 June 1922, NLI, ms. 23 627.
58. D. A. Kennedy, 'The Big House in Irish Literature', in *Irish Georgian Society Bulletin*, 1989, p. 17.
59. Earl of Ossory, 'The Attack on Kilkenny Castle', *Journal of the Butler Society*, I, 4 (1972), pp. 259–60.
60. Ibid., pp. 275–9.
61. R. B. Seigne to Lord Donoughmore, 16 Feb. 1923, TCD, K/20/134.
62. 6th Marquis of Lansdowne, *Glanerought and the Petty-Fitzmaurices* (Oxford, 1937), pp. 205–9.
63. W. T. Cosgrave to Granard, 2 Mar. 1923, PRONI, T/3765/K/15/2/9.
64. Lansdowne, memo, 'Irish land purchase', n.d. [June 1922], PRO, 30/67, 51/3020–5.
65. Midleton to Collins, 13 June 1922, ibid., 50/2984.

66. Courtown to Midleton, 10 Nov. 1922, ibid., 52/3096.
67. Castletown to Griffith, 1 Mar. 1922; Secretary to Adjutant-General, Mar. 1922, NA, H5/5.
68. P. T. Harrington to the Secretary of the Local Government Board, 8 June 1922, NA, H5/135.
69. H. P. Maxwell to the Minister of Home Affairs, 9 June 1922, ibid.
70. Ibid., 10 June 1922.
71. William Rochfort to the Minister of Home Affairs, 30 Oct. 1922, ibid.
72. Runaidhe to William Rochfort, 12 Dec. 1922, ibid.
73. Rochfort to Minister for Justice, 23 Dec. 1924, ibid.
74. Mr Hayes to the Secretary of the Chairman of the Provisional Government, 15 Jan. 1922, ibid., H5/395.
75. Seigne to Donoughmore, 13 Feb. 1922, TCD, K/20/123.
76. Ibid., 14 Feb. 1922, K/20/135.
77. Coimisinéir Garda Síochána to Minister for Home Affairs, 23 Nov. 1922, NA, H5/560.
78. Coimisinéir Garda Síochána to Minister for Home Affairs, 15 Jan. 1923, NA, H5/575.
79. Leas Coimisinéir Garda Síochána to Dept. Home Affairs, 5 May 1923, NA, H5/560.
80. Runaidhe to Coimisinéir Garda Síochána, 14 Nov. 1923, ibid.
81. Miss V. Magan to the Secretary of the Land Settlement Commission, 5 Dec. 1923, NA, H5/1114.
82. NA, H5/174, H5/389 and H5/405.
83. Lansdowne, *Glanerought and the Petty-Fitzmaurices*, p. 202.
84. 'Land agitation in Queen's Co.', 1922, NA, S566.
85. Garda Commissioner to Minister for Home Affairs, 23 Nov. 1923, NA, H5/560.
86. Bandon to Midleton, 13 Feb. 1921, PRO, 30/67, 44/2555.
87. Midleton to HM the King, 30 Apr. 1922, ibid., 50/2944.
88. R. B. MacDowell, *Crisis and Decline: The Fate of the Southern Unionists* (Dublin, 1997), p. 122.
89. 'Land agitation in Queen's County', NA, S566.
90. Castletown to Minister of the Interior [*sic*], 14 Nov. 1922, NA, H5/174.
91. P. Hart, *The IRA and its Enemies* (Oxford, 1998), pp. 273–315.
92. James Douglas to Monteagle, 1 July 1920, NLI, ms. 13 417.
93. Resolutions passed by the standing committee of the Irish Peace Conference, 27 Sep. 1920, ibid.
94. D. G. Boyce, *Englishmen and Irish Troubles* (London, 1992), p. 193.
95. Belton to Midleton, 16 Sep. 1921, PRO, 30/67, 46/2721.
96. Belton to Midleton, 24 June 1921, PRO, 30/67, 46/2721.
97. *Irish Times*, 14 July 1921.
98. Letter to Lloyd George, 21 Jun. 1921, PRO, 45/2641; *The Times*, 22 Jun. 1921.
99. MacDowell, *Crisis and Decline*, p. 107.

100. *Irish Times*, 11 July 1921.
101. Belton to Midleton, 8 Aug. 1921, PRO, 30/67, 45/2698A.
102. Ibid., 12 Sep. 1921, 46/2720.
103. P. Buckland, *Irish Unionism, 1: The Anglo-Irish and the New Ireland, 1885–1922* (Dublin, 1972), p. 246.
104. Midleton the Earl of K. P., *Records and Reactions: 1856–1939* (New York: Dutton, 1939), p. 263.
105. Oranmore to Midleton, 3 Dec. 1921, PRO, 30/67, 48/2818.
106. Lansdowne to Midleton, 9 Dec. 1921, PRO, 30/67, 48/2832.
107. Lansdowne to Midleton, 19 Dec. 1921, PRO, 30/67, 48/2850.
108. Lord Dunraven, *Past Times and Pastimes* (London, 1922), vol. II, p. 91.
109. Ibid., p. 156.
110. Lord Dunraven to William O'Brien, 15 Dec. 1921, NLI, ms. 8554.
111. Mayo to Midleton, 13 Jan. 1922, PRO, 30/67, 48/2868–71.
112. T. Dooley, 'The Decline of the Big House in Ireland, 1879–1950', Ph.D thesis (NUI, Maynooth, 1997), vol. I, p. 270.
113. Mayo to Midleton, 13 Jan. 1922, PRO, 30/67, 49/2868–71.
114. Castletown to Griffith, 1 Mar. 1922, NA, H5/5.
115. Memorandum, 28 and 29 Apr. 1922, PRO, 30/67, 50/2935–40.
116. Lansdowne to Midleton, 10 May 1922, PRO, 30/67, 50/2964.
117. Ibid., 14 May 1922, PRO, 30/67, 50/2975.
118. Midleton, memorandum of meeting with Griffith in Nov. 1921, 29 May 1922, PRO, 30/67, 50/2979.
119. Midleton to Churchill, 13 June 1922, PRO, 30/67, 50/2982.
120. Ibid.
121. Memorandum of meeting of Midleton, Desart and Donoughmore with Cosgrave, Hogan and O'Higgins, 9 Nov. 1922, PRO, 30/67, 52/3088.
122. Memorandum 'Meeting of Irish peers and others', 16 Nov. 1922, PRO, 30/67, 52/3089–90.
123. Midleton to Jameson, [17?] Nov. 1922, PRO, 30/67, 52/3101–4.
124. Desart to Midleton, 23 Nov. 1922; W. Guinness to Midleton, 26 Nov. 1922, PRO, 30/67, 52/3122.
125. Buckland, *Irish Unionism, 1*, p. 225.
126. Desart, memorandum of conversation with Cosgrave, 18 Oct. 1922, PRO, 30/67, 51/3070.
127. D. O' Sullivan, 'Early Days in the First Senate', in *Irish Times*, 8 Oct. 1964.
128. Seanad Debates, 1922–3.
129. Seanad Debates, 12 Apr. 1923, 798. See also N. Brennan, 'A Political Minefield: Southern Loyalists, the Irish Grants Committee and the British Government, 1922–31', in *IHS*, XXX (May 1997), pp. 406–19; and Dooley, *The Decline*.
130. H. Nicolson, *Diaries and Letters, 1939–45* (London, 1970), p. 214.

11

Gender: Gendering the Irish Revolution

Margaret Ward

Considering female agency

In June 1932, a few months after the election of the first Fianna Fáil Government and also a few days after Amelia Earhart, the first woman to fly solo across the Atlantic, had landed her plane in County Derry, Nora, daughter of James Connolly, wrote a bitter reflection on the current poor position of revolutionary women in Ireland. In Nora's eyes, the past had been very different. In the period before the 1916 Rising she remembered her father's encouragement of women:

> The more active part women took in a movement the greater his pleasure; by his advice and counsel he encouraged them; more, he gave them often that little extra push forward they needed. He saw nothing incongruous in a woman having a seat on an army council, or preferring to bear arms to winding bandages.[1]

In the Ireland of 1932, with Eamon de Valera in power, those who had not wanted women anywhere near the barricades of the Easter Rising were in the ascendant. It is not difficult to understand why Nora Connolly wrote as she did, remembering a time when women had 'won the right to share in the dangers of war', only to have 'relinquished their right to share in the dangers of peace'. However, those to whom she directed her comments were not her former male colleagues, but those women whom she accused of again showing a 'damnable patience' by being content to be 'the drudges of the movement'. Why did men escape censure? How could a radical woman like Nora Connolly ignore the misogyny inherent in the revolutionary movement she had been a part of for almost 20 years? Was it that her experience of a movement – in the form of the Irish Citizen Army and its efforts to promote a gender-based egalitarianism – blinded her to the realities of everyday life, and in particular to the almost total exclusion of women from the public sphere? Was this the reason why she concluded that if women occupied a subordinate position politically or militarily, the explanation must lie with them and with their failure to speak up or fight for their rights?

With a daughter's loyalty to her father's memory and despite her own activism, Nora Connolly unwittingly colluded with the silencing of women's agency. Her statement of disillusion echoed the presumptions of the male historical narrative, where women, if they did appear, were defined in male terms and without recognition of their efforts to become agents of change.

Most histories of the 'Irish revolution' have expressed a gender conservatism that has confined women to the role of reproducer, not as agents in their own right. Another version of history – initially written by those who had been active in some of those events, and later elaborated upon by certain historians – has acknowledged some agency on women's part – but only in order to justify their subsequent exclusion from the public world of nation-building. This was by producing 'demonised images of the deviant non-domestic woman', as Louise Ryan has described the 'furies' of P. S. O'Hegarty's post-Civil War frenzied rhetoric.[2] In not dissimilar vein to O'Hegarty, Tom Garvin's analysis of the 1922 period highlights what he calls the 'Mammy's boy' syndrome as a contributing factor to civil war:

> much of the unreality of republican political ideas seems to have been derived from the political emotionalism of inexperienced girl-friends, wives and mothers filtered through psychologically intimidated young warriors and politicians.[3]

Nancy Curtin and Marilyn Cohen have urged a reclaiming of gender as a central tool of analysis for historians.[4] While women are sometimes added on to narrative accounts there has been little if any modification of the privileging of the male subject – 'psychologically intimidated' or not. To understand the processes that led to 1932 and to the virtual exclusion of women from the body politic, we need to understand the Irish revolution in terms of gendered systems of power and social organisation.

American historian Linda Kerber reminds us that the word 'citizen' has carried military overtones since the days of the Sparta Republic and the citizen warrior.[5] A connection between the obligation to take up arms to win independence and a subsequent construction of citizenship has defined classical republicanism throughout history – and not simply its Irish variant. Kerber's analysis has parallels with the Irish experience of distinct male and female roles in the long-standing struggle to win independence from British rule. During debates over voting qualifications in the early Republic, a connection was expressed between the physical defence of the Republic and the right to participate in governance. The implicit distinction between those who bore arms and those who did not ensured that the rights of women to citizenship would be deeply contested by the next gener-ation of American men. It would also lead, eventually, to some suffra-gists feeling they had to justify their claim to the vote by equating the dangers of childbirth to the dangers endured by soldiers in war.

Nancy Curtin has extended Kerber's analysis of manly virtue and the citizen-soldier to the classical republicanism of the United Irishmen of the 1790s, characterised as a 'homosocial paramilitary organisation'. The gender-based division of labour implicit in the republican tradition meant for men 'active participation in liberating an abused and feminised nation from dishonour', while citizenship for women involved 'republican motherhood – sacrificing husbands, brothers and sons to the national struggle'.[6] That passive form of cit-izenship consigned women to the private sphere, their duty to 'incul-cate their menfolk with civic virtue and prepare them for the mother nation's service' – a role of 'heroic subordination' which continued to have both male and female adherents in the revival of republicanism during the early years of the twentieth century.

By the nineteenth century, full inclusion into the nation would be measured by access to suffrage rights. Catholic emancipation, as Catherine Hall has analysed so brilliantly, meant that 'Irish Catholics were both within and without the nation: some were political citizens but their subjecthood was framed by Irishness'.[7] Irish women, denied suffrage, remained outside even the putative nation, but with the advent of the female suffrage movement a new discourse of nationhood began. Feminist understanding of the political and social inequalities suffered by women encouraged a minority of politically active women to develop a sustained critique of the political repercussions of the public and private distinctions confining them to the domestic sphere. Within Ireland, and from a nationalist feminist perspective, Hanna

Sheehy-Skeffington criticised the roles performed by women within the broad nationalist movement, where they were valued only 'in (their) capacity as mother and housekeeper, not as individual citizen'.[8] Her critique was directed at those conservative forces impeding the development of female agency. It was not a criticism of women who undertook such roles. Sheehy-Skeffington could see that women were forced to seize whatever meagre opportunities were available.

Conflicting views regarding the role to be performed by women in the Irish nationalist revival of the early twentieth century were clearly evident. As a militant republican, Constance Markievicz foreshadowed the attitudes of Nora Connolly in her conviction that will-power would cut through the restrictions confronting women. She argued that women, 'though sincere, steadfast Nationalists at heart', had been 'content to remain quietly at home, and leave all the fighting and the striving to the men'. Enjoying a privileged economic independence, Markievicz was not constrained by domestic demands. Her words and actions echoed the masculine equation of citizenship and militancy: 'Fix your mind on the ideal of Ireland free, with her women enjoying the full rights of citizenship in their own nation. ... And if in your day the call should come for your body to arm, do not shirk that either'.[9]

Markievicz was a member of Inghinidhe na hÉireann, a nationalist feminist organisation containing many members who insisted that the opportunity to take up arms could not be denied to women. By 1909, their paper, *Bean na hÉireann*, was arguing that physical force was the only remedy for 'the upholding of our Nation', because a movement 'that stops short of shedding blood ... cannot be taken very seriously'.[10] As militant separatism challenged constitutionalism, the differing conceptions of women's role in a war of national liberation were clearly evident in the pages of the various nationalist journals. By 1913, the IRB paper *Irish Freedom* carried an article assuring its readers that there was nothing 'unwomanly' about active patriotism, urging women to consider the possibility of bearing arms for the nation:

> It is assumed by a great many people, as a matter of course, that women cannot fight, but the merest glance backwards at history shows that there is not a country in the world, Ireland included, where women have not fought, and fought well at one time or another ... when the day comes for which 'Northman' in his article bade the young men of Ireland to prepare themselves, there will be women as well as men, ready to answer the call.[11]

This was a minority view. Women's right to participate in war remained a deeply contested issue and woman as citizen was not yet part of the discourse. From a feminist perspective, Sheehy–Skeffington declared war to be 'the negation of the feminist movement'.[12] She did not believe that the opportunities provided for women could compensate for the loss of life entailed. However, as a nationalist she did – crucially – insist upon the maintenance of a distinction between the imperialist war being fought by Britain and Germany in 1914, and a war of national liberation: 'If I saw a hope of Ireland being freed forever from British rule by a swift uprising, I would consider Irishmen justified resorting to arms in order that we might be free'.[13] The assumption that it would be 'men' who would resort to arms could be taken to mean that not even the most outspoken of feminists would contemplate the arming of the female section of the population; unlike the militants of Inghinidhe, who would assert women's right to be given training in the use of firearms.

Heroic subordinates? The role of Cumann na mBan

The formation of the Irish Volunteers in 1913, as a militarised riposte to the anti-nationalist Ulster Volunteer Force, was accompanied with assurances that membership would help recruits to 'realise themselves as citizens and as men'.[14] Mary Condren has, rightly, described this period of constitutional crisis as one in which the discourse on 'manhood' reached 'almost pathological proportions'.[15] The corollary of all this was a renewed emphasis upon woman as heroic subordinate. Competing discourses jostled for dominance. Would women be more than passive citizens in this new bid to realise the republic? An article in the *Irish Volunteer*, written to coincide with the inaugural meeting of Cumann na mBan in April 1914, called upon women to 'form ambulance corps, learn first aid, make all the flags to be carried by the Volunteers, do all the embroidery that may be required, such as badges on the uniforms, etc.' In a rhetorical flourish the writer concluded, 'To a patriotic Irishwoman could there be any work of more intense delight than that?'[16]

Cumann na mBan was intended as a female auxiliary to the male military organisation, but without representation on the executive of the Volunteer movement. Its primary aim was to advance the cause of 'Irish liberty' through arming and equipping Irishmen for the defence of Ireland. The issue of whether this 'liberty' would include the enfranchisement of women (as Irish and British women were voteless) was avoided, despite the repeated queries of the suffragist paper the *Irish Citizen*. The IPP had refused the feminists' plea to challenge the Liberal government on the terms of the Home Rule Bill: under its provisions it would be home rule for Irish men but not for Irish women. Constitutional and physical-force nationalists were equally concerned not to allow the issue of female franchise to split nationalist ranks, so women were ignored. The remnants of Inghinidhe na hÉireann preferred to join the egalitarian Irish Citizen Army, where women and men were at least treated equally with regards to arms training. James Connolly was also someone who declared he supported, without reservation, the militant suffragettes. The gendered nature of franchise remained controversial and unresolved in the period before the Easter Rising.

Kathleen Clarke, member of a well-known Fenian family, wife of leading IRB member Tom Clarke, and herself a member of the executive of the central branch of Cumann na mBan, exemplified the ideal wife of a revolutionary. She had wanted to march out with the insurgents on Easter Monday, but was forbidden by her husband from doing so. Although she had 'begged' him, she said, to allow her to march with him he 'absolutely refused' her request. Her orders were to ensure the well-being of the dependants of those involved in the Rising.[17] The Clarke marriage, although a partnership, became a military hierarchy based upon gender. It was, as Curtin has characterised the marriage of Matilda and Wolfe Tone, 'a division of republican labour'.[18] While public and private worlds appeared separate, their interpenetration was such that female support was crucial to future success. However, that symbiosis posed no challenge to those public/private binaries. After the Rising, from her sickbed, the widowed Clarke disbursed the funds left to her, as instructed. The subordinate and domestic nature of women's contribution ensured the continued primacy of the male role, with an attendant high status accorded to those who took up arms.

The names appended to the Proclamation of the Republic were exclusively male, a product of this hierarchical division of labour. None the less, the declaration of equal rights and equal opportunities it contained provided a defining moment in women's struggle for citizenship. Hanna Sheehy-Skeffington made an explicit comparison between the Easter Rising and the earlier American and French Revolutions. The Irish example, she declared, was 'the only instance I know of in history where men fighting for freedom voluntarily included women'.[19] Despite its lack of female signatures the Proclamation was of immense importance to women, providing, as Maryann Valiulis has stated, 'formal recognition to their place in the nationalist movement'.[20] From this moment on, female activists were able to refer to it on every occasion they believed themselves denied the right to equal participation. For example, Margaret Skinnider, a member of the Irish Citizen Army, argued successfully during the Rising of her entitlement to throw a bomb attached to an eight-second fuse through the window of the Shelbourne Hotel. Women 'had the same right to risk (their) lives as the men' now that they were 'on an equality with men' in the Constitution of the Irish Republic.[21]

Mary Condren's exploration of the 'sacrificial discourse' within the Irish nationalist tradition concludes that the masculinist 'festival paradigm' of the Easter Rising was instrumental in reinforcing gender boundaries. The treatment of Constance Markievicz illustrates her argument. Markievicz was the only woman to be court martialled by a military tribunal as a consequence of her participation in the Rising. However, instead of her following her companions to the firing squad, her sentence was commuted, on the grounds of her sex, to penal servitude for life. Asquith's decision was influenced by the public uproar surrounding the wartime execution of Edith Cavell, condemned as a German spy, but it possessed a deeper symbolic resonance. While Irish nationalists 'might temporarily have relaxed the prohibitions against women, the imperialist British knew better than to allow a woman to enter any patrilineage, albeit an Irish one'.[22] To have granted Markievicz the status of martyr would have been to undermine the foundations of a patriarchy that benefited all men, regardless of nationality.

In the post-1916 period, when nationalist organisations grew dramatically in size as a result of renewed enthusiasm for the cause, and Sinn Féin reorganised to become the political expression of Irish nationalism, the male leadership encouraged recruitment to Cumann na mBan. It was a deliberate strategy. This would ensure that women remained confined to a politically marginal, woman-only sphere. They could demonstrate against conscription, raise funds, and offer shelter, first aid and food to the men on the run, but there was no suggestion that these services would confer the rights of citizenship upon women who were still, prior to 1918, denied the right to vote. The promise of the Republican Proclamation that women would have equal status with men had yet to be translated into reality. David Fitzpatrick, tracing the wave of popular sentiment that characterised the post-Rising reorganisation of Sinn Féin in County Clare, has described local branches as taking on the character of social clubs. The separation of the sexes characteristic in Irish social life was reflected in a gendered conception of Sinn Féin as a male-only organisation:

All men aged between 14 and 90 were invited to join up. Lady supporters were tactfully advised to channel their energy into the fast-growing Cumann na mBan, though for the time being their subscriptions would be gladly received.[23]

This segregation meant that comparatively few women were mobilised. For County Clare, in March 1919, there were 31 Volunteer companies, with roughly the same number of Sinn Féin clubs. At the same time, police reported only nine branches of Cumann na mBan. Police guesswork might not be entirely reliable, yet Marie Coleman has discovered a similar pattern for County Longford, where there were approximately 12 branches for a total membership of 300 women.[24] The auxiliary nature of Cumann na mBan ensured that they could only be 'strongest in areas where the Volunteers were strongest'.[25] Nevertheless, the overall strength of the organisation had increased to a total of 600 branches by 1918.

The majority of its members were young and single. When the War of Independence began in 1919 they were free to act as couriers, to tend to men on the run, or to accompany the flying columns as first aid support. This was dangerous, exciting and essential work. The majority of branch members also performed more mundane activities. All shared the experience of involvement. Optimistic visions of a future 'new Ireland' were partly an outcome of this agency. Many women believed that their ability to participate would be further enhanced once independence was achieved. However, this kind of participation was not the norm. Other women, who also played a part in the Irish guerrilla war, did so from the confines of the domestic sphere. Their experiences were more typical of the majority and served to confirm an image of a suffering Mother Ireland. Mary MacSwiney, a member of Cumann na mBan and deputy in the Second Dáil, described their hardships during the Treaty debates:

> it is the women suffer the most of the hardships that war brings. You can go out in the excitement of the fight and it brings its own honour and its own glory. We have to sit at home and work in more humble ways, we have to endure the agony, the sunshines, the torture of misery and the privations which war brings, the horror of nightly visitations to our houses and their consequences.[26]

Such psychological pressures experienced by women trapped within the home, at the mercy of the British forces of occupation, might provide an explanation for why the Treaty was accepted by a majority of the population: the relief that such brutalities would no longer be visited upon them. Yet for some who rejected the Treaty, such as Mary MacSwiney, the Irish home was a site of active resistance to British rule, and women within the home were at the heart of that resistance. It was an acceptance of women's role as heroic subordinate that unintentionally reinforced, rather than challenged, gender divisions.

Gender equality within Sinn Féin

A minority of women were more confident that they had a right to voice their demands. In the aftermath of the Rising a small group of women organised to challenge their subordinate position within the nationalist movement. Their existence provides compelling evidence for women's determination to ensure that the pledges of the Proclamation would be translated into reality – and equally compelling evidence for a continuing deep-rooted resistance to their presence within the political movement.

The League of Women Delegates, formed in April 1917, was an expression of the unease of prominent republican women (some bereaved by the Rising, some who had participated in it, and other members of the Citizen Army, Cumann na mBan and Sinn Féin) concerning their lack of representation within the regrouping nationalist organisations. During the six months prior to the all-important Sinn Féin Convention of October 1917 the League exerted determined pressure upon the male leadership. When it was discovered that provision would be made for the co-option of (male) prisoners being released, a request was made for Cumann na mBan, as the female equivalent of the Volunteers, to be co-opted onto the Sinn Féin executive committee: 'Seeing that you are enlarging your Council to include ... six prisoners to be elected by the prisoners, the time seems opportune to include also six women, elected by women'.[27] The petition submitted by the League made clear that it was understood that the right to political representation was linked to participation in the military opposition to British rule. They stated that their claim was 'based on the risks women took, equally with the men, to have the Irish Republic established'. There was no demand for the principle of natural justice to apply. Women had fought alongside men for the establishment of the Republic and their argument upheld the link between the bearing of arms and the right of citizenship. Of course, that might have been no more than a strategic calculation. Of perhaps more significance was the warning of the necessity of having the 'organised co-operation' of women 'in the further struggle to free

Ireland and the advantage of having their ideas on many social problems likely to arise in the near future'. An underlying assertion of gender equity can be discerned here.

None of these arguments for equality of status convinced the men. After a further three months of fruitless persuasion, a delegation of senior republican women to Sinn Féin offices finally extracted a promise that four women could be co-opted onto the executive. None were to represent any organisation other than Sinn Féin. Cumann na mBan, an expression of the aspirations of many republican women, remained excluded, despite the ambiguity surrounding male membership of Sinn Féin and the Volunteers.

The eventual co-option of female representation was highly significant, enabling an executive motion on the issue of female equality, framed by the women and spoken by them, to be put to the Sinn Féin Convention in October. The League had also hoped that this gathering of Sinn Féin delegates from all over the country would provide an opportunity to establish an all-Ireland organisation of women. The difficulties in persuading local Sinn Féin branches to take seriously their female members was evident in the attendance figures: out of 1,000 delegates, only 12 were women. Agreement on the proposal that 'the equality of men and women in this organisation be emphasised in all speeches and leaflets' was a triumph under the circumstances, although the formation of a women's organisation proved impossible.[28]

Contributions to the debate on female equality revealed a difference in conceptions of women's role. Dr Kathleen Lynn, who had served as medical officer for the Citizen Army during the Rising, argued for women's superior moral probity:

> We see all around us a system rotten with corruption and intrigue. If women have their place it will be much easier to keep it honest and open and straight. There would have been no Easter Week had it not been for the women who urged the men to take action boldly.

In contrast, Jenny Wyse Power, who had not taken part in the rising, rejected any suggestion of female superiority:

> I think we are all clearly satisfied that the same status must be given to women as to men in Ireland. I do not agree with what Dr Lynn said, that only for the women of Ireland you would have no Easter Week. The women cheered and encouraged the fighting, but the men went out and fought.

Sean T. O'Kelly expressed the views of many men in disclaiming any culpability for women's unequal status. British rule had ensured that they had so far been powerless on the matter. However, as he argued, 'our Gaelic civilisation' would only be restored if 'the full status of our women' was restored, one could conclude that the general attitude of delegates did support a greater integration of women into public life.

Four women were elected onto the 1917 Sinn Féin executive and over time considerable numbers of women were co-opted onto the various organisations established by Sinn Féin as part of its developing resistance to British rule. This was partly a response to pressure from women, but it was also a pragmatic response to the hazards of well-known IRA men undertaking political roles that made them vulnerable to arrest.

Cumann na mBan, militarism and suffrage

When the War of Independence began, deteriorating conditions made it impossible for the League of Women Delegates to continue. Its final meeting took place in January 1919. Their last concerns had been to pressurise Sinn Féin to include more women as candidates for election and to organise classes in public speaking in order to encourage more women to put forward their names. There was an evident assumption amongst the wider nationalist community that women (unless they demonstrated to the contrary) would continue in the role of heroic subordinate. In the general election of 1918 Constance Markievicz and Winifred Carney were the sole female candidates. Both had proved their credentials by bearing arms for the Republic. Kathleen Clarke, imprisoned in Holloway Jail, had wanted to be selected as a candidate. As a 'patriot widow' she had, like Matilda Tone before her, 'acquired authority to venture ... in the public sphere',[29] only to discover that she was a victim of internal machinations, displaced by a more desirable male candidate.[30] Hanna Sheehy-Skeffington, who also wanted to stand in the first election where women had the vote, discovered that the only constituencies offered to her were ones where Sinn Féin had no chance of success.[31] Six women were elected to the Second Dáil in May 1921, but the improvement was marginal. Tom Garvin's assessment of these elections makes plain the reason, 'the selection itself was made from lists of proposed candidates sent up from the constituencies by local Sinn Féin branches, often controlled by the local IRA; the nomination was commonly in gift of the local IRA leader'.[32]

Cumann na mBan, emboldened by the 1916 Proclamation, altered its constitution. It now committed itself to 'arming and equipping the men and women of Ireland' and to ensuring that members followed 'the policy of the Republican Proclamation by seeing that women take up their proper position in the life of the nation'.[33] Constance Markievicz was elected President. From this point onwards she occupied the dual role of Sinn Féin politician and leading representative of resurgent Irish womanhood. Considerable tensions shaped her relations with male colleagues. After she was appointed Minister for Labour, Kathleen Clarke asked how she had managed this, 'as I had noticed that the present leaders were not over-eager to put women into places of honour or power'. For Clarke, women had earned the right, as well as the men had, 'having responded to every call made upon them throughout the struggle for freedom'. Markievicz replied that 'she had had to bully them' through threatening to go over to the Labour Party.[34] Her demotion from the Cabinet, following restructuring during the period of the Truce in July 1921, symbolised the later exclusion of women from decision-making.

The ambiguity inherent in how women were regarded as participants was encapsulated in the Sinn Féin election address of 1918. In emotionally-calculated prose, women able for the first time to vote found themselves, in the public space of politics, cast both as symbols and as saviours of the nation. They were women who would 'stand by their tortured sister Rosaleen', that 'mystical woman in captivity' who had provided inspiration for generations of nationalist poets. The reasons advanced for women voting for Sinn Féin ranged from a traditional endorsement of their role as transmitters of national culture, to an implicit promise that active support now would receive future rewards:

> We appeal to the women voters all over Ireland to vote with Sinn Féin because the physical safety of the race depends upon our immediate freedom; because Sinn Féin carries on the tradition of independence which, thanks to the Gaelic Mother still lives in Ireland; because in every generation Irish women have played a noble part in the struggle for freedom; because finally as in the past, so in the future the womenfolk of the Gael shall have a high place in the Councils of a freed Gaelic nation.[35]

When Sinn Féin urged the electorate to 'vote as Mrs Pearse will vote', there was an emphasis upon nationalist women in the role of 'bereaved mother', rather than as wives who had sacrificed their sexual partners in defence of the nation.[36] These competing discourses were significant. Women in the leadership of the movement resisted attempts to lessen their status as independent individuals. Those who

were widows assumed an agency previously unattainable and latent
abilities became manifest. Aine Ceannt, an Easter Week widow and
leading figure in the League of Women Delegates, was appointed
Secretary to the Children's Relief Association of the White Cross. In
a preface to Crissie Doyle's *Women in Ancient and Modern Ireland* (published the year after the Rising), she had written of a 'glorious past'
where women had taken 'their rightful place in Arts, Literature,
Legislation and even in the making of War'.[37] A totality of future
interests and influences was expressed in unambiguous terms.

In rural Ireland, women struggled to establish their right to participate in the different organisations of the republican movement as
they continued to find themselves directed to their local Cumann na
mBan and away from Sinn Féin. In 1922 the *Freeman's Journal*
declared 'there is no sex bar in Sinn Féin, and women are on exactly
the same terms as men'. In explaining why few, if any, of the women
delegates to the 1922 Ard Fheis were from country clubs, the newspaper too readily proffered the explanation that 'sex antagonism' was
not the case. The reality of daily life meant that 'farmers' wives and
daughters have to work too hard and continuously on the farms to
have time for politics'.[38] The most plausible explanation, as Hanna
Sheehy-Skeffington in her capacity as Sinn Féin Director of
Organisation acknowledged, was that sex antagonism *was* a factor.
Sinn Féin branches did not welcome women. Her instructions for the
period 1921–2 confronted the difficulties:

> An impression exists in some districts that membership of Cumainn is con-
> fined to men. This is a mistake and every effort should be made to secure [sic]
> that women shall not only be on the roll of members, but take an active share
> in the work of Cumainn and the Sinn Féin movement generally.[39]

For their part, Cumann na mBan activists resented being regarded
as a Sinn Féin women's club. They were part of the military section
of the nationalist movement and young militants within it pressed
hard, although unsuccessfully, for the adoption of a wholly military-
style organisation, with a command structure modelled on that of the
Volunteers. It would have resulted in greater operational autonomy, at
the expense of harmonious working relations with their male counterparts. A desire to participate on a more equal basis with their male
comrades undoubtedly widened their sphere of activities far beyond
the conventional 'bandage rolling' of the early years, but could this, as
claimed by Marie Coleman, be said to have 'revolutionised the role of
women in the republican movement'?[40] Peter Hart believes the

evidence demonstrates that Cumann na mBan 'did not apparently feel belittled or marginalized',[41] despite testimony from many of their male comrades which revealed a conception of women's role as little more than one of 'helping' the men. Sarah Benton, critical of women's participation in a military movement, argues that 'The abandonment of women's interests is the price women had to pay for the right to belong'.[42] The evidence surely is that their experience gave them the confidence to articulate their demands. By 1921 the nationalist discourse was heavily militarised. The polling booths had elected those regarded as the best of the fighting men. In order to prove their credentials, nationalist women found themselves asserting their militant capabilities, arguing that they had earned the right to vote and to stand for election because they had undertaken a full part in the struggle.

An important indicator of women's continued efforts to maintain a voice in political life is evident in the concerted attempt to extend the franchise to women between the ages of 21 and 30. After the vote on the Treaty had been taken in the Dáil, Mrs Kate O'Callaghan presented a Bill on the franchise issue, arguing that the Treaty could not be put to the people until this was agreed. Representatives from the different suffrage societies still in existence petitioned the Dáil to vote on their behalf. As a past member of a suffrage society, O'Callaghan claimed a continuing commitment to the welfare of women, reinforcing her plea for equality with a reminder that women 'did their own part in the war during the last five years'. Having taken their share in the dangers, young women had 'purchased their right to the franchise and they have purchased their right to a say in this all-important question before the country'. The slippage in argument from a general principle of individual rights to one that linked participation in war with the right to the franchise is evidence that these were republican women, not suffragists, who were now fighting for their rights. This is seen too in the contribution of Constance Markievicz, who began with a denunciation of 'one of the crying wrongs of the world, that women, because of their sex, should be debarred from any position or any right', before changing ground to the argument that participation in war had conferred upon women the rights of citizenship: 'Today, I would appeal here to the men of the IRA more than to any of the other men to see that justice is done to these young women and young girls who took a man's part in the terror'.[43]

Through support for the military campaign against British rule, women had become the idealised republican citizens. In the process, they had transformed themselves. They had taken a 'man's part', and consequently had earned the right to be treated as equals. To her sister, the feminist Eva Gore-Booth, Markievicz was convinced that women's role in the War of Independence had proved a turning point. Their consciousness of their capabilities had altered and they found their lack of vote 'humiliating. ... They say they must have a say as to the Treaty, and that if they are good enough to take part in the fight, they are good enough to vote'.[44] Although the franchise was extended eventually to women over the age of 21, this was not done until after the Treaty had been voted upon, for fear that women would 'torpedo' the Treaty by voting against. After all, Cumann na mBan had been the first organisation to declare its rejection.[45]

Returning to the private sphere

A small group of women, associated with the feminist movement that had existed prior to 1914, were involved in local government in the early years of the new state. While some accepted the Treaty, at least initially, all were to become critical of the Free State's policies regarding women. Diversity in terms of political allegiances existed alongside a fundamental unity on the right of Irish women to full citizenship. As hostility towards female activism intensified, solidarity based upon necessity developed between the different female organisations.

In the aftermath of the Civil War, women became convenient scapegoats for their former male colleagues, appalled by the enormity of that war of 'brother against brother'. P. S. O'Hegarty spoke for many in government when he wrote of 'the furies' who had been turned into 'unlovely, destructive-minded, arid begetters of violence' by the revolution.[46] With women in political power, claimed O'Hegarty, 'there would be no more peace'. The consequence was, as Valiulis has said, that a negative perception was translated into legislation in 'an effort on the part of successive Free State governments to define women out of politics'.[47] Those in the male leadership who had proven unwilling to allow equal participation during the War of Independence were, once in government, vociferous advocates of measures designed to return women to the private sphere. Women's participation as justices in the Republican Courts had been a signifier of the egalitarian credentials of republicans, yet by 1924 the Cosgrave government had introduced legislation to restrict their right to serve on juries. In 1932, when the losing side in the Civil War came to power, there was considerable agreement between pro- and anti-Treatyites that women's primary role should be that of wife and mother. De Valera, in a telling moment, eulogised Mrs Pearse at her funeral in 1932; but stated that but for the fame of her sons, her 'modesty would have kept her out of the public eye'. Once again women could be no more than 'a living vessel through which the dead may speak'.[48] His constitution in 1937 explicitly defined women's contribution to the state solely in terms of hearth and home. The Irish revolution had come full circle. Despite the valiant efforts of women to claim agency for themselves, the public world and mainstream nationalism were as heavily gendered as they had been prior to the First World War.

Notes

1. N. Connolly, 'Women's Part in the Revolutionary Struggle', in M. Ward (ed.), *In their Own Voice* (Dublin, 1995), pp. 155–6.
2. L. Ryan, 'Negotiating Modernity and Tradition: Newspaper Debates on the "Modern Girl" in the Irish Free State', *Journal of Gender Studies*, VII, 2 (1998), pp. 181–97.
3. T. Garvin, *1922: The Birth of Irish Democracy* (Dublin, 1996), p. 99.
4. M. Cohen and N. J. Curtin (eds), *Reclaiming Gender: Transgressive Identities in Modern Ireland* (Basingstoke, 1999), pp. 1–9.
5. L. Kerber, 'Military Obligation and Citizenship in the Construction of National Citizenship in the United States', unpublished paper presented to the conference 'Gendered Nations: Nationalisms and Gender Order in the Long 19th Century', Berlin, March 1998.
6. N. J. Curtin, 'Matilda Tone and Virtuous Republican Femininity', in D. Keogh and N. Furlong (eds), *Women of 1798* (Dublin, 1998), pp. 31–4.
7. C. Hall, 'The 1832 Reform Act', in I. Blom, K. Hagemann and C. Hall (eds), *Gendered Nations: Nationalisms and Gender Order in the Long Nineteenth Century* (Berg, 2000), p. 117.
8. H. Sheehy-Skeffington, 'Nationalism and Feminism', *Bean na hÉireann*, 1909, in Ward, *Own Voice*, p. 33.
9. C. Markievicz, 'Women, Ideals and the Nation', 1909, in Ward, *Own Voice*, pp. 31–2.
10. Ibid., p. 29.
11. Southwoman, 'To the Young Women of Ireland', *Irish Freedom*, Nov. 1913, in Ward, *Own Voice*, pp. 35–6.
12. Quoted in M. Luddy, *Hanna Sheehy-Skeffington* (Dublin, 1995), p. 26.
13. H. Sheehy-Skeffington to L. Bennett, undated fragment, NLI, ms. 24 134. For further discussion on this, see M. Ward, 'Nationalism, Pacifism, Internationalism: Louie Bennett, Hanna Sheehy-Skeffington and the Problems of "Defining Feminism"', in A. Bradley and M. G. Valiulis (eds), *Gender and Sexuality in Modern Ireland* (Amherst, MA, 1997).

14. M. Ward, *Unmanageable Revolutionaries: Women and Irish Nationalism* (London, 1983), p. 91.
15. M. Condren, 'Work-in-progress: Sacrifice and Political Legitimation: the Production of a Gendered Social Order', *Journal of Women's History*, VI, 1, p. 167.
16. C. de Brun, *Irish Volunteer*, 4 Apr. 1914, in Ward, *Own Voice*, p. 37.
17. Kathleen Clarke, *Revolutionary Woman: Kathleen Clarke, 1878–1972, An Autobiography*, ed. H. Litton (Dublin, 1991), p. 78.
18. Curtin, 'Matilda Tone', p. 45.
19. M. Ward, *Hanna Sheehy-Skeffington: A Life* (Cork, 1997), p. 154.
20. M. G. Valiulis, ' "Free Women in a Free Nation": Nationalist Feminist Expectations for Independence', in B. Farrell (ed.), *The Creation of the Dáil* (Dublin, 1994), p. 82.
21. M. Skinnider, 'Doing my Bit for Ireland', in Ward, *Own Voice*, p. 69.
22. Condren, 'Work-in-progress', p. 172.
23. D. Fitzpatrick, *Politics and Irish Life, 1913–1921* (Cork, 1998), p. 122.
24. M. Coleman, ' "They also served": the Role of Cumann na mBan in the War of Independence – the evidence from County Longford', *Pages: Arts Postgraduate Research in Progress*, V (University College, Dublin, 1998), p. 33.
25. Ibid., p. 34.
26. M. MacSwiney, in Dáil Éireann Private Session (17 Dec. 1921), in Ward, *Own Voice*, p. 113.
27. Minute book of Cumann na Teachtaire (League of Women Delegates), NLI, ms. 21 194. For further details see Margaret Ward, 'The League of Women Delegates and Sinn Féin', *History Ireland*, 4, 3 (Autumn 1996), pp. 37–41.
28. Minutes of the 1917 Sinn Féin Convention, NLI, ms. 21 523.
29. Curtin, 'Matilda Tone', p. 45.
30. Clarke, *Revolutionary Woman*, p. 164.
31. Ward, *Sheehy-Skeffington*, p. 226.
32. T. Garvin, *Nationalist Revolutionaries in Ireland, 1850–1928* (Oxford, 1987), p. 145.
33. Ward, *Unmanageable Revolutionaries*, pp. 126–7.
34. Clarke, *Revolutionary Woman*, p. 170.
35. Sinn Féin, *An Appeal to the Women of Ireland*, 1918, in Ward, *Own Voice*, pp. 78–9.
36. A point made by S. Benton, 'Women Disarmed: the Militarization of Politics in Ireland, 1913–23', in *Feminist Review*, 50, p. 161.
37. C. M. Doyle, *Women in Ancient and Modern Ireland* (Kilkenny, 1917), p. 4.
38. Quoted in Garvin, *1922*, p. 99.
39. Ward, *Sheehy-Skeffington*, pp. 230–1.
40. Coleman, ' "They also served" ', p. 40.
41. P. Hart, *The IRA and its Enemies* (Oxford, 1998), p. 257.

42. Benton 'Women Disarmed', p. 169.
43. For women's contribution to the Treaty debate and the franchise question, see Ward, *Own Voice*, pp. 111–22.
44. Ibid., p. 122.
45. Ward, *Unmanageable Revolutionaries*, p. 175.
46. P. S. O'Hegarty, *The Victory of Sinn Féin* (Dublin, 1924), p. 105.
47. Valiulis, ' "Free Women" ', p. 86.
48. M. G. Valiulis, 'Neither Feminist nor Flapper: the Ecclesiastical Construction of the Ideal Irish Woman', in M. O'Dowd and S. Wichert (eds), *Chattel, Servant or Citizen* (Belfast, 1995), pp. 169–70.

12

Commemoration: 'Shows and stunts are all that is the thing now' – the Revolution Remembered, 1923–52

Anne Dolan

Fighting stopped on 24 May 1923; this chapter begins on the 25th. Allowance is made for the years prior to 1916; they have purpose, give context, maybe even cause for the changes that followed. The years after 1923 are different. Cut adrift as the 'Free State', as 'Independent Ireland', they seem irrelevant to the revolution that created them; the work of another conference, another book, 1916–23, 1923–32 and so on: like Mussolini's trains our history always seems to run on time.

The nature of the Irish revolution means nothing without consideration of the nature of Irish revolutionaries. To stop because the fighting stopped takes too much for granted. Stopping assumes that revolutions remain unchanged; that they stay untouched and untarnished until a clutch of historians trouble themselves to muse. It cannot be assumed that on a given date revolutionaries just stop being revolutionary. It is not a disease cured simply by the cessation of violence, nor a subject grown bland because the guns have been hidden away. After 24 May 1923, revolution is possibly at its most revolutionary for it is then that the manipulation, the interpretation begins.

It is the nature of revolution to evolve: it is the nature of revolutionaries, particularly those divided by civil war, to claim it and abuse it, even to fight to belong to it. This chapter is about one side's memory of revolution; about the history of one monument to the revolutionary dead.

In August 1923, the Free State Government erected a 40-foot cross on the lawn of Leinster House, the seat of Parliament, to mark the first anniversaries of the deaths of President Arthur Griffith and General Michael Collins. Crowds watched the lengthy pageant, the arrival of ministers and dignitaries. Doubtless they were impressed by the marching bands, the armoured cars, the fighter planes; by the swagger of what was called the 'Bothar Buadh' parade, 'the Road to Victory' that sounded with every step that this was triumph and strength and stability. It was a pageant of power and independence; it was a celebration of republican defeat.

But the monument was a sham. Made of wood and plaster and covered in cement, its medallion portraits of the two dead men were merely painted to look bronze. By December 1923, the paint had already started to peel. Unveiled 14 days before polling in the state's second general election, it had begun to show signs of wear just like any other forgotten election poster.

Like London's Cenotaph, the monument on Leinster Lawn was to be a short-lived centrepiece of a victory march; sincerity would replace it with something more permanent as soon as possible. But in Dublin's case minds were changed for different reasons; there was none of the popular regard that altered London's opinion of Lutyens' evocative work.[1] 'A monument of the very lightest structure ... to remain in position for only a short time' became instead 'a structure sufficiently durable to withstand climatic conditions for some years'.[2] 1923 promised the highest honour of the state. By 1939, the cross teetered 'one foot out of the perpendicular' and prey to the whims of the next gust of wind.[3] Seven years of Fianna Fáil power cannot really be blamed. Cumann na nGaedheal had had nine years to keep their promise.

Civil war's debt was a genuine excuse but penury's pleas make a rather hollow ring when £25,000 was allotted to the care of British military graves that held the bodies of 1919–21's enemies, when £50,000 went to the commemoration of the Great War dead at Islandbridge.[4] It would be nice, but a little naive, to believe that this National War Memorial was funded by hearts sorrowing for the men who had died for the rights of small nations. However, a government that feared the shadow that a Great War memorial would cast from the once mooted Merrion Square site on to Leinster House and possibly on to the Cenotaph, did not make such donations.

Vice-President Kevin O'Higgins' comments in the Dáil were proof of that:

> You have a square here, confronting the seat of the Government of the country. ... I say that any intelligent visitor, not particularly versed in the history of the country, would be entitled to conclude that the origins of this State were connected with that park and the memorial in that park was connected with the lives that were lost in the Great War in France, Belgium, Gallipoli and so on. That is not the position. The State has other origins, and because it has other origins I do not wish to see it suggested, in stone or otherwise, that it has that origin.[5]

O'Higgins' two brothers had fought in the Great War; he had insisted on laying a wreath at the Cenotaph in London when President W. T. Cosgrave did not attend.[6] He was possibly more sympathetic than most in the Dáil to the War Memorial cause. The more volatile outside the Dáil, were unquestionably worse. Yet even he could still utter these words. He could utter them because even the seemingly mild-mannered Cumann na nGaedhealers were dissatisfied, complaining that too 'many Irishmen are showing their admiration of the late Earl of Ypres and his supporters in the English Army'.[7] But the conveniently remote Islandbridge site was also a type of appeasement, a generous kind of thank you to Andrew Jameson and Henry Guinness, one a leading member of the Memorial Committee and, more importantly, director and governor of the Bank of Ireland, respectively. The government remembered the bank's loans of £100,000 a fortnight, of £2,750,000 that had kept the desperate Free State afloat in 1922.[8] Judging from O'Higgins' statement, it remembered the money more, more than the men who had given their lives in 'France, Belgium, Gallipoli and so on'. When the donation was eventually made, republicanism jumped eagerly to the obvious conclusions:

> the old English Garrison, pampered and nursed by the present Free State Government, have votes; and it is through them Mr Cosgrave hopes to secure another five years in office. The secret circular from the Unionists to their fellow-Masons soliciting funds to return Mr Cosgrave at the next election, and Mr Cosgrave's grant of £50,000 out of the Irish people's money for their English Memorial Park, throws off the mask of Irish Nationality under which the members of the Free State Government have hitherto tried to deceive the Irish people in their platform utterances.[9]

On the basest of levels, the government had more to gain from Islandbridge; settlement of favours past, the prospect of favours still to come. A new Cenotaph would merely be a costly sermon to the converted.

But whatever the cost the will to build had gone. Year after year an awkward pageant returned to the rotting Cenotaph. Embarrassed by the army mutiny and the Boundary Commission, the government preferred the safety of the dominion shore to Collins' slippery stepping-stone approach.[10] Reverence at this cross only recalled just how much the professing faithful had blasphemed. In 1925 only nine out of 105 deputies bothered to come.[11] By 1926, even *An Phoblacht* was making uncomfortably apposite condemnations, denouncing the ceremony as 'a piece of political humbug as threadbare as it is shockingly out of place'.[12] But 1927 brought reprise. The murder of O'Higgins called for another show of strength, another return to the totem of Free State sacrifice. The following year added a plaque for the dead Vice-President, but there was not even a speech, just the image silently uncovered. There were too many Count Plunketts calling the ceremony 'a demonstration against the people',[13] and Fianna Fáil had assumed its thorny place in the government's side. In 1929 only four ministers and five deputies came. The President did not deign to attend.

With 1932 'official' ceremonies ended, there were no more soldiers, no more dignitaries, no more marching bands. It was possibly foolish to expect a republican government subscribe to a '*Bothar Buadha*' that celebrated its defeat in civil war, that enshrined a state it intended to dismantle. But there was no 'Cenotaph Ceremony Ban' as was writ large by *The United Irishman*. Thousands of people still witnessed a procession to the Cenotaph, thousands watched a wreath laid to the honour of the three dead men.[14] Organised by the Association of the Old Dublin Brigade IRA and held 'with the concurrence of the Oireachtas authorities', an illustrious procession made its way to the foot of the Cenotaph.[15] Former soldiers walked with relatives and a former President; apathy gone in the heightened sensibilities of opposition.

> Strange that the State you founded
> Should even by seeming, spurn you,
> Humbly we lay these flowers
> That Ireland may know we mourn you[16]

was the only message on the wreath; pique more than heartfelt emotion or distress, an ache for the pomp and circumstance that was inherent in leadership and ceremony. A Mass in every military barracks was dedicated to the memory of the three men; that never changed. It was just never public enough. They had grown used to government, had taken for granted the authority that could command an army to march. The Cenotaph was their symbol of power and victory, it ill behove them to ask permission to visit it. They may have grown tired of it, even embarrassed by it, but now it symbolised their powerlessness. The impotence of opposition made ceremony important again; the shabby monument staked their claim to the state. The dead were emotive, useful, political again.

The plans for 1933 were made early; the Blueshirts prepared.[17] Groups were to descend on Dublin in tens and twenties, in hundreds and thousands.[18] The indignity of 1932 was not to be repeated. The prospect of 30,000 Blueshirts marching Mussolini-like on the capital while the remainder targeted the towns of Ireland, did little to reassure the Fianna Fáil Government.[19] De Valera knew all about codified orders to parade; Easter 1916 must have played heavily upon his mind. By Eoin O'Duffy's own admission, the Gardaí had grown 'up in the belief, because of circumstances, that they were servants of the Government Party rather than of the State itself'.[20] They could not be trusted. With the 'eruption from the rat holes of the country of an usurping army', it had gone beyond commemoration; it was possible rebellion, promised civil war.[21] In the Blueshirts' own words, it was 'the march of a nation against Fianna Fáil'.[22]

1933 was about political chaos; it was to be the culmination of a festering collection of sporadic incidents with IRA men, of tussles at election booths and dances and cattle sales, of bigger marches to republican graves. It was anger at the election result of January 1933, when De Valera was returned with an overall majority, when the irate sister of Michael Collins, Margaret Collins-O'Driscoll, a TD for Dublin North since 1923, had failed to be re-elected. As much as she may have mourned her brother, as much as the banning of the parade may have seemed like an affront to the memory of Griffith, Collins and O'Higgins, the politicisation, the abuse of memory by the Blueshirts, and by Cumann na nGaedheal who abetted them, did more to dishonour these men than anything the supposedly demonic De Valera could have conceived. Because of Fianna Fáil 'the ceremony is denuded of meaning': there was a convenient hypocrisy in Cosgrave's hollow words.[23] He never mentioned that his own government had considered abandoning the ceremony in 1927. That the years that followed provoked nothing more than predictable Masses and marches; that they were peaceful, innocuous, inoffensive, explained what 1933 was all about.[24] As civilised as the hand over of power may have reputedly been in 1932, there were elements of pro-Treatyite support who could not countenance defeat in any form; defeat in itself, by the enemies of 1922, by the socio-economic alternatives of 1932. The dead were a means to an end, cherished and vigorously championed maybe, but still an emotive and evocative rallying cry that had come to sound sickeningly shrill.

Having become a danger to the lives of passing deputies, Fianna Fáil initiated discussions with Fine Gael about the tottering Cenotaph in July 1939. Within days the Minister for Finance instructed the OPW to submit 'a design for a permanent memorial including a cross'.[25] All was apparently peace and reconciliation; former enemies discussing a memorial to the figures that once divided them. In less than 100 words, a statement informed the press that the memorial was to be replaced; dignity tripping from these terse few words that seemed to say that civil war politics were at an end. But just as the scaffolding erected at Leinster Lawn was merely there to 'indicate that work is in hand or is contemplated',[26] there was something false about the meeting and the statement, something contradictory about Fianna Fáil's entire approach to the memorial. To begin with, the meeting between Eamon de Valera, Sean Moylan, Michael Hayes and Desmond FitzGerald was held privately. Voters were never told because cries of '77'[27] still carried too much weight at election hustings to risk the revelation. Voters had no need to know because news of collusion with the enemy over the bones of Collins, Griffith and O'Higgins would have fallen on stony ground in the Ballyseedys, at the Masses on 8 December, in the Rory O'Connor Fianna Fáil Cumann; in the extremes of Fianna Fáil, which did not share their leader's opinion of the IRA.

Although the motives for this secrecy might explain the brevity of the press statement, they do more to explain something of the nature of civil war bitterness in Ireland. Behind closed doors politicians could discuss the Civil War, ruminate over the commemoration of one side's dead. Outside, in the Dáil, in the streets, it was different; a memory to be 'burnished and polished', fostering 'the illusion that fundamental differences remained between the parties'.[28] But if politicians preserved their friendships, as Michael Hayes believes,[29] if de Valera, FitzGerald and Hayes could discuss the past, the people that they, amongst other men, had once charged with the actual fighting of the war did not have the luxury of such pliant memories. For many there was nothing but silence; the quiet return to a republican or an unmarked army plot that could never speak of horrors seen and horrors done.

But memory was not as malleable as the noble leaders might pretend. Gestures were made with one hand, then tightly reined by the other. De Valera took control. He discounted the notion of a competition for the design. That was all right for the Garden of Remembrance with its neutral promise to honour all who died for Ireland. This was Leinster Lawn, the seat of power; the men honoured were once the enemy. Nor would it be relocated; the dangerously public and popular St Stephen's Green was no place for a monument to the leaders of a Free State; the new Constitution said it was Éire after all. De Valera discussed the matter personally with the Chairman of the Board of Works, the virulently republican former Fianna Fáil minister Joseph Connolly.[30] Stipulating, deciding, de Valera presented Fine Gael with a design only after he had altered it to his own tastes.[31] Fine Gael could have its monument but only on de Valera's terms. Commemoration would be conceded but only without the clamour of ceremony, only if Fianna Fáil was seen to give and Fine Gael submissively and silently to receive.

Throughout, the Taoiseach was consistent in this apparent inconsistency. He completed Cosgrave's initiative to provide busts of Collins and Griffith for the privacy of the Taoiseach's office but stopped the state ceremony at the Cenotaph;[32] he permitted the Collins family to erect a monument over the grave of Michael Collins, but only with restrictions on the materials, the inscription, the amount spent, and the promise that there would be no public subscription, no publicity and no one present at the blessing.[33] Coogan puts it all down to bitterness, a personal paranoia that kept de Valera trembling in the shadow of Collins for the rest of his life, but this does nothing to explain the concessions, however grudging. It does not ask why a Cumann na nGaedheal government let the Cenotaph rot or why after almost ten years of power, Collins' grave was still unmarked.

Although de Valera commemorated his enemies with an asceticism that undermined the gesture, although he had to wait until the Anglo-Irish Agreement of 1938 had torn the last sentences of Collins' and Griffith's Treaty to shreds, his actions, however shaped by bitterness, defied bitterness. The decision to rebuild the Cenotaph may have been a nod in the direction of the cross-party unity which 'the Emergency' demanded, its manifest maturity a sign of statesmanship, but the decision bespoke something more than a mere accommodation of a possibly troublesome opposition. The decision seemed to encode the end of bitterness.

An anti-Treatyite government may have made its first recognition of the legitimacy of pro-Treaty memory, but ingrained in some political hearts and minds was a bias that continued to 'burnish and polish'. While any efforts to begin work on the monument were vetoed by a Department of Defence fearful of giving 'a particular advantage to an attacking body of troops', German or English,[34] certain members of Fine Gael took the opportunity to exploit the inactivity for all its political worth. P. S. Doyle, a Fine Gael TD for South Dublin, raised the matter four times in the Dáil between June 1944 and October 1947.[35] Abetted by a *Sunday Independent* article,[36] and resolutions from Dublin City Council and Fine Gael Central Branch,[37] Doyle found his greatest ally in a fellow Fine Gael TD, John A. Costello. Having put an aggressive question to the Minister for Finance, Costello was dismissively told to take the matter up with his own Chief Whip.[38] The public urgency of Doyle and Costello, their impatience with the excuses of war and finance and lack of materials, belied the real feelings and direct involvement of the Fine Gael Party, whose representatives 'did not indicate that the erection of a new Cenotaph was regarded by them … as a matter of urgency',[39] and whose leader had just sent written acceptance of the new design.[40] Costello did not heed the hidden meetings, the concessions; Fianna Fáil's rejection of a plan to site the monument on Merrion Square simply because Mulcahy 'and his colleagues were opposed to the erection of the Cenotaph on any other site than Leinster Lawn'.[41] Costello continued to play to the gallery.

Apart from acceding to Fine Gael's wish to maintain its symbolic colonisation of the seat of power, de Valera and his Cabinet made one parting bequest. On 16 September 1947 a decision was made to alter the design of the monument. Orders for 'a column or obelisk, including provision for a cross and for portrait plaques of Griffith, Collins and O'Higgins' were made.[42] A design that traditionally implied power,[43] it might, given Fine Gael's insistence on the siting, mute the associations with the party's martyrs. Art historians claim that the change was prompted by a report claiming that a Celtic cross was out of place on Leinster Lawn, and that it was no longer possible to produce such crosses to the standard of their ancient predecessors.[44] It is difficult to believe that Fianna Fáil only grasped the ramifications of an artist's misgivings eight years after its ringing endorsement of the design in 1939. The circulation of a memorandum to the Cabinet on 10 September 1947,[45] a mere six days before the decision was taken, recalling Fine Gael's affinity with the Leinster Lawn site, seems, even accounting for Fianna Fáil's appreciation of the aesthetic, a little more plausible. A petty rebuke of the opposition perhaps, but the bequest of an obelisk by a party buoyed by the success of neutrality and the satisfaction of such a public moral victory over Churchill, thwarted Fine Gael's attempt to continue to assert its own version of political legitimacy. It was an image of power and statesmanship, not mourning: 'a symbol of state authority which any Dáil could endorse'.[46]

Presented with a Dáil question from P. S. Doyle[47] and a resolution from the Cork Central Branch of Fine Gael,[48] Costello, the leader of the new inter-party Government, was reminded of what was once the urgency of his own opposition. Yet once prompted, Costello readily recalled his crusading zeal. Not to be outdone by de Valera, he insisted on handling the issue personally, answering Dáil questions and circulating memos.[49] He tussled with an indolent Finance, sending minutes 'in rather stiff terms'[50] demanding that 'that the matter should be dealt with as one of the greatest urgency at every stage'.[51] Pressed by 'several complaints regarding the delay',[52] it was the Taoiseach who met the Commissioner of the OPW, the Taoiseach who scrutinised the designs, the Taoiseach who restored the inscribed dedication which Fianna Fáil had dared, in its eagerness to neutralise the monument, to erase.[53] In truth the Cenotaph was to be Costello's monument.

Set in the centre of a re-landscaped Leinster Lawn a slender, 60-foot granite obelisk, capped by a gilt bronze flame, would stand on a circular sloping base adorned with four bronze wreaths that framed medallions of Griffith, Collins and O'Higgins and an inscription tablet bearing the words '*Do Chum Glóire Dé agus Onóra na hÉireann*' (For the glory of God and the honour of Ireland).[54] A gold inlaid cross would be the only other feature of Raymond McGrath's austere design.[55] Costello and his inter-party Cabinet promptly sanctioned the scheme: the design, the re-planning of the garden, the estimate of £20,000. Clann na Poblachta, the coalition partner that balked at Richard Mulcahy and his civil war record, now acquiesced in the honour of the men who had supposedly caused the war, forgiving, it would seem, under the guiding hand of a reputedly impartial Taoiseach. But Costello's purity is not enough to explain this peaceful concord. Sean MacBride and his republican ilk may have been moved to honour by a genuine respect for the dead men, a respect that can be traced to *Poblacht na hÉireann* obituaries of 1922,[56] to the grudging gestures of Fianna Fáil. MacBride had clearly come a long way since his days of hearty objections to a treacherous Fianna Fáil daring to commemorate Cathal Brugha. But while esteem could apparently remember what Griffith once inspired, what Collins had once achieved, it could never forgive the Richard Mulcahy of 1923. Alternatively, the Clann may have thought little of honour and esteem, capitulating instead to the whims of a stronger partner in government who insisted on including the less popular Kevin O'Higgins. Whatever the reason for the Clann's consent, the Cenotaph conspires to question Costello, at least Costello as the man 'untainted by civil war memories'.[57]

Between the acceptance of the design on 26 July 1948 and the completion of the monument in October 1950, Costello had shown a degree of haste that, with regard to the Cenotaph, could only be considered indecent. On every level the urgency bespoke purpose: 16 years of Fianna Fáil and de Valera, 16 years scavenging in a political wilderness that yielded nothing more than the futility of Blueshirtism, had taken its toll on Fine Gael. Rising like a trophy of power, the Cenotaph bellowed Fine Gael's return; the shout all the louder because of the indignity of coalition. Powerful parties build monuments, in this case with a haste that hoped Fine Gael would still be in office to reap the benefits of its completion. But if haste denoted the party's will to reassert its claims on power, the urgency also registered Costello's personal claims to power and recognition. Without the baggage of 1916 and reprieved executions, without the mystery or the provocation of de Valera, the relatively anonymous and uncontroversial Costello had to manufacture tangible bequests to the nation. He left a monument which associated him with a time of power and opportunity, a monument that linked his name with the oft spoken greats of more exciting years who shared his distinction of defeating de Valera. But even if the Cenotaph was not erected out of a sense of inferiority and personal aggrandisement, Costello's urgency links the monument to his other great bequest to the nation: the declaration of a Republic.

In September 1948, the leader of Fine Gael, the supposedly conservative and commonwealth party, declared that Ireland would become a republic. In the months that followed he scrutinised plans, approved inscriptions, beseeched and implored for the erection of a monument to the men who had supposedly signed away the republic: to Griffith the Dual Monarchist, to O'Higgins the advocate of commonwealth. In many ways his urgency seemed to associate these men with his action, adding their imprimatur to that of the men of 1916 which the appropriation of Easter Sunday 1949 had guaranteed for his somewhat premature and contentious declaration. Here at last was the Republic, declared by a Fine Gael man, a man of the 'party' of Griffith, Collins and O'Higgins. Now they could be republicans again instead of 'traitors' and 'Free Staters'; only now appropriately honoured with their permanent memorial, which had fittingly relegated the statue of Prince Albert with a truly republican zeal;[58] only now recognised as the men who had bequeathed the freedom to achieve this long-awaited freedom.

Spurious though the connection may be between the declaration of
the Republic and the erection of this beleaguered monument, a question mark over Costello as the man 'untainted' by civil war bitterness
remains. While the apparent vindication of his predecessors raises a ten-
tative doubt, other questions asked both in and outside the Dáil evoke
greater misgivings. Notwithstanding a quibble as to the pagan origins
of the obelisk design, quickly dissipated by a photograph of the Pope in
close proximity to the obelisk in St Peter's Square,[59] and an objection
made by Con Lehane, a Clann na Poblachta TD and one-time IRA
man, to the extravagance of £20,000 when 'want and destitution could
still be found in many places in Dublin',[60] bitterness was the main
charge. The first assault was made on 2 May 1950. Sean MacEntee contrasted the activity on Leinster Lawn to the postponement of work on
the Rotunda Garden of Remembrance designated by Fianna Fáil, on
the prompting of the Old IRA, to commemorate all who died for
Ireland.[61] Encouraged by the Fianna Fáil TD, Lehane suggested that
the Cenotaph be rededicated to 'all those who gave their lives to break
the connection with England'. He was ignored, but his departing 'all
you are concerned with is instigating and maintaining bitterness' pre-
saged the tone of the exchanges which followed.[62] A debate on the
estimates for the Office of Public Works on 12 July 1950 provided a
forum for the virulence that had been incited by articles in the *Irish
Press*.[63] M. F. Kitt, Fianna Fáil TD for Galway North, provided a fitting
prologue to the onslaught of deputy Henry Colley.[64] Recalling
MacEntee's earlier theme, Kitt spoke of 'conniving' to erect a memorial to Fine Gael 'leaders' while 'forgetting the men who died for the
Republic',[65] grist to a mill which Colley would grind with all the pas-
sion of 1922. Angered by the erection of a temporary infants' clinic on
the site of the proposed Garden of Remembrance, Colley began:

> It has surely come to a pretty pass if we have to hide behind infants' swaddling
> clothes to protect ourselves when we are trying to let down the memory
> of the 1916 men … there has been no hesitation about the memorial on
> Leinster Lawn to the founders of a partitioned State while the memorial
> to the real founders of the State, the 1916 men, about whom there should be
> no questions whatever has been deferred, to use the Parliamentary Secretary's
> expression. … The erection of the Cenotaph is going ahead. Immediately the
> Government took office they saw to that. In fact it looks like a deliberate
> attempt to try to recreate the whole civil war spirit.[66]

Next he attacked the republicanism of Clann na Poblachta; the shame of
'people who protested to be staunch republicans' erecting monuments

to 'the founders of a partitioned State'.[67] Bowing out with the charge of extravagance, he compared the original Fianna Fáil provision of £2,700 for the monument with the £30,000 to £35,000 figure which various deputies and press articles now associated with the Cenotaph.[68] Taking Colley's place, Lehane rose and began his epilogue – a plague on both your houses:

> I deplore that decision [to erect the Cenotaph] because the memorial is purely sectional in its significance, erected to the three leaders of one Party in the British-engineered civil war. I deplore the decision because it is calculated to recreate the bitterness engendered by that civil war. ... Unfortunately, on too many occasions from members of the Party opposite [Fianna Fáil] have we seen deliberate attempts to provoke that bitterness, to maintain it and to intensify it. I deplore the decision, and I think the Government by that decision have, to an extent, played into the hands of those sections of the Fianna Fáil Party who realise that they have no political existence other than that based on the bitterness they can create.[69]

Questioning the sincerity of Fianna Fáil opposition in the light of the party's decision to erect the Cenotaph while in power, Lehane's pleas to abandon past bitterness, naïvely heralded the Taoiseach's more realistic response.

Without mention of the extravagance of his own party bias or the hospital building programmes that his government repeatedly postponed, Costello stressed that he was just innocently carrying out plans initiated by the previous Fianna Fáil Government.[70] Virtuous, he vigorously renounced bitterness: 'So far from endeavouring in any way to foment the feelings or the spirit of the civil war or to revive bitterness, the whole policy of this Government, and the real reason for its foundation, has been to put an end to that bitterness and to this personal strife'.[71] While Richard Mulcahy might have had something else to say about this motley union of the dissatisfied, convened to dethrone de Valera, the Taoiseach had politely pointed out what Lehane had been trying to say. Colley, while undoubtedly aggrieved by the delay of the Garden of Remembrance, was playing politics with the Garden and the Cenotaph. He was 'burnishing and polishing' the bitterness to the detriment of the maverick Dr Noël Browne, whose temporary infant care units erected on the precious Rotunda Gardens were undoubtedly causing dead republicans everywhere to spin in their unsettled graves.

Following an unsuccessful attempt by Colley to engage the Taoiseach in a second round two days later, MacEntee stepped into the breach. A bastion of apparent magnanimity, he spoke of the good faith of

Griffith, Collins and O'Higgins, of how the 'good they did this country entitles their memory to our honour and respect', of how his party
sanctioned the erection of the memorial because the party was big
enough to recognise that:

> the Irish people and the Irish nation is one, and that there has to be an ele-
> ment of give and take in these matters; so that what is dear to one heart, not
> so dear to another, nevertheless might be realised in order to preserve the
> essential unity of our nation. It was in that spirit that men whose brothers had
> been done to death, that men who had been deprived of the right to earn a
> livelihood because they would not take the test under the old Free State
> Constitution, decided to give effect... to the decision of the Cumann na
> nGaedheal Government which they had displaced in 1932.[72]

With the simple 'it is regrettable... that our successors were not
inspired with the same feelings',[73] MacEntee advanced his charge for
the high moral ground. In a haze of Pearses, Brughas and conjured
images of an idyllic Garden of Remembrance where the young might
contemplate the cost of their freedom, he bemoaned the precedence
that the Cenotaph had taken over the Memorial Garden 'to the men
who had died faithful to the Republic'.[74] That the Garden had been
overlooked by Fianna Fáil from 1935 to 1948 seemed to have slipped
the deputy's mind. Because Fine Gael was not being seen to return the
favour of Fianna Fáil's grudging concession of the Cenotaph, because
it had allowed Noël Browne to put sick children before dead republicans, the party was pursuing the 'republican dead with malevolent
hatred even beyond the grave'.[75] But Sean MacEntee did 'not wish to
create any bitterness'. He spoke not as a politician, 'not because we
want to make Party political capital out of this', but as a 'friend' and a
'comrade' of the republican dead; 'the men with whom we had chat-
ted and joked'.[76] Yet whoever he was pretending to be, MacEntee was
ignored. Nothing was said, just the damning, and still fitting, indict-
ment of deputy Lehane: 'I do not think I ever listened to anything so
nauseatingly dishonest in all my life.'[77]

Other voices were raised. Republican 'friends' and 'comrades'
undoubtedly biased but free of the slur of party politics, which
maligned the sincerity of MacEntee's objections, gathered and issued
resolutions. To the veterans of the Nortons Malthouse Garrison (1922)
the Cenotaph was a 'deliberate attempt to distort history', a danger to
unity in the days ahead.[78] The Committee of the Four Courts Garrison
and the National Executive meeting of the IRA Veterans' Association
decried the party political monument, calling for the grounds of the
'People's Parliament' to be adorned with a memorial to the men who

had died for the republic.[79] None were as critical as T. P. Murphy, a Mayo man who wrote to the editor of the *Irish Press*. Attacking the Taoiseach for 'simulating sweet reasonableness' and for playing upon the 'decency and propriety' of Fianna Fáil, he accused the Cenotaph and its builders of injuring the memory of the republican dead by honouring the two men 'whose names … spell the last act of a tragedy for Ireland'.[80] All spoke with the zeal of bias, some suggesting the inclusion of the men 'who so nobly carried on the fight to 1947', men who had conspired against the law of the state since the banning of the IRA. All spoke of unity, but a unity based on submerging Free State memory. While the *Irish Times* praised the good example of party leaders on both sides of the Dáil, these perhaps more sincere reactions vindicated the article's other conclusion.[81] For many of the men who had fought in the Civil War, 30 years was still a short time in the memory of a nation.

On 9 July 1952, Fine Gael's Liam Cosgrave asked the new Fianna Fáil Minister for Finance when the Cenotaph was due to be completed.[82] The terse response, that work had been finished since October 1950 when Cosgrave's own party was in power, was somehow a fitting epilogue to the history of this troubled monument. None of the deputies who had so eagerly brandished names of martyrs and claims of honour and dishonour could even bother to look out of the window of their own parliament building. The chance to play politics had passed.

Of the Cenotaph, Maud Griffith wrote in 1924: 'shows and stunts are all that is the thing now'.[83] Two years after her husband Arthur's death the government had not paid the £5 10s it had taken to bury him; when it did, departments quibbled over who should bear the pitiable cost.[84] In 1925 she finally received the deeds to his unmarked grave. She had to threaten to exhume his body. Maud Griffith had come to know something of the nature of revolution.

After 1923 commemoration was war by other means. Fianna Fáil, Cumann na nGaedheal and Fine Gael had repeatedly gone to the polls with more than a glorified encore of the Treaty debates, but in Leinster House civil war and revolution were the reliable retorts in their limited repertoires. Although they knew that in time 'some 200,000 people are on the register who never saw a Tan, never lived under the Cosgrave regime and who don't care one damn about where anyone was in '16, '22 or '39',[85] they preferred not to heed it. They could bait each other at convenience's command with the vehemence of 1922, with the names and the massacres of men many never even knew.

It is the nature of revolutionaries to reinvent their revolution, and the dead were 'prostituted to the polemics of the present, and the gravediggers drag[ged] out the corpses with the sole purpose of hawking them around present battlefields'.[86]

Notes

1. J. Winter, *Sites of Memory Sites of Mourning: The Great War in European Cultural History* (Cambridge, 1996), pp. 103–4.
2. Office of Public Works (OPW) to Finance, 4 June 1924, NA, DF (Dept. of Finance), 930.
3. Report by J. Connolly, OPW, submitted to government, 28 May 1939, NA, S5734a.
4. Departmental memorandum (May, 1931), NA, DF S004/0013/24.
5. Dáil Éireann *Proceedings* (29 Mar. 1927).
6. NA, DF S200/0024/26; NA, S3370a. Cosgrave did not attend as he felt his role in the 1916 Rising might cause offence. K. Jeffery, *Ireland and the Great War* (Cambridge, 2000), pp. 125–6.
7. John Sweetman, to the 'Government', 10 Aug. 1925, NA, S4156.
8. R. Fanning, *The Irish Department of Finance* (Dublin, 1978), pp. 84–7.
9. *The Republican File*, 9 Jan. 1932.
10. The Boundary Commission was established by the Treaty to review the boundary between North and South. After a leak to the press of its recommendations that some southern territory be ceded to the North, its final report was set aside and the existing boundary was left unaltered.
11. *An Phoblacht*, 21 Aug. 1925.
12. *An Phoblacht*, 27 Aug. 1926.
13. *Kerry News*, 22 Aug. 1927.
14. *Irish Times*, 22 Aug. 1932.
15. NA, S5734E, 99/1/35.
16. *Irish Press*, 22 Aug. 1932.
17. The first announcement was made in the *United Irishmen*, 13 May 1933.
18. *The United Irishman*, 3, 10 and 17 June 1933; 15, 8 and 29 July 1933; *The Blueshirt*, 5 Aug. 1933.
19. M. Cronin, *The Blueshirts and Irish Politics* (Dublin, 1997), p. 22.
20. Memo from General Eoin O'Duffy, Commissioner of the Garda Síochána to the government, 1931, UCDAD, P24/488.
21. *Catholic Bulletin*, XXIII, 2 (Feb. 1933), p. 96.
22. *The United Irishman*, 19 Aug. 1933.
23. *Connaught Telegraph*, 19 Aug. 1933.
24. Parades were held by Blueshirts in 1934 and 1935.
25. Minister for Finance to OPW, 31 July 1939, NA, S5734a.
26. P. J. Raftery, Assistant Secretary, OPW, to the Secretary, Ministry for Finance, 11 Aug. 1939, ibid.
27. '77', the number of republicans executed during the Civil War, was often used as a catch-cry in the Dáil and during campaigns.

28. J. J. Lee, *Ireland, 1912–1985* (Cambridge, 1989), p. 69.
29. M. Hayes, 'Dáil Éireann and the Irish Civil War', *Studies*, LVIII (Spring 1969), p. 22.
30. Maurice Moynihan to the Minister for Finance, 31 July 1939, NA, S5734a.
31. De Valera reduced H. G. Leask's three-panelled design for a limestone monument to 20 feet 9 inches. The Taoiseach also stipulated the removal of the lettering. Costs were estimated at £2,700. Report by H. G. Leask, 19 Aug. 1940; memo of the meeting between J. Connolly, OPW and de Valera, 24 May 1940, NA, S5734a.
32. J. Hill, *Irish Public Sculpture* (Dublin, 1998), p. 153.
33. T. P. Coogan, *Michael Collins* (London, 1990), pp. 428–30.
34. Comdt. L. Ó hÉigeartaigh, Officer in Command of Defences, to T. S. C. Dagg, Department of Finance, 22 July 1940, NA, S5734a.
35. Dáil Éireann, *Proceedings* (28 June 1944); (11 Oct. 1945); (21 May 1946); (15 Oct. 1947).
36. *Sunday Independent*, 5 July 1942.
37. *Irish Independent*, 18 Sept. 1944; T. McNeill, Clerk of the City Council, to the Government Secretary, 8 Jan. 1946, NA, S5734b.
38. Dáil Éireann, *Proceedings* (28 May 1947).
39. J. E. Hanna, Department of Finance, to the Secretary of Department of an Taoiseach, 18 Feb. 1946, NA, S5734b.
40. Richard Mulcahy to an Taoiseach, 7 July 1947, ibid.
41. Memorandum for the government from the Office of the Parliamentary Secretary to an Taoiseach, 10 Sept. 1947, ibid.
42. Memorandum of Cabinet meeting, 16 Sept. 1947, ibid.
43. Hill, *Irish Public Sculpture*, p. 153.
44. Ibid.
45. Memorandum to Cabinet from the Office of the Parliamentary Secretary to an Taoiseach, 10 Sept. 1947, NA, S5734b.
46. Hill, *Irish Public Sculpture*, p. 155.
47. Dáil Éireann, *Proceedings* (12 May 1948).
48. W. G. Kennefick, Secretary, Fine Gael Cork Executive, to J. A. Costello, 3 May 1948, NA, S5734c.
49. Memorandum for the Government by Department of an Taoiseach, 5 May 1948, ibid.
50. Memo, N. S. Ó Nuallain to the Taoiseach's Secretary, 4 Feb. 1949, ibid.
51. Memo, M. Ó Muimhneachain, Taoiseach's Office, to Department of Finance, 9 Feb. 1949, ibid.
52. Secretary, Department of an Taoiseach, to Secretary, Department of Finance, 4 Feb. 1949, ibid.
53. Office of an Taoiseach to OPW, 27 Feb. 1950, ibid.
54. B. Farrell, OPW, to Department of an Taoiseach, 20 July 1949, ibid.
55. McGrath was principal architect at the OPW.
56. *Poblacht na hÉireann War News*, 39 (15 Aug. 1922); ibid., 47 (24 Aug. 1922).
57. Lee, *Ireland*, p. 299.

58. The new design for the lawn and monument required the removal of the Prince Albert statue to a less intrusive location. Department of Finance memo, 15 July 1948, NA, S5734c.
59. Hill, *Irish Public Sculpture*, p. 155.
60. Dáil Éireann, *Proceedings* (15 Dec. 1949); *Irish Times*, 23 Jan. 1950.
61. Ibid., 2 May 1950.
62. Ibid.
63. *Irish Press*, 12, 15 and 26 July 1950.
64. Fianna Fáil TD for Dublin North-East.
65. Dáil Éireann, *Proceedings* (12 July 1950).
66. Ibid.
67. Ibid.
68. Report by H. G. Leask, 19 Aug. 1940; memo of meeting between J. Connolly, OPW and E. de Valera, 24 May 1940, NA, S5734a. Files relating to the final cost are withheld. Estimates amounted to £20,000, Dáil Éireann, *Proceedings* (15 Dec. 1949).
69. Dáil Éireann, *Proceedings* (12 July 1950).
70. N. Browne, *Against the Tide* (Dublin, 1987), p. 114.
71. Dáil Éireann, *Proceedings* (12 July 1950).
72. Ibid. (14 July 1950).
73. Ibid.
74. Ibid.
75. Ibid.
76. Ibid.
77. Ibid.
78. *Irish Press*, 12 July 1950.
79. Ibid., 15 July 1950; National Executive of IRA Veterans' Association resolution, 29 July 1950, NA, S5734c.
80. *Irish Press*, 26 July 1950.
81. *Irish Times*, 15 July 1950.
82. Dáil Éireann, *Proceedings* (9 July 1952).
83. Transcript of note from M. Griffith, 10 Aug. 1924, UCDAD, P7/b/330.
84. Unsigned Finance memo (18 Aug. 1924), NA, DF S004/0013/24.
85. Fianna Fáil Head Office to S. Fitzgerald, CAI, PR/6/521.
86. *Sunday Tribune*, 25 Jan. 1998.

13

Socialism: Socialist Intellectuals and the Irish Revolution

Richard English

Writing to his London publisher about his 1933 play, *Wrack*, Peadar O'Donnell opened with typical impishness: 'Dear Mr Cape, I am glad to hear you like *Wrack*; I like it myself!' Later in the same epistle O'Donnell commented, in a slightly dismissive tone, 'I really can't say when I may have other plays – I have to break up my time a good deal to do hack work for badly paying working class journals.'[1] If his words here echo Karl Marx's lament about newspaper work ('the continual journalistic muck annoys me'),[2] then they appropriately point towards one of O'Donnell's main intellectual influences. Like James Connolly, he drew heavily on Marx, whom it appears he first encountered during the Irish revolutionary period itself. According to one close associate, somebody 'gave him Marx to read. He just could-n't get over this.'[3] And O'Donnell himself presented this period as one of intellectual awakening: 'I was absolutely flabbergasted to find how ignorant I was. I read omnivorously, day and night, attended lectures, and prepared for the road.'[4]

But in reflecting some light on O'Donnell's attitudes towards post-revolutionary intellectual work, his letter to Cape also helps to intro-duce the subject of this chapter. For the relationship between socialist intellectuals and the Irish revolution involves not only the participa-tion of such figures in the 1916–23 period, but also their subsequent (re)writing and reconstruction of those revolutionary years. My focus is primarily on what Eunan O'Halpin has recently referred to as 'the interesting though implausible proposition that revolutionary socialism and Irish republicanism were natural bedfellows'.[5] My subjects are revolutionary socialist republican intellectuals, and I will explore their engagement with the Irish revolution in three interlinked sections. These will scrutinise: first, the years of the revolution itself; secondly, the subsequent generation up until the early 1960s; and thirdly, the period from the 1960s onwards. A conclusion will discuss some of the broader implications of the material covered.

1916–23

Socialist intellectuals offered intriguing arguments to explain and justify the Irish revolution. Their thesis, put crisply, was this. The struggle between the oppressed nation (Ireland) and the oppressor nation (England) was necessarily interwoven with the struggle within Ireland between those classes oppressed under capitalism and those oppressor classes which benefited from it. England's control over Ireland had the purpose of economic exploitation. The means of such exploitation was the capitalist system; therefore, English control of Ireland ensured the sustenance of that system. Those classes in Ireland that benefited from capitalism thus had an economic imperative to support some form of subservient political connection with England; those classes that suffered under capitalism (the working classes, urban and rural) possessed an equally compelling economic motivation to be separatists. If one wanted to establish socialism in place of capitalism in Ireland then one had to end English rule; and if one wanted to end English rule then the only truly reliable forces on which to depend were those with an economic compulsion to see the struggle through: namely, the working class (James Connolly's 'incorruptible inheritors of the fight for freedom').[6] It was not simply that both causes (those of class and nation) were desirable; rather, they were organically linked, inextricably interwoven. To quote Connolly again: 'The cause of labour is the cause of Ireland, the cause of Ireland is the cause of labour. They cannot be dissevered.'[7] Thus the revolutionary impulses behind true republicanism grew out of anti-capitalist social conflict. In the heat of 1922, O'Donnell (the pre-eminent socialist republican diva of the post-Connolly generation) attempted to explain the emergence of the independence movement in precisely these terms:

> It was as Connolly's Union that the Irish Transport and General Workers' Union gripped the country. The Irish political struggle came under a new light. Out of the ranks of workers and peasants the Irish Republican Army grew. The imperialism of the gombeen man was plain to the workers from

their new class-viewpoint, and the national inspiration merged into the social longings and hopes of the workers. The workers became the insurrectionary nation.[8]

Connollyite impulses were held to motivate the working classes, who simultaneously embodied sincere, uncompromising republicanism and provided the primary momentum behind the revolutionary movement.

Those holding to such a thesis *were* revolutionaries: in Connolly's view, 'The day has passed for patching up the capitalist system; it must go.'[9] Drawing on Marx and Engels, socialist intellectuals held the politics of each period to be determined by its particular economic relations; and this materialism enabled them to explain the revolution – and its failure. For while the working class had been identified as the authentic Irish nation, other classes fought against the simultaneous uprooting of capitalism and English rule, and it was these anti-republican forces that won the day in the early 1920s. Socialist republican intellectuals condemned the 1921 Treaty and the state that emerged out of it. 'The Free State', declared Peadar O'Donnell in February 1923, 'is a British institution, and has the right of the British Empire. That is: the Free State has no right in Ireland.' 'British rule', he continued, 'in this country was founded on a crime. The Free State is a British rule and is founded on the same crime. Its every function is a crime.'[10] The Treaty was seen as a betrayal, with class interests having determined the treachery of those who had deserted the republic.

There were clear problems with this analysis. James Connolly's career reflected many of the difficulties which his subsequent celebrants would themselves face. His participation in the 1916 Easter rebellion – a gesture sitting awkwardly with much of his earlier philosophy – marked the degree of desperation which he had come to feel during the First World War. Rather than representing the triumph of his socialist republican ideology, his 1916 involvement reflected the inadequacy of his central argument when set against the actual Irish people's attitudes and actions. The early years of the First World War underlined the hollowness in Connolly's claim that the working class were the incorruptible inheritors of the fight for (his version, at least, of) Irish freedom. And, contrary to the O'Donnellite thesis, the revolution, which Connolly helped to inaugurate, further demonstrated the inadequacy of his central argument.[11] The social composition of the revolutionary republican movement was in fact broadly reflective of Irish Catholic society as a whole, representing a broad class spectrum (with least representation at the very highest and lowest

extremes).[12] Revolutionary republicanism cannot, therefore, be deci-
sively explained by reference to working-class, anti-capitalist class
conflict. Various classes were sincerely, committedly involved; and
working-class republicans themselves were only very rarely motivated
by O'Donnellite anti-capitalist thinking.[13]

So anti-capitalist class conflict was not the central dynamic of the
Irish revolution. Indeed, the picture which emerges is complex rather
than monocausal, the forces behind the revolution including: Gaelic
and Catholic idealism; Catholic revanchism, assertiveness and sectarianism; specific educational influence; a number of possible socio-
economic dynamics (by no means necessarily radical or relating to the
working classes); the psychological and other direct rewards of revolutionary activity; and the absorption – from a variety of sources – of
romantic nationalist assumptions (see also Chapter 7). The striking
feature about this list is the extent to which many of these forces were
capable of transcending class background. It is vital also to recognise
the importance of variation, regional as well as individual: any blanket
explanation applied to the revolution as a whole is likely to smother
the real nature of the conflict. Indeed, it is arguable that the best way
of explaining 1916–23 is to look at the particular ways in which individuals reached their decisions. Each of the forces mentioned above
could operate differently upon different people, and the interaction
between these forces again varied from person to person among the
revolutionaries.[14]

This variation suggests the need for close scrutiny of the distinctively individual ideas of socialist intellectuals themselves during the
revolution. For some, socialist ambition was one of a range of goals,
with a widely committed character such as Hanna Sheehy-Skeffington
providing a striking example. She was, as her nephew Conor Cruise
O'Brien put it, 'a strong republican',[15] and was also an enthusiast for
socialism, pacifism and (particularly) feminism. Like other activist
intellectuals of the left in these years, she was strongly influenced by
James Connolly. And, like others supportive of Sinn Féin's nationalist
revolution, she was to find that her other commitments were liable to
become eclipsed in political practice. Most importantly, perhaps, one
might consider the effect upon her thinking of the appalling violence
of these years. Her husband's famous and distinctive death during
the 1916 rebellion surely gave added urgency and intensity to her pursuit of her various idealistic goals. As with so many other people in
the Irish revolution, she was simultaneously scarred, motivated and
destined to greater disappointment as a consequence of violence.[16]

1924–61

Was 1916–23 a revolution? According to the aspirations of the socialist intellectuals under scrutiny here, it clearly was not. Indeed, they were in subsequent years to experience a particularly sharp dose of disappointment. Again, Hanna Sheehy-Skeffington proves a telling example. Nationalism in Ireland overwhelmed her other (feminist, socialist, pacifist) ideals, and these post-revolutionary difficulties were implicit in the obvious tension between her various causes during the mythic period itself. This was, after all, an enthusiast for James Connolly's socialism who yet endorsed Sinn Féin during the Anglo-Irish War. And her problems became more sharply defined during the subsequent generation. Having lost her religious faith and ceased to be a practising Catholic, she had also failed to recognise the revolution as a profoundly Catholic one. Thus this 'unrepentant pagan' felt exasperated that the young independent Ireland was 'rapidly becoming a Catholic statelet under Rome's grip'. She identified such a development as the result of 'a failure in revolution'[17] and, from her perspective, clearly it was. But, equally clearly, most Irish nationalists did not see it that way and had not done so during 1916–23 either. Again, feminism, like socialism, had to be nationalist or unionist (and became eclipsed by whichever ideology it sided with); nationalisms devoured all, and feminists who had supported the Irish revolution were predictably disappointed by the independent Irish state which subsequently emerged.

In some of these experiences the lads had similar tales to tell, especially about Eamon de Valera's Ireland. The flinty, melancholic George Gilmore later observed that, 'he [De Valera] was one of the ones that I really got to know pretty well and I know that he was anti-feminist'. One of the few non-Catholics to have been in the IRA, the socialist Gilmore also commented that, 'if I had to divide the people I knew into goodies and baddies, I'd put de Valera among the goodies, but it'd be with very great reservations because he had that very sectarian attitude'.[18] Indeed, Gilmore was painfully distressed at the conservatism which Irish sectarianism cloaked in the post-revolutionary years:

> we have *two* partitionist groups, nominally hostile, actually mutually helpful… one supporting in the six counties a 'Protestant parliament for a Protestant people', the other striving to create in the twenty-six counties the idea of a Roman Catholic nation in place of the non-sectarian republican idea, both working in defence of conservative politics.[19]

All of this fitted in with the 'revolution betrayed' thesis. Gilmore celebrated the United Irishmen as having embodied non-sectarian ambitions worthy of true Irish republicanism. From such a viewpoint, the 1916–23 episode had by contrast taken on a depressingly Catholic flavour, and the next generation of socialists repeatedly condemned this trend.

Yet they still managed to read the revolution as having validated rather than refuted the logic of their political philosophy. A key focal point here was their interpretation of 1916, James Connolly's place in Valhalla earning subsequent socialists the right to sing out. Gilmore captured neatly the post-revolutionary left's view of the great man's achievement, writing that, 'The oneness of the struggle against national subjection and social oppression in a subject nation has been stressed by James Connolly. ... The failure to make that essential one-ness a basis for political action has been the great weakness in the republican movements of the nineteenth century and right down to our own day.'[20] In 1936 Peadar O'Donnell highlighted another key theme in socialist intellectual argument here, proclaiming that 'Connolly and Pearse brought the republican and labour forces into a united front in Dublin in 1916, and this is the crowning achievement of both their lives.'[21] The belligerent Frank Ryan had, some years earlier, claimed that Connolly and Pearse shared the same 'ideal',[22] while a leading communist agitator, Sean Murray, claimed: 'A national independence movement allied to the working class with its ultimate goal a socialist republic: such was the doctrine of Connolly.'[23] But the 1916 rebellion did not have as its ultimate goal a socialist republic, and the marked differences between the respective ideas of Pearse and Connolly (even in 1916 itself) are clear and well known.[24]

Post-revolutionary socialists castigated both sides in the Treaty split of the early 1920s, and attempted to draw sustaining lessons from the mistakes of each. In 1932 Peadar O'Donnell argued that Michael Collins had suffered from 'the weakness for intrigue and conspiracy that secret societies breed', and stated his own preference for mass revolutionary politics over 'the cult of armed men' which Collins had epitomised.[25] This might be considered peculiar from one who spent most of the post-revolutionary decade on the IRA's Army Council, but it reflected a genuine concern that the next phase of struggle be moved onto a clearly anti-capitalist, mass-movement basis. And if Collins was condemned, then so too was his anti-Treaty giant of an opponent; Fafner may have outlived Fasolt, but neither properly understood the dynamics of the operatic plot unfolding around them.

De Valera was criticised by the socialist republican left for the nature of his post-revolutionary Ireland, and often such attacks were explicitly related to the 1916–23 revolution. In 1936 Peadar O'Donnell complained that there were 'no monster demonstrations raising the independence issue in the clear slogans of 1920–21'. Fianna Fáil were narrowing down the national struggle to serve party ends, and this echoed failings of the early 1920s: then de Valera had dropped the republic for his document number two, and instead of sounding the appropriate call to the nation had 'merely attempted to improve the terms of the bargain between the Irish middle class and British imperialism'. The people were consequently bewildered: 'the independence fight lost its impetus in 1921 because the standard was lowered and the masses could not see where to rally'.[26] Bewildered and implicitly radical masses, missed opportunities, class-determined pusillanimity (or worse) on the part of national leaders: through such themes the revolution provided the key to understanding the nature of all subsequent political developments.

Three other conflicts help illuminate the ways in which the next generation of socialist intellectuals utilised the revolution: the Ulster Question, competition with the Blueshirts, and the related fight in Spain. Socialist intellectuals of republican persuasion assumed, with Marx and Engels, that Irish nationalism was a progressive political force. Unionism was read as a sub-national reactionary ideology, and its working-class adherents were thought to be buried deep in false consciousness. The revolution was held to have failed all workers in the north-east, and it was casually assumed that a one-island, unitary framework was the only appropriate one to accept. But let us, as Marx would say, consider the matter a little more closely. One recent scholarly study of the 1880–1925 period has suggested that: 'in many important ways the developing working-class culture of Belfast had more in common with Glasgow, Manchester or Bristol than with Dublin, Cork or Galway'.[27] Occasionally, socialist republicans would seem themselves to have recognised the validity of this British context for Belfast working-class culture. In 1934 O'Donnell himself noted that, 'Some people [say] that the basis of partition is religion. The things that mark off the six counties from the rest is imperialistic finance and factory workers such as you have in Manchester.'[28] Three years earlier he had observed that, 'Partition arises out of [the] uneven development of capitalism in Ireland.'[29] Yet he typically mingled acute observation (that economic realities helped shape different politics in different parts of Ireland) with a rigid adherence to socialist republican orthodoxy. One might have expected the latter to have been shaken by the former, but not in O'Donnell's mind. This is something which later commentators have sometimes emulated: recognizing that divergent economic development lay behind partition but maintaining none the less a rigid, all-Ireland, republican orthodoxy. The argument that class unity could transcend confessional allegiance, and the conviction that the tensions between Protestant workers and Protestant employers could produce a fissure which would allow republican radicalism to flourish, had proved equally illusory during the revolution. But they were none the less also retained after it.

The 1930s battle of socialist intellectuals against Irish fascism was also held to relate to the 1916–23 revolution. Eoin O'Duffy's stance in the Civil War did not go unnoticed, while George Gilmore referred to the Blueshirts as 'a dangerous regrouping of the enemies of the republic'.[30] This argument was doubly useful: their pro-Treaty past delegitimised the Blueshirts in republican thinking, while fascism delegitimised the pro-Treatyites from the perspective of the left. Whichever eye one looked through, these were therefore illegitimate figures. If one looked through both eyes at once, as did socialist republicans, then the image was even clearer. Just as, in the revolution, socialist intellectuals called for violence against those considered traitors. Where in 1922 Peadar O'Donnell had called for Labour leader Tom Johnson to be forcibly ejected from Ireland,[31] a decade later he and Frank Ryan were sanctioning violence as a means of silencing again their pro-Treaty opponents: Ryan – 'No matter what anyone said to the contrary, recent events showed that while they had fists, hands and boots to use, and guns if necessary, they would not allow free speech to traitors.' O'Donnell – 'The policeman who put his head between Mr Cosgrave's head and the hands of angry Irishmen might as well keep his head at home.'[32]

But it was in Spain that the Irish socialist fight against fascism gained its most famous moment, and intellectuals were again prominent. The intellectual left identified the struggle against tyranny in Spain with that in Ireland, thus necessitating the well-known Spanish gesture by Ryan and his comrades. The Spanish Civil War also offered a kind of Irish Civil War rematch, and with it a possible vindication of that earlier, unsuccessful republican struggle. There were, therefore, Irish revolutionary dimensions to the Spanish adventure. Two figures, perhaps, stand out: Frank Ryan and Charlie Donnelly. The latter, a kind of Connollyite Shelley for the 1930s, epitomised the romance, poignancy and intellectual charm of this celebrated period.

Impecunious while in London, this County-Tyrone-born poet preferred to spend his meagre resources on cigarettes and books than on
food; and he supposedly uttered poetic words even shortly before his
youthful death in Spain in 1937.[33] Echoes of the revolution might
be expected to be less clear here, as Donnelly had only been born
in 1914. But he too looked back to the heroic period, with admir-
ing glances towards the 'essentially internationalist' Connolly and
Casement.[34]

Ryan's case is more famous, and arguably more telling. He held that
there was an automatic bond between Irish republican politics and the
fight against tyranny elsewhere in the world; revolutionary Ireland was
linked with Spain's anti-fascist struggle as with all such defences of liberty. Yet his sad, famous journey from anti-fascist Spanish volunteer to
distinguished guest in Nazi Germany shows the fatuity of assuming
that Irish republicanism is necessarily allied to fights for liberty rather
than against them. My argument here is not, as one recent author has
mistakenly suggested, that Ryan's amiable relationship with Nazi
Germany 'clinches the argument of radical republicanism's inherent
lack of progressiveness'.[35] My claim is rather that this episode demonstrates, not socialist republicans' inherent lack of progressiveness, but
rather their lack of inherent progressiveness – a very different point
indeed, but one which certainly subverts socialist republican thinking
in this area.[36]

1961–2000

In 1961 Desmond Greaves published a brilliant, though ultimately
unpersuasive, biography of James Connolly. This celebrated Connolly's
recognition of the dual (national, socialist) quality of the Irish struggle,
and argued that, 'The juxtaposition of two ideas, socialism and national
independence, is at the heart of Connolly's contribution to Irish history.'[37] There is, as so often, a measure of poignancy about aspects of
such a socialist approach; Greaves's confidence in a 'world-historical
mainstream of scientific socialist thought'[38] certainly seems a trifle
pathetic today. But he has his modern-day supporters, Anthony
Coughlan's eulogistic essay on this 'extraordinary man'[39] providing an
(at times, moving) example. Coughlan too defends Connolly, in particular accusing academic detractors of tending to forget the context –
'the work-burden and immediate concerns' – within which Connolly's
ideas and writings developed. Such people 'ignore such contexts when
offering criticism of a particular text or drawing some academic

conclusion from minor contradictions in argument or detail'.[40] In fact, appreciation of Connolly's personal setting is not absent from the extensive modern academic literature;[41] and Coughlan's argument appears to contain a certain circularity, attempting as it does to excuse the inadequacy and incoherence of an historical figure's ideas on the ground that they were too busy acting upon those ideas to be able to appreciate their inadequacy or incoherence. Nor, as some post-Greavesian socialist intellectuals came increasingly to point out, were Connolly's inconsistencies minor. The ghost of Sean O'Casey lived on, with people of leftist pedigree offering some of the fiercest attacks on Connolly and his legacy.[42]

But despite powerful assaults, from the left and elsewhere, Connollyite republicanism possesses a continuing allure for some socialist intellectuals, and there are still scholars who adhere to a Connollyite approach to Irish politics. W. K. Anderson in 1994 confidently asserted, in almost Greavesian manner, that 'There is no doubt that Connolly's greatest and most enduring legacy to Irish socialism lies in his recognition that the struggle for national independence was an inseparable part of the struggle for socialism, and that by combining the forces of socialism and nationalism both would be strengthened.'[43] In particular, there are still those who hold that the years of the Irish revolution offered the possibility of a radically oriented, anti-capitalist, social revolution. Typically here one finds again the argument that a rank and file with militant inclinations was betrayed by pusillanimous, self-interested, conservative leaders during the revolution; and that had those on the radical left only built the correct kind of revolutionary workers' party, then things might have turned out very differently.[44] Frequently one finds here the confusion of poor social background with sympathy for social radicalism, membership of the working class being taken to indicate some form of affinity with socialist republican political philosophy.

This politics of the 'if only' assumes that bourgeois, conservative elements were handed the leadership of the revolution; that the possibility existed for a radical, anti-capitalist leadership to seize the day; and that the lessons of this missed opportunity remain relevant. Kieran Allen, for example, espouses that brand of Marxist argument which holds that if only there were a political alternative in Ireland 'that roots itself in the struggles of workers',[45] then a radical picture might have been (and might yet be) painted.

It is also true that a long tradition of socialist intellectuals, looking back to Marx and including Desmond Greaves, has looked in hope for an Irish radical revolution to provide the stimulus to similar change in Britain.[46] Moreover, the most famous conflict (Irish *or* British) in the post-1961 period, the Northern Irish troubles, has also seen prominent socialist intellectuals draw significant lessons from the Irish revolution. These have included figures as diverse as Eamonn McCann, Michael Farrell, Bernadette Devlin, and eminent members of the modern Sinn Féin movement; and they require some comment since they bring us to one of the main connections between our three episodes. The boisterous Bernadette was not only convinced by the arguments of Connolly, but offered a familiarly leftist reading of the unfinished revolution: 'Since the Treaty of 1921 ... the republican target has been a reunited, socialist Ireland.'[47] Like numerous other influential figures in the northern descent into turmoil, Devlin had a vision of Irish history built upon a socialist republican interpretation of the Irish revolution.

This is not to blame socialists for the modern troubles. But their role, among others, should surely be recognised. It is clear, for example, that Anthony Coughlan and the Dublin Wolfe Tone Society played a seminal role in precipitating civil rights agitation in Northern Ireland.[48] This socialist republican grouping looked for intellectual and theoretical guidance from ageing veterans of the revolution, O'Donnell and Gilmore,[49] and Coughlan was a great admirer of both men. The Trinity College, Dublin academic was central to the Wolfe Tone Society initiative, and has himself suggested that 'there is a good case for regarding Desmond Greaves as the intellectual progenitor of the civil rights movement of the 1960s. For it was he who pioneered *the idea* of a civil rights campaign as the way to undermine Ulster unionism.'[50] Greaves was an admirer of O'Donnell and Gilmore,[51] as well as the eulogistic biographer of their hero James Connolly, and their leftist comrade Liam Mellows.[52] In turn, Connolly's influence was crucial in relation to other leading civil rights activist intellectuals of the left.

In 1966 Michael Farrell endorsed Connolly's views, arguing that 50 years after the latter's death, 'his dream of an Irish workers' republic has still to be achieved. Only the united action of working-class people north and south, Catholic and Protestant, in a single labour and trade union movement can achieve Connolly's aim.'[53] These combined objectives (uniting the Protestant and Catholic working classes, and establishing a Connollyite united Ireland) were shared by participants in the Wolfe Tone Societies, and were central to the socialist interpretation of the unfinished revolution. There were, therefore, significant ideological and personal connections between our three episodes, connections which played a pivotal role in igniting the turbulence of 1960s Ulster. Connolly, O'Donnell and Gilmore fought in the revolution; the latter two flew the socialist republican flag during the subsequent generation; they then passed it on to a 1960s generation of activist intellectuals who were themselves dedicated to finishing the revolution which Connolly had begun. Socialist republicanism has cast a larger shadow over Irish history than one might expect either from the number of its committed adherents or from the cogency of its arguments. The connections just discussed provide a sharp example of this, and remain one of the most significant, unfortunate features of the socialist intellectual dimension to the Irish revolution.

Conclusion

While Coughlan, Greaves, Devlin, Farrell and their comrades did help to change history through the destabilisation of Ulster, they did so in ways that were profoundly different from those which their ideology had led them to anticipate. Civil rights activism resulted not in Protestant–Catholic working-class unity, but rather in the intensification of sectarian tension and the retaliatory descent into lengthy bloodshed. Desmond Greaves considered the Provisional IRA campaign mistaken, but he had played his part in creating a context within which this appalling phenomenon had emerged. Like others who think that they understand history's strict teleological dynamics – and that as a consequence they can predict and control what will happen after they have created turbulence – socialist republicans repeatedly contributed to great change of a kind they neither expected nor sought. Connolly helped produce a Rising which sanctified precisely the kind of cross-class, bourgeois-led, conservative nationalism that he had spent most of his career deploring. O'Donnell ignited a significant 1920s land annuities campaign with the intention to overturn the defeat of 1921, complete the revolution and establish a radical 'republic of the poor'.[54] In fact his land annuities campaign helped into power the leading conservative, Catholic nationalist of modern Ireland. And 1960s socialist intellectuals deliberately provoked disorder in Northern Ireland with the intention that working-class Protestants would join ranks with working-class Catholics in republican radical unity; in reality, working-class Protestants proved far more likely to respond by joining the UVF. In trying to create (and subsequently to complete) the Irish revolution, socialist intellectuals did change the world, but never as they intended or hoped.

At root, this is because they were so profoundly, demonstrably wrong about so much. Just as the socialists of 1916–23 misread historical figures like Tone, Lalor, and the Fenians, so too, post-revolutionary socialists misinterpreted the lessons of the revolution itself. The assumption that true republicanism sprang from anti-capitalist, class-struggling impulses is simply not validated by serious inquiry into the revolutionary or pre-revolutionary periods. To mis-readings of history can be added those of religion, land, the state; and underpinning it all lay the misunderstood link between Irish nation-alism and economic interests. Such a link plainly existed, but did not necessarily have anything to do with socialism at all. Socialist intel-lectuals identified a key issue when they addressed the material basis to Irish nationalism. But they exaggerated the mechanical influence of economic interest, and further assumed that anti-capitalist class con-flict defined the Irish people's struggle for national independence. Yet during, as after, the revolution it was cross-class expectation of (eco-nomic and other) rewards which made Irish nationalism so powerful a force. The left's crude economic determinism was too inflexible to respond to, or to account for, the complex ways in which social dynam-ics moulded and drove attitudes towards nationalism. Middle-class ambition could direct people towards committed Irish republicanism every bit as effectively as could working-class instincts; indeed, it might be more fruitful to seek a telling explanation of authentic Irish repub-licanism in these years in a battle between different sections of the capitalistic middle classes.

Certainly, there prevailed in the revolution itself the idea that class struggle would disrupt – rather than strengthen, clarify or define – the national struggle; and from this orthodoxy, socialist intellectuals were ineffectual dissidents. Moreover, the working classes were not neces-sarily anti-capitalist anyway. This was true of Ulster unionist workers as of their Irish nationalist counterparts, and socialist republicans failed to grasp that economics might indeed help to determine the attitude of working-class Protestants in Ulster, but in an emphatically non-republican direction.

Yet, implausible though their arguments were, socialist intellectuals remain profoundly interesting to the historian of the revolutionary period. They did, as noted, contribute to historical change; and it should be remembered that they could seem to contemporaries more dangerous than they eventually turned out to have been. The authori-ties were, at times, anxious lest social and national agitation coalesce;[55] and although most of the strike activity in this period was aimed at the amelioration of conditions rather than at any O'Donnellite destruction and re-creation of society, there seemed enough life in the socialist threat to alarm governments for some years to come.

The sources of socialists' ideas were complex and, at times, exotic. Peadar O'Donnell combined Marx with a distinctive reading of Tone, Lalor and the Fenians, and with a Donegal-inflected socialism as distinctively intriguing as it was unsuccessful. Socialists could, as with O'Donnell and his Larkinite mother, have parental inspiration; or, like Charlie Donnelly and George Gilmore, they could rebel against parental piety and propriety. Non-ideological influences could have a decisive impact on their intellectual trajectory, as with the partial disintegration of Donnelly's pre-Spanish life in Ireland, or the personal links (or enmities) forged for some within the radical camp. Such figures still remain absorbing, despite the general collapse of their claim to be swimming with the historical tide. Indeed, a certain glamour attaches to the republican left of revolutionary vintage, some of whom were charismatic and highly intelligent. Some indeed have reached significant cult status: Peadar O'Donnell, Frank Ryan and George Gilmore never reached the standing of James Connolly,[56] but all did come to enjoy reasonably impressive prominence. One scholar has even claimed recently that, with the exception of Michael Collins, Ryan is now 'the most admired political figure of modern Ireland'.[57]

Moreover, the forces to which these people gave articulate voice (a socialism heavily influenced by the thought of Karl Marx, and a nationalism drawing sustenance from ethnic and religious roots) are arguably the most important in modern world history. Just as, in the British case, it is stimulating to approach history by considering how people have reflected on class,[58] so too in Ireland. And in their interrogation of romantic nationalist assumptions, from within the republican camp, Irish socialist intellectuals could achieve a, sometimes surprising, degree of iconoclasm; Gilmore's reference to Patrick Pearse as a 'backward-looking romantic'[59] serves as a telling example. Light can, at various angles, be reflected back onto the revolution using these dissident figures as a mirror. What kind of revolution do they show it to have been?

As already noted, they might question its very definition as a 'revolution' at all. Through the dramatic failure of their truly radical project, they demonstrated precisely how conservative a period 1916–23 actually was. These *were* revolutionaries, seeking what O'Donnell termed 'the complete change of society'.[60] The quality and energy of their efforts, and the extent of their failure, underline the truly conservative nature of the revolution. Not only did their failure reflect the impact of economic background on the political ambitions of people from a variety of classes; but class struggle was seen by most republicans in these years as disruptive of the national harmony they sought to foster between all classes: precisely the kind of approach which O'Donnell and his comrades abhorred.

It was also a very Catholic episode, as the socialists' provision of an alternative (and their exasperation at its failure) eloquently demonstrated. Socialist intellectuals proclaimed the possibility of class unity overcoming sectarian divisions; the revolutionary years in fact demonstrated the degree to which sectarian self-definitions gave meaning to Irish people's lives. And it was also a revolution strikingly characterised by conspiratorial violence. If there was a dialectic at the heart of these years, it was a dialectic not between classes but between violence and counter-violence,[61] and socialist intellectuals were unable to displace such a preoccupation from republican thinking. Formally eschewing the idea that physical force should be central to the republican struggle, they in practice endorsed vanguardist violence as a key tactic in 1916, between 1919 and 1923, and again later when offering didactic and propagandist readings of the revolution. They were wedded to a truly aggressive form of Irish nationalism; even the pacifist Hanna Sheehy-Skeffington helped to edit the IRA's newspaper for a time in the 1930s. Connolly, O'Donnell and comrades sanctioned violence by practising it in the revolution, and then by celebrating it on frequent occasions subsequently. They recognised that mass politics, focused on social issues, was their true home, but were forced by republican expectation to live in a more violent and less accommodating abode. If nationalism eclipsed socialism, then it was in the form of a violent, revanchist, emotionally satisfying anti-politics that it did so during these years.

Conservatism, Catholicism and the centrality of violence are shown by these people to have been particularly important because they themselves provided serious alternatives in each case; socialist intellectuals undermine counterfactual readings of 1916–23 that seek to downplay the degree to which revolutionary republicanism was defined by such themes. Historiographical fashion here might be thwarted,[62] for the claim that these years were full of socially revolutionary possibility which can be reclaimed through counterfactual speculation, seems less persuasive given the existence at the time of such able, energetic, articulate and inventive radicals. We know how conservative, Catholic and bloodily vengeful the revolution was, because the option of radical, non-sectarian mass politics *was* there.

Consideration of the counterfactual leads to other questions, concerning scholarly methodology. Certainly, the unravelling of socialist intellectuals' explanations of the revolution should caution against any mechanically schematic, or monocausally deterministic, accounts of these years. And reflection upon the usefulness of comparative reflection might also be productive. Comparative analysis suggests itself at numerous points in our study of socialist intellectuals. It was clearly convenient for the left to identify the working class as the authentic political community, and then itself as the representative or embodiment of that class. The leftist self could thus experience solipsistic conflation with the nation, and there are clearly resonances here between Irish and other settings. E. P. Thompson's patriotism sought authentic England in a distinctively indigenous radical heritage; and important sections of the French left have presented the proletariat as the leading element within the French nation. If it is tempting to consider the historiographical experience of such English and French socialist intellectuals, then such experience does not offer much comfort for their Irish comrades. Even from admirers, E. P. Thompson has received polite censure as an historian.[63] And the French intellectual left's celebration of their Revolution (as the initiation of a process which would develop from bourgeois beginnings towards socialist completion) has been powerfully challenged by a very different reading (according to which the Revolution was an event whose completion was embodied in stable democracy itself).[64] Echoes here might be heard in the way that Irish socialist intellectuals have seen their interpretation of their own revolution subverted by scholars such as Tom Garvin, with 1916–23 being presented not as an episode of unfinished radical reconstruction, but rather as the birth of a conservative democracy stabilised in subsequent years.[65]

Such comparative reflections are potentially illuminating, but ultimately, I suspect, more in demonstrating difference and particularity than in producing general patterns of explanation. Just as the revolution's socialists might undermine counterfactual possibilities and deterministic certainties, they arguably also suggest that it is in pursuit of explanations of the unique that comparative work might be most profitable. Despite the beguiling resonances between E. P. Thompson and Peadar O'Donnell, for example, each man can only be understood if one closely scrutinises that which distinguished them from one another, that which made their ideas and careers unique.[66] And the point concerning the differences – in context, origins, dynamics, and world-historical consequences – between the French and Irish revolutions is clearer still. This is not to proscribe comparative reflection, but to encourage it as a means of understanding why each event or person is unique.

There is a related point here concerning what might be called the Gellnerian approach to human change. Brilliantly and famously, Ernest Gellner studied the origins of nationalism in terms of the emergence of a world phenomenon;[67] his interest lay not in what made different nationalists, at different times and in different places, think in divergent ways. Study of even such a small cult as the socialist revolutionary left in Ireland indicates some dangers in such an approach. With their socialist dissidence, they show that even within a comparatively small movement such as Irish revolutionary republicanism there was room for profoundly different versions of nationalism; indeed, even *within* this socialist sub-group there were important divergences.[68] There is clearly, then, a danger that many colours will be blurred into one if we adopt a Gellnerian perspective. Indeed, it is conceivable that even theorists' more valuable generalisations will match no individual's experience exactly, their ideal-type depictions being illuminating but, ultimately, imprecise in each specific case.

And yet the avoidance of antiquarian purposelessness requires that historians' particularising tendencies complement rather than replace Gellnerian grand visions. There is considerable value in considering the theses of theorists of nationalism, such as Gellner, in relation to modern Ireland. His arguments concerning modernisation, or education, are of powerful relevance; and other scholars of this type also offer stimulating reflections, some of which might fruitfully be applied to Irish nationalism. Liah Greenfeld's arguments concerning prestige, *ressentiment*, international emulation and shifting national elites, for example, all resonate clearly with the Irish revolution.[69] It is in the tension between the two approaches – closely focused (ultimately, individual) scrutiny, and large map-drawing – that the Irish revolution will most effectively be studied. Despite his wonderful admission of political failure ('I never was on the winning side in any damn thing ever I did'),[70] Peadar O'Donnell and his fellow socialist intellectuals deserve their distinctive, eccentric place in history, and may yet have implications wider than their eccentricity would initially suggest.

Notes

1. O'Donnell to Cape, n.d. [1933?], Jonathan Cape Archives, University of Reading.
2. Marx, quoted in D. McLellan, *The Thought of Karl Marx* (Basingstoke, 1980), p. 69.

3. Nora Harkin, interview with the author, Dublin, 4 Feb. 1988.

4. P. O'Donnell, *Monkeys in the Superstructure: Reminiscences of Peadar O'Donnell* (Galway, 1986), p. 10.

5. E. O'Halpin, *Defending Ireland: The Irish State and its Enemies since 1922* (Oxford, 1999), p. ix.

6. J. Connolly, *Collected Works, I* (Dublin, 1987), p. 25.

7. J. Connolly, *Collected Works, II* (Dublin, 1988), p. 175.

8. *Workers' Republic*, 26 Aug. 1922.

9. Connolly, *Collected Works, II*, p. 442.

10. *Workers' Republic*, 3 Feb. 1923.

11. For detailed discussion of these points, see R. English, *Radicals and the Republic* (Oxford, 1994), pp. 15–29.

12. Ibid., pp. 1–65; P. Hart, 'The Social Structure of the Irish Republican Army, 1916–1923', *Historical Journal*, 42, 1 (March 1999).

13. It is tempting here to argue that Irish experience resembled British, bearing in mind McKibbin's observation, regarding the 1880–1950 period, that 'It is plain that the British working class was never a revolutionary one' (R. McKibbin, *The Ideologies of Class: Social Relations in Britain, 1880–1950* (Oxford, 1994), p. 295).

14. For detailed exposition of this argument in relation to one leading IRA man, see R. English, *Ernie O'Malley: IRA Intellectual* (Oxford, 1998). For discussion of the causes behind the revolution as a whole, see P. Hart, *The IRA and its Enemies* (Cork, 1998), and J. Augusteijn, *From Public Defiance to Guerrilla Warfare* (Dublin, 1996).

15. C. C. O'Brien, *Memoir: My Life and Themes* (Dublin, 1998), p. 340.

16. An interesting letter of H. Sheehy-Skeffington's, to E. O'Malley in 1936, demonstrates her own sadness in face of the revolutionary violence. Having just read O'Malley's 'absorbing' account of the Anglo-Irish War, *On Another Man's Wound*, she lamented in relation to this era that 'militarism breeds hatefulness as reprisal and counter-reprisal succeed each other' (Sheehy-Skeffington to O'Malley, 25 Sep. 1936, Cormac O'Malley Papers, private possession).

17. M. Luddy, *Hanna Sheehy-Skeffington* (Dundalk, 1995), pp. 38, 52. On Sheehy-Skeffington, see also M. Ward, *Hanna Sheehy-Skeffington: A Life* (Dublin, 1997).

18. G. Gilmore, interview with Jennifer FitzGerald, 27 May 1985.

19. G. Gilmore, 'The Republic and the Protestants', *The Bell*, XVI, 5 (Feb. 1951), p. 14.

20. G. Gilmore, *The Irish Republican Congress* (Cork, 1978), p. 3.

21. *Irish People*, 11 Apr. 1936.

22. Writing as Seachranaidhe, *Easter Week and After* (Dublin, [1928?]), p. 15.

23. S. Murray, *The Irish Revolt: 1916 and After* (n.d.), PRONI, D2162/J/96, p. 13.

24. English, *Radicals*, pp. 12–18.

25. P. O'Donnell, *The Gates Flew Open* (London 1932), pp. 31, 168.
26. P. O'Donnell, 'The Irish Struggle Today', *Left Review*, Apr. 1936, pp. 297–8.
27. J. Lynch, *A Tale of Three Cities: Comparative Studies in Working-Class Life* (Basingstoke, 1998), p. 1. For illuminating treatment of the Scottish connection, see G. Walker, *Intimate Strangers: Political and Cultural Interaction between Scotland and Ulster in Modern Times* (Edinburgh, 1995).
28. Peadar O'Donnell, minutes of IRA General Army Convention (17 March 1934), UCDAD, P67/525.
29. *An Phoblacht*, 7 Feb. 1931.
30. Gilmore, *Republican Congress*, pp. 12, 17.
31. *Workers' Republic*, 26 Aug. 1922.
32. Both comments made at the same meeting, in Dublin on 10 Nov. 1932; quoted in English, *Radicals*, p. 109.
33. Behind an olive tree, during a break in the firing shortly before he was killed, Donnelly apparently mused – while squeezing olives – that 'Even the olives are bleeding.' Celebrations of this now include even a poem by M. Longley, 'In Memory of Charles Donnelly', in *Gorse Fires* (London, 1991), p. 48.
34. C. Donnelly and Ajax, 'Connolly and Casement', *Left Review*, Apr. 1936, p. 293.
35. E. Staunton, 'Frank Ryan and Collaboration: a Reassessment', *History Ireland*, 5, 3 (Autumn 1997), p. 50.
36. See English, *Radicals*, pp. 245–51. My arguments here have also been misrepresented in F. McGarry's excellent *Irish Politics and the Spanish Civil War* (Cork, 1999), pp. 107, 279. I did not, in fact, dispute that the republican left was sincerely anti-fascist; indeed, I explicitly argued that 'the anti-fascist cause was strenuously supported' by the Republican Congress (*Radicals*, p. 203). My point was rather that, in terms of *international* alliances and attachments, competing impulses within the republican left might lead its adherents to involve themselves with causes which were far from anti-tyrannical. Ryan's amiable relationship with Germany is hard to reconcile with the republican left's own view that there was a *necessary* connection between Irish socialist republicanism and the international fight for freedom and against tyranny. If, as in this case, republicans' British enemies were themselves opposed by genuine tyrants, then there was at least the possibility of Irish socialist republican involvement with the latter.
37. C. D. Greaves, *The Life and Times of James Connolly* (London, 1986), p. 425.
38. Ibid., p. 426.
39. A. Coughlan, *C. Desmond Greaves, 1913–1988: An Obituary Essay* (Dublin, 1991), p. 17.
40. Ibid., p. 20.
41. D. Howell, *A Lost Left: Three Studies in Socialism and Nationalism* (Manchester, 1986), p. 86.

42. P. Bew, P. Gibbon and H. Patterson, *The State in Northern Ireland, 1921–72* (Manchester, 1979); A. Morgan, *James Connolly: A Political Biography* (Manchester, 1988); H. Patterson, *The Politics of Illusion: A Political History of the IRA* (London, 1997).

43. W. K. Anderson, *James Connolly and the Irish Left* (Blackrock, 1994), p. 41.

44. For a recent example, see C. Kostick, *Revolution in Ireland: Popular Militancy, 1917 to 1923* (London, 1996). Kostick cites IRA leader Dan Breen as typifying a lower-class republicanism frustrated during the revolution (pp. 31, 49). But Breen's case in fact offers Kostick's argument little support. Peadar O'Donnell – who had, if anything, an interest in presenting the most radical possible reading of the revolution – recalled Breen telling him that 'if in the 1919–21 period someone had talked of dividing up estates in his area, he would have had him shot', see J. P. McHugh, 'A Study of *An Phoblacht*: Irish Republican Thought in the Post-Revolutionary Era, 1923–37', MA thesis (University College, Dublin, 1983), p. 34.

45. K. Allen, *Fianna Fáil and Irish Labour: 1926 to the Present* (London, 1997), p. 13.

46. D. Reed, *Ireland: The Key to the British Revolution* (London, 1984), pp. xii–xiii.

47. B. Devlin, *The Price of My Soul* (London, 1969), pp. 13, 88.

48. B. Purdie, *Politics in the Streets: The Origins of the Civil Rights Movement in Northern Ireland* (Belfast, 1990), pp. 130–2.

49. P. Bishop and E. Mallie, *The Provisional IRA* (London, 1988), p. 52.

50. Coughlan, *Greaves*, p. 8.

51. C. D. Greaves, 'Epilogue', in T. A. Jackson, *Ireland Her Own: An Outline History of the Irish Struggle for National Freedom and Independence* (London, 1971), pp. 446–7.

52. C. D. Greaves, *Liam Mellows and the Irish Revolution* (London, 1971); for O'Donnell's ingenious reading of Mellows, see English, *Radicals*, pp. 52–4.

53. Purdie, *Politics in the Streets*, p. 230.

54. P. O'Donnell, quoted in English, *Radicals*, p. 90.

55. 'War Cabinet: Sinn Féin Activity' (24 Feb. 1918), in *Sinn Féin Activities, 1915–20: British Government Reports*, NA, S14049; Ross to Long, 19 Feb. 1919, HLRO BL 96/10/8.

56. Compared with the prominence of Connolly, all three played minor roles in the revolutionary fighting. O'Donnell joined the First Northern Division's Second Brigade in east Donegal, becoming its OC in 1921; he reached the rank of Brigadier-General during the Anglo-Irish War, and was one of the senior IRA officers who opposed the 1921 Treaty; but he saw comparatively little military action. Gilmore was, by his own account, a minor figure during the revolution; his IRA involvement was in County Dublin. Ryan too was an obscure figure, with the East Limerick Brigade.

57. R. A. Stradling, *The Irish and the Spanish Civil War, 1936–1939* (Manchester, 1999), p. 2.
58. D. Cannadine, *Class in Britain* (New Haven, 1998).
59. Gilmore, *The Irish Republican Congress*, p. iii.
60. O'Donnell, *Monkeys*, p. 9; the 1922 programme of his then party, the Communist Party of Ireland, provides contemporary evidence that such was indeed his aim (see *Workers' Republic*, 16 Dec. 1922).
61. This point is brought out very well in Hart, *The IRA*.
62. For a stimulating attempt to put flesh on counterfactual bones, see N. Ferguson (ed.), *Virtual History: Alternatives and Counterfactuals* (London, 1997).
63. D. Eastwood, 'E. P. Thompson, Britain and the French Revolution', *History Workshop Journal*, 39 (1995).
64. For sophisticated treatment of this theme, see S. Khilnani, *Arguing Revolution: The Intellectual Left in Postwar France* (New Haven, 1993).
65. T. Garvin, *1922: The Birth of Irish Democracy* (Dublin, 1996).
66. Both were radical, authenticist patriots; witty and brilliant writers and speakers; wide-ranging public moralists; and latter-day enthusiasts giving their blessing to anti-nuclear and other radical causes. But compare their arguments and intellectual formation as described, respectively, in M. Kenny, 'Edward Palmer (E.P.) Thompson', *Political Quarterly*, 70, 3 (1999), and English, *Radicals*.
67. For statement and refined restatement see, respectively, E. Gellner, *Nations and Nationalism* (Oxford, 1983); E. Gellner, 'Nations, States and Religions', in R. English and C. Townshend (eds), *The State: Historical and Political Dimensions* (London, 1999).
68. Even Connolly's, O'Donnell's, Ryan's and Gilmore's politics differed significantly, in origins and nature, from one another. In terms of regional, class, family, professional and intellectual background, there were great differences between these men; differences of emphasis also emerge in their politics, O'Donnell being, for example, more rurally focused than Connolly, more optimistic about political change than Gilmore, less in tune with physical-force practice than Ryan. See English, *Radicals*, and also the chapters respectively examining O'Donnell, Gilmore and Ryan in R. English, 'Radicals and the Republic: Socialist Republicanism in the Irish Free State, 1925–37', Ph.D thesis (University of Keele, 1990).
69. L. Greenfeld, *Nationalism: Five Roads to Modernity* (Cambridge, 1992).
70. Peadar O'Donnell, speech in Belfast's Conway Street Mill, 7 Apr. 1984.

14

Revolution? Revolutions are what Happens to Wheels – the Phenomenon of Revolution, Irish Style

Tom Garvin

Theories of revolution have gone out of fashion, more or less in tandem with the fashionability of the actual phenomenon itself. Trotsky's notion that war was the locomotive of history now gives us images of some appalling third-world train-crash rather than the brushing aside of an effete old order so as to usher in the new, some blood being inevitably spilt on the way. Ironically, the most recent large phenomena which looked something like revolutions were the collapse of the so-called revolutionary regimes in Russia and its satellites in Eastern Europe and Asia ten years ago. Essentially these events represent the philosophical bankruptcy of Leon Trotsky and his theory of history. Similarly, Barrington Moore's well-known historicist thesis of the late sixties that the coming of the modern world could not occur without some essentially violent break with the political and social past ('the destruction of feudal society') looks a little tired, in the year 2001.[1]

In Ireland, 'red' IRA people of the 1968–85 period are now respectable bourgeois politicians, decent defenders of democracy, criminals, retired informers, dead, or some curious combination of two or several of the above. The death of the romantic cult of the revolutionary, coupled with the concomitant scepticism about the political efficacy of violent action, has reinforced this change of mood. This ideological or philosophical death has, curiously, happened with a resounding accompanying silence in Irish academia and journalism. There are honourable exceptions to this generalisation, but I suspect that the Irish intelligentsia's flirtation with revolutionary Marxism a generation ago now causes some embarrassment to their older and possibly wiser selves.[2]

Moore was a brilliant and fashionable Marxisant scholar in the 1960s and early 1970s. What happened? He was not defeated by intellectual argument, but rather seems to have been by-passed by the verdict of history, or the facts of real life. It sometimes seems as though the social sciences and contemporary history, rather than being sciences with some kind of claims to predictive capacity, were rather a chorus of commentators on a huge natural experiment called 'Real History'.[3]

Certainly, in the case of Ireland, Hegel's Owl of Minerva seems invariably to fly at dusk, or even in the middle of the night, as in the case of certain ultra-republicans. Irish theories of revolution were entertained by would-be practitioners of revolution, and usually had the bad habit of being lifted from essentially irrelevant pre-war European or post-war third-world models; it was only when they got shipwrecked through the actions of the revolutionaries themselves that these theories got criticised or pulled apart. Furthermore, the purveyors of these theories tried to use the general forgetfulness of the culture to put behind them their earlier programmes so that they might embark on new ones. Thus, in the Republic, the once-communist and pro-Soviet Workers' Party-cum-IRA 'Stickies' has become a highly respectable component of the Irish Labour Party. Again, in Northern Ireland, the treasonable Ulster Volunteer Force (UVF) of 1912, armed by the German Government, evolved into the stalwart scions of unionism and loyalism. The traitors of 1912 became the heroic martyrs of the Somme in 1916. Yet again, to give an early example of Irish political metamorphosis, De Valera's would-be martyrdom of 1916 was followed, as time and times went by, by his merciless and very effective treatment of IRA men in the 1940s.

The idea of revolution

We have had a fair few would-be revolutionaries in Ireland since 1789 or even 1776; they are a little like the weather; something you talk about a lot but can do little about personally. The word 'revolution' is itself a curious one. As David Fitzpatrick has famously put it in his classic *Politics and Irish Life*, revolutions are what happens to wheels; the word suggests that society can be seen as a wheel that can be turned so that you are where I am and I am where you are. Implicit in the metaphor is a zero-sum style of thinking, where you must suffer if my suffering is to cease, or my suffering must continue if you are to continue to prosper. Douglas Hyde found this idea extant among the Sligo peasantry of a century ago, possibly partly in the form of a joke, but there all the same. It is a metaphor deep in European popular culture, certainly going back to classical times, and was tapped into very successfully by, for example, the early Christian church.[4]

Revolution is also notoriously difficult to define as a political or sociological concept. The *Oxford English Dictionary* defines it as 'a complete overthrow of the established government in any country or state by those who were previously subject to it: a forcible substitution of a new ruler or form of government'. The trouble with this second definition is that any coup d'état, take-over by a junta or stolen election victory might qualify as a 'revolution'. Evidently the word has rather grander and deeper cultural resonance than this; Lenin's revolution in Russia was somehow a greater, more important and more terrible event than (say) Pinochet's take-over in Chile. It was also, I would argue from intuition, a different type of event.

Thus, revolution involves not only a more-or-less forcible change of regime, but also a change in social relations, class structure, possibly property relationships, and perhaps also drastic changes in the country's relationships, with the rest of the world, in particular the great powers of the period. Thus, Russia's relationships with Germany, France and Britain were revolutionised in the period after 1917, as were Cuba's with the United States in 1959–60 and China's with the United States after 1949. Similarly, England's Glorious Revolution did not only involve a new religious settlement, much transfer of property and a new dynasty, it also involved a marked hostility to France compared with the Stuart kings' friendliness toward that power.

Foreign policy changes commonly accompany the internal upheaval, and foreign powers become part of that process of upheaval itself; France meddles in the English and American revolutions; the Allies intervene in revolutionary Russia; the Soviet Union and the United States both interfere on opposite sides in the Chinese and Cuban revolutions. Here in Ireland, anti-British foreign powers have fished in their enemy's troubled Irish waters for several centuries – Spain, France, the United States, Germany and the Soviet Union all succeeding each other in trying to make political capital out of the Irish bog.

This is by way of offering a set of 'marks' or characteristics that a true revolution should exhibit, rather like the 'marks of the true church' offered Catholic schoolchildren in Ireland a generation ago. Despite the somewhat doubtful provenance of this empiricist approach to definition, it has some heuristic utility. In summary, revolution is a series of events involving rapid domestic political and social change, often involving considerable violence and the participation of large numbers of people, and drastic changes in foreign relations.

A distinction that is commonly drawn is that between 'social' revolutions and 'national' revolutions, a distinction that occasionally breaks down in practice. The Chinese revolution of 1912–49 was, for example, not only a great social revolution, it also involved the riding to power of a communist movement on the back of a scandalised and ancient Chinese national pride, seeking redress for a century of bullying and humiliation by the western powers and Japan. Even now, the behaviour of Chinese elites displays a classic late-nationalist determination not to be pushed around by old enemies or ex-enemies. Again, Fidel Castro, undoubtedly a revolutionary, is also equally undoubtedly a nationalist.[5]

Revolutions involving the separation of a putatively national territory from a larger state, or imperial confederation of states and semistatal territories, are, however, commonly seen as a distinct class of events ('nationalist revolutions'). The secession of the United States from the British Empire would be regarded as a classic example of such an event, perhaps even a particularly 'pure' example. Again, the protracted series of wars that resulted in the secession of the Protestant Republic of the Netherlands from the Hapsburg Empire in the seventeenth century might be another such.

In each of these cases considerable changes occurred in property and social relations. In the American case, something like one-third of the pre-revolutionary population had to leave the country and forfeit their property, a fact quickly forgotten when the United States was opened up to a huge flood of land-seekers from western Europe after the Peace of Paris in 1783; the American Tories were compensated by the British Government with cash and land in Canada, Britain or Ireland. In the Netherlands, what was possibly the first purely bourgeois and mercantile state came into being in the seventeenth century as the Dutch rid themselves of Hapsburg, Spanish and Catholic aristocratic rule. The Dutch revolution also sparked off an imperial expansion which displayed an energy and effectiveness remarkable in so small a country.

Famously, Marxist political thinkers over the past century and a half pinned their hopes for a transformation of human society on two great historical social classes: the industrial workers and the peasantry. By and large, the former class has proved to be wanting and has fairly consistently backed away from any thoroughgoing revolutionary upheaval. Bismarck and other leaders of capitalist states found it relatively easy to attach the working classes to their national states' causes by means of welfarism, patriotic rhetoric and militarism; the catastrophe of August 1914 symbolised the end of the classic period of workers' revolutionism. The twentieth century's greatest revolutions, in the sense of revolutions involving the most numbers of people, have been peasant-driven at crucial points; cases in point are the Chinese revolution, the Mexican revolution, the Vietnamese revolution and, until the Bolsheviks nipped it in the bud after the Civil War, the Russian revolution.

An Irish perspective

Whether there has really been an Irish revolution, failed, successful, betrayed or unbetrayed, is a moot point. What is certainly the case is that some people, many of them significant or at least noticeable political actors at various junctures in Irish political history, thought that there is, or has been, an Irish revolutionary process. Supporters of the traditional cause of an Irish-speaking, 32-county, vaguely socialist workers' and farmers' republic regarded the settlement of 1921 as a great betrayal and the defeat of the IRA in both parts of Ireland as a British-engineered Irish Thermidor.

Similarly, Patrick Pearse, in the run-up to the First World War, repeatedly heralded the coming Irish revolution in increasingly strident and sometimes hysterical tones. Again, a strange assortment of Trotskyites, Narodniks, Stalinists and anti-communists have commonly come up with a similar picture of an island somehow ripe for revolution Cuba-style and somehow escaping it narrowly through the treachery or alternatively the bravery of a small group of determined men and women, often including such unlikely groups of allied villains or heroes as Carson, Cosgrave, de Valera and Brookeborough.[6]

Evidently these people saw Ireland either as a country going through a revolution that had been betrayed by an alliance of imperialists and the local comprador bourgeoisie and their working-class lackeys, or as a country that had been saved from the communist menace. I do not see Ireland this way at all, although I immediately admit that it is a view held by many in the past and even now. Ireland is a country that has been increasingly stable politically since the period of the Great Famine; its last chance at a true revolutionary upheaval, I would argue, was in the period of the French Revolution, when a properly organised United Irish insurrection, aided determinedly by the French, just might have brought it off. Ever since then, the possibilities of an Irish revolution have waned and the main Irish political tendencies have been a democratic nationalism, as originally formulated by Daniel O'Connell, and an equally democratic popular unionism, created partly in response to O'Connell's mass movements; there has been a long war between two rights, both popular, neither truly revolutionary and both democratic. The trouble was, they did not seek the same democracy.

Ironically, the Great Famine, which provoked the formation of the Fenian movement, also confirmed the primacy of O'Connellism, by changing the sociological profile of rural Ireland in such a way as to eliminate the cottier class and weaken the landless labourer or rural proletariat. At one blow the possibility of an Irish rural Maoism was eliminated forever. An equal irony accompanies the fact that the Davitt–Parnell alliance, which passed the land of Ireland from mainly Protestant landlords to mainly Catholic small farmers, also strengthened the cause of popular unionism, by removing the last bone of contention that remained between Protestant tenantry and Protestant landowners in Ulster and elsewhere.

Ever since, Irish revolutionary republicanism and its allied opinions has had a strange and rather unreal revivalism about it, and commonly has based itself rhetorically on non-existent or certainly non-allegiant classes: for example, the 'Gaelic' core of Ireland (which has not existed since 1800 or thereabouts); the Irish working class (which scarcely exists, or ever has existed, outside Belfast as a classic industrial working class, and nowadays not even there); the Irish small farmers, a now dying class who were deeply conservative, even reactionary in their political and social thinking; and for a while in the sixties in a *reductio ad absurdum*, the students (who are in reality the pioneers of Irish suburbia, north and south).

There are two periods in which insurrectionist Irish revolutionary republicanism apparently 'got lucky' in this increasingly inhospitable political environment: 1912–21 and 1969–75. In each case they were less lucky than they imagined themselves to be, as their movements were less united internally and less popular than they appeared to be. The events of the first period are well known, but I would like to make a few small points: 1916 was not a popular rebellion; the vote for Sinn Féin in 1918 was as much a vote against conscription and British Government bullying as it was for independence; the Sinn Féin movement was mainly conservative, non-Bolshevik and very much in favour of low taxes; in Ireland it was disproportionately financed by the anti-tax prosperous farmers of Munster; Collins was milking the anti-welfarist sentiments of the Irish rural bourgeoisie. After the Treaty settlement, the suppression and even occasional killing or even murder of the extremists by the Free State Government was quietly consented to by the majority of the population. Many of these extremists were, in effect, agrarian and sectarian in their motives, and wished to drive loyal Protestant and Catholic families off the land by intimidation, forced sale and, occasionally, murder. Protestant and loyal households in Munster were guarded by the National Army of Michael Collins, Richard Mulcahy and Peadar MacMahon for over a year after the end of the Irish Civil War in May 1923. These facts were later airbrushed out of history by 'green' and 'red' propagandist revisionists of Fianna Fáil and various Sinn Féins.[7]

The second period when revolutionaries saw a window of opportunity was 1969–75. These years saw an attempt at the destabilisation of both regimes in Ireland by a small and unrepresentative armed clique ('the IRA') who fantasised themselves to be representatives of the 'real' Ireland, a 'real' Ireland which does not exist. Their 'revolutionary war' rapidly turned into a race war within Northern Ireland and was deeply unpopular in both parts of the island. In both periods, the sheer weight of unsympathetic or even hostile public opinion wore down the extremists and either permitted acquiescence in their extermination or forced them to convert themselves into moderates. Both movements were defeated by the people, or peoples, of Ireland; divided we stand, united in nothing but our joint hostility to revolutionary politics and a wish for peaceful electoral democratic government. Irish revolutionary purpose has perished because of an overwhelming sense of its pointlessness.

The Irish problem has been, for a long time, a problem for constitutional engineers to solve rather than a problem for revolutionary heroes or revolutionary murderers. This diagnosis is essentially that of the New Zealand oceanic historian of the English-speaking peoples, J. G. A. Pocock, in a lost article written in 1966. Entitled 'The Case of Ireland Truly Stated: Revolutionary Politics in a Context of Increasing

Stabilisation', it argued that the romantic and visionary character of Irish nationalist thought and rhetoric disguised an increasingly realistic and pragmatic style of politics, and has done so for over a century.[8]

This dichotomy between the windy rhetoric of politicians and priests on the one hand and dusty reality on the other explains, for example, the acceptance of Partition by men who had fought bravely for a united independent Ireland between 1916 and 1922. It explains the quiet acceptance of an English-speaking Ireland; the equally quiet acceptance of EU membership, if not all of its implications, as demonstrated in the 2001 vote against the Treaty of Nice; the demilitarisation of the Free State and, later, the Republic; the ruthless treatment of the IRA by both William Cosgrave and Eamon de Valera; the provisional, but real, acceptance of Northern Ireland by most northern Irish nationalists before 1969; the huge nationalist votes in 1998 in both parts of Ireland in favour of an agreement which, in effect, states that there can never be Irish unity without majority consent in Northern Ireland and the Republic of Ireland. It also explains the ready acceptance of the 1999 power-sharing executive in Northern Ireland, and Dublin's quiet, and even happy, jettisoning of the irredentist Articles Two and Three of the 1937 Constitution in their De Valeran forms.

Thus, I would argue that there has never been a completed Irish revolution, merely a series of attempts to create one against a backdrop of a classic process of democratic reformism in both parts of Ireland, both before and since 1922. Admittedly, the new polity set up in the 26 counties in 1922 did involve the formation of a new ruling class or stratum. However, it can be argued that this group would have gained power by peaceful means sooner or later. I wrote years ago that the Irish revolution has been a long time dying; perhaps I should have written instead that the Irish revolution has been a long time being stillborn.

This 'shadow of a revolution', to adapt Sean O'Casey's well-known phrase, did follow the classic chronology of true revolutions. Jaroslav Krejci's well-known study of the phenomenon of revolution portrayed it as a process lasting several generations, with a long run-up to the revolutionary process and a long aftermath or collective hangover afterwards.[9] The Czech revolution lasted from 1403 to 1458 (55 years); the English 'puritan' revolution from 1628 to 1689 (61 years); the French Revolution from 1751 to 1873 (122 years). The Russian Revolution he puts at over 150 years, from the Decembrists to the Fall of the Wall, or roughly 1818 to 1989 (171 years). In the Irish case,

I would suggest the beginnings lie in the formation of the Fenian or IRB Society in Dublin in 1858, and the end of the process was marked by the Omagh bomb of 1998 and the Good Friday agreement. Whatever the validity of this suggestion, we have certainly been in endgame since 1994. A revolutionary or pseudo-revolutionary process which has been with us, like it or not, for a century and a half, is finally becoming obsolete.

Notes

1. B. Moore Jr, *The Social Origins of Dictatorship and Democracy* (Harmondsworth, 1969). I wish to thank the participants in a conference on the Revolution in Ireland in Queen's University, Belfast, on 6–7 Dec. 1999 for their helpful, friendly and occasionally devastating comments on an early draft. I wish in particular to thank Dr J. Augusteijn of Leiden University for his help with the redrafting.
2. One of the honourable exceptions is Eoghan Harris, whose journalism is often admirable.
3. This view of the social sciences has been put forward formally by, among others, Anthony Giddens.
4. An excellent survey of the literature is provided in A. S. Cohan, *Theories of Revolution: An Introduction* (London, 1978).
5. I explore the alliance between social radicalism and nationalism in Tom Garvin, *Mythical Thinking in Political Life* (Dublin, 2001).
6. W. A. Phillips, *The Revolution in Ireland, 1906–1923* (London, 1926); see also T. Garvin, *Nationalist Revolutionaries in Ireland, 1858–1927* (Oxford, 1987).
7. The agrarian and sectarian streak in the movement in the 26 counties apparently expressed itself most openly in Cork. See P. Hart, *The IRA and its Enemies* (Oxford, 1997).
8. I cite here from memory a typescript version of the article lent to me briefly 30 years ago and subsequently lost. Professor Pocock has informed me that he has lost the original (correspondence).
9. J. Krejci, *Great Revolutions Compared* (Brighton, 1983), passim.

Chronology

1912   11 April: First reading of third Home Rule Bill
1913   31 January: Foundation of Ulster Volunteer Force
          26 August: Start of Dublin Lock-out
          24 September: Provisional Government of Ulster formed
          19 November: Foundation of Irish Citizens Army
          25 November: Foundation of Irish Volunteers
1914   2 April: Foundation of Cumann na mBan
          24–5 April: Larne gun-running
          26 July: Howth gun-running
           3 August: Outbreak of First World War
          18 September: Third Home Rule Bill enacted but suspended
          20 September: Redmond's Woodenbridge speech
          24 September: Split in Irish Volunteers
1915   May: Military Council of IRB founded
1916   January: IRB Military Council decides on rising
          24–9 April: Easter Rising
          3–12 May: Executions of leaders of rising
          Christmas: Release of internees of Easter Rising
1917   2 February: North Roscommon by-election
           9 May: Longford by-election
          10 July: East Clare by-election
          25 July: Opening of Irish Convention
                     Release of convicted prisoners of Easter Rising
          25 September: Death of Thomas Ashe
          25–6 October: Sinn Féin Ard-Fheis
          27 October: Irish Volunteers Convention
1918   April: Conscription Crisis
          17–18 May: German Plot, arrest of republican leaders
          11 November: Armistice in First World War
          December: General election victory by Sinn Féin
1919   January: Versailles Peace Conference
          21 January: First Dáil established
          April: Limerick Soviet
          June: De Valera starts tour in USA
          18 June: Founding of Sinn Féin arbitration courts

           4 July: Sinn Féin and IRA proscribed
           20 August: Dáil introduces oath to Republic and the Dáil
           12 September: Sinn Féin and Dáil declared illegal
           11 November: *Irish Bulletin* first published
1920   1 January: Start of Anglo-Irish War
           15 January: Municipal elections
           May: Rural council elections
                   First Dáil Land Court
           July: Sectarian riots in Belfast
                   Belfast Boycott instigated
           August: Restoration of Order in Ireland Act
           September: Establishment of Ulster Special Constabularies
              1 November: Hanging of Kevin Barry, first official execution
                   of the war
           21 November: Bloody Sunday
           28 November: Kilmichael Ambush
           December: Mediation visit to Dublin by Archbishop Clune
           11 December: Sacking of Cork City
           12 December: Martial law declared in south-west Ireland
           23 December: Government of Ireland Act passed
1921   May: Formation of Second Dáil
              5 May: Craig and de Valera meet in Dublin
           24 May: General elections in Northern Ireland
           25 May: Burning of Custom House, Dublin
           22 June: Opening of Northern Irish Parliament by King
                   George V
           11 July: Truce
           14 July: De Valera meets Lloyd George in London
           11 October: First meeting of Irish and British negotiation
                   teams
              6 December: Signing of the Anglo-Irish Treaty
1922   7 January: Ratification of Anglo-Irish Treaty by Dáil
           14 January: Establishment of Provisional Government
           30 March: Craig–Collins Pact
           20 May: De Valera–Collins Pact on elections
           12 June: British make final changes to new Free State
                   Constitution
           16 June: Elections in southern Ireland
           22 June: Sir Henry Wilson killed
           28 June: Start of Civil War
           27 September: Special Powers Act passed in Dáil

25 October: Constitution of Irish Free State passed by Dáil
    Formation of Republican Government by
    de Valera
6 December: Official establishment of Irish Free State
7 December: Northern Ireland votes itself out of Free State
1923   30 April: Unilateral ceasefire by republicans in Civil War
24 May: Ending of all military activities by republicans in
    Civil War
27 August: First general election in Irish Free State
1924   6–19 March: Army Mutiny
1925   3 December: Boundary Agreement
1926   May: Foundation of Fianna Fáil
1927   10 July: Assassination of Kevin O'Higgins
12 August: Fianna Fáil enters Free State Dáil
1932   9 February: Foundation of Army Comrades Association
    (Blueshirts)
9 March: Fianna Fáil forms government in Irish Free State
1933   13 May: Blueshirts formally announced
1934   8 April: Founding Republican Congress
1937   14 June: New constitution accepted in referendum
1938   25 April: Return of Treaty ports
1939   16 January: Start of IRA bombing campaign in Britain
2 September: Ireland declares neutrality in Second World War
1946   6 July: Founding of Clann na Poblachta
1948   February: First Inter-Party Government
1949   Easter: Calling of Republic of Ireland
1956   12 December: Launch of IRA border campaign
1962   26 February: border campaign called off
1967   January: Founding of Northern Ireland Civil Rights
    Association
1969   Start of 'Troubles'
December/January 1970: Spilt in republican movement,
    formation of Provisional IRA and Provisional Sin Féin
1998   10 April: Good Friday or Belfast Agreement signed
15 August: Omagh bomb explodes

Index